SPORT PSYCHOLOGY
FOR WOMEN

SPORT PSYCHOLOGY FOR WOMEN

Robert A. Mechikoff
San Diego State University

with Virginia Evans
Wellesley College

HARPER & ROW, PUBLISHERS, New York
Cambridge, Philadelphia, San Francisco, Washington,
London, Mexico City, São Paulo, Singapore, Sydney

1817

Executive Editor: Judy Rothman
Project Coordination, Cover Design, Text Art: BMR,
   David Crossman
Compositor: Recorder Typesetting Network
Printer and Binder: R.R. Donnelley & Sons Company

Sport Psychology for Women

Copyright © 1987 by Harper & Row, Publishers, Inc.

Library of Congress Cataloging-in-Publication Data

Mechikoff, Robert A., 1949-
   Sport psychology for women.

   Bibliography: p.
   Includes index.
   1. Sports for women—United States—Psychological aspects.
2. Sports for women—United States—Coaching.   I. Title.
GV706.4.M4 1987   796'.01'940973   86–33714
ISBN 0–06–044445–2

87 88 89 90   9 8 7 6 5 4 3 2 1

I dedicate this book to my daughter, Kelly Lee Mechikoff, an aspiring basketball and volleyball player, and to the coaches and women athletes of yesterday, today, and tomorrow.

R.A.M.

Contents

section II
APPLIED PSYCHOLOGICAL COACHING METHODS

CHAPTER 7
BASKETBALL

CHAPTER 8
FIELD HOCKEY

CHAPTER 9
GYMNASTICS

Preface

The growth and popularity of sport in general and women's sports in particular will no doubt continue for decades. Along with the popularity of women's sports, the field of sport science (sports medicine) continues to enjoy phenomenal growth and a promising future. Prior to 1973, the scope and status of major sports competition for women was severely limited. As a result of the suffocating economic position and societal status accorded to women athletes prior to the early 1970s, the overwhelming majority of time, money, effort, and exposure within sport went to the promotion and scientific support of men's athletics.

Perhaps the single most important factor in providing opportunity and access to major athletic competition for women was Title IX. Although initiated less than 15 years ago, the scope and impact of Title IX upon sport in America as a vehicle for opportunity and access propelled women's sports into the 21st century. However appealing and promising the current state of affairs in women's sports appears, a significant amount of talent and opportunity has been forever lost over the past 75 years because of the secondary status assigned to would-be women athletes by the socio-political thinking of that bygone era.

There exists an enormous void of useful information about the psychological preparation of women athletes when compared to their male colleagues. Information regarding the psychological makeup and preparation of women athletes from the perspective of applied sport psychology is very limited in terms of research interest, scope, and content. The literature available on applied sport psychology for women is primarily experimental in both design and application, which is appropriate and necessary for research but does not lend itself to immediately helping coaches and athletes who are preparing *right now* for competition. *Sport Psychology for Women* was written to provide a much-needed learning tool and resource guide for coaches who are working with women athletes on the club, high school, and college level. This is the only book that incorporates basic psychological theory and applied sport psychology as practiced by many of the best head coaches of women's sports in the United States. The book takes the reader from an introduction to sport psychology in Section I to a major coaching clinic devoted exclusively to applied sport psychology and women athletes in Section II. There is currently no other published reference like it anywhere.

The text can be used in a variety of physical education classes at the undergraduate and graduate level, i.e., psychology of sport, team sports for women, coaching the elite athlete, coaching theory, methods of applied sport psychology, psychological preparation of women athletes, and as a text for short-term intensive coaching clinics conducted by private enterprise or universities and colleges that offer college credit. In addition, the book may be integrated into the curriculum in both women's studies and psychology departments.

Section II of the book is organized into sport-specific units, i.e., basketball, volleyball, etc. The reader is strongly encouraged to read and digest all of the tools and techniques presented by these outstanding coaches regardless of his or her athletic expertise, knowledge, or interest. For example, a tennis coach will learn much from Coach Carol Plunkett of San Diego State University but should be able to utilize additional tools and techniques that Linda Sharp, basketball coach at the University of Southern California, or Bill Neville, volleyball coach at Montana State University, present.

After exhaustive data collection and analysis, the evidence indicates that highly successful coaches and athletes incorporate the tools and techniques of applied sport psychology as an integral part of their program. Most coaches have a sincere interest in their athletes and want them to grow and become successful as a result of participation in sports. To this end, the coaches endeavor to "work hard" and encourage their athletes to do likewise. Working hard does not insure success; however, working hard *and* smart as a coach and athlete will provide the edge that can easily make the difference between victory and defeat. Becoming knowledgeable in the area of applied sport psychology is the cornerstone of working smart.

Robert A. Mechikoff
Virginia Evans

Acknowledgments

I am deeply indebted to Mrs. Bessie Lockhart, who typed and retyped this manuscript at my request more times than I care to remember. The critical reviews and suggestions of Dr. Bill Kozar of Texas Tech University, Dr. Russell Lord of Eastern Montana College, and Karen Kenney and Dr. Paula Rogers Lupcho of the University of California, Berkeley, were invaluable in terms of organization, content, and direction. My gratitude and respect for Fred Henry, my editor at Harper & Row, is beyond words. The faith and encouragement of my parents, Alex and Aileen Mechikoff, are much appreciated. I wish to dedicate this book to my daughter, Kelly Lee Mechikoff. Her innocence, ever-smiling face, and boundless enthusiasm and joy provide my inspiration and purpose. The expertise of Dr. Virginia Evans was crucial in obtaining the original material that comprises Section II of the book. Although the material in Section I originated from my desk alone, the critical comments and chapter reviews supplied by Dr. Evans were of great benefit. My deepest appreciation is extended to the outstanding coaches who provided the crucial information contained in Section II.

Robert A. Mechikoff

section I

INTRODUCTION AND APPLICATION OF SPORT PSYCHOLOGY

chapter *1*

Psycho-Socio Foundations of Performance

WOMEN IN SPORT

One of the most frequently asked questions about sports in general and women athletes in particular is *when* will the human factor as a limitation and absolute end regarding athletic performance finally be realized? Humans seem to run faster, jump higher, excel and surpass existing records each year. When and where will it end? This question is best answered by a brief look at the recent rise of women's athletic competition from second-class status to that of legitimate varsity—elite recognition. Until the mid 1970s, before the implementation of Title IX and the Women's Movement, the opportunity for American women who sought to excel in the competitive sports arena was limited and restricted primarily as a result of traditional gender roles and expectations in terms of the way women were to be properly perceived by society. With few exceptions, women and girls were channeled into acceptable sports such as ice skating, gymnastics, field hockey, swimming, and tennis. Prior to the mid 1970s, athletic participation for aspiring young women in general was not encouraged by parents and society. With few exceptions, "tomboys" and serious athletic competition for women athletes were not considered socially acceptable. Depending upon geographic region, this unfortunate perception may continue to operate today, although at a reduced level.

The birth of competitive women's athletics is usually identified with the mid 1970s, which gave birth to the Association of Intercollegiate Athletics for Women (AIAW) and the implementation of Title IX. The AIAW was a significant factor in the enormous growth and support of women's sports programs in the nation's colleges and universities. Unlike their male counterparts who can historically trace their athletic activity and social acclaim and acceptance to prior to the turn of the 20th century, contemporary women athletes have had the access, expertise, and opportunity for varsity competition approaching the level of the established men's programs for only approximately ten years! The overall results in terms of performance and growth have been exceptional. However, the reader must take into consideration the following:

1. The vast majority of physiological research and findings relative to sports performance has been directed toward the male athlete.
2. The overwhelming majority of sport psychology research findings and applications has been concerned with male athletes.
3. The primary thrust in social science research relative to sociology of sport and social psychology of sport has been focused on the male athlete.
4. Since minimal research in sport psychology has been conducted on women athletes, the quality and quantity of future contributions and applications of applied sport psychology hold significant promise for the immediate present and the future.
5. Where would the level of women's athletics be today if women athletes had the same or similar opportunities and support that men enjoyed at the turn of the century (e.g., if women athletes had the same status and support as men had at the turn of the century)?
6. The second-class status with which women's athletics were identified for a number of decades resulted in a minimal amount of scholarly and professional interest by many sport scientists in particular and the coaching profession in general.

The vast amount of research data available for male athletes as compared with information on women athletes is indicative of a recent and, hopefully, bygone era. Because of the enormous strides made in women's athletics in terms of recognition, ability, and resources within the past ten years, the future of women's athletics, especially at the elite level, is very promising. Because of the lack of all-around support women athletes had to contend with until recently, the research gap between men and women athletes remains significant. However, it seems reasonable to conclude that the state of the art as it currently exists in sport science and sports medicine may enable us to greatly increase the athletic performance in women and eventually fill this gap.

As a research discipline and practice, the interest in and study of traditional, orthodox psychology is primarily concerned with behavior of the animal kingdom in general and with human behavior in particular. The discipline of psychology is unique in that it is considered both a biological *and* social science. The topic and parameters of behavior are very broad in scope and definition. The study of behavior in terms of origin, influence, prediction, and control is an area of psychology that has tremendous potential for use in all aspects of athletic competition. *Human behavior* as reflected in a single athlete, or an entire team, and the resulting effect upon athletic performance comprise but one area of applied sport psychology.

Psychology as a social science has an interest in social problems and seeks to understand and initiate positive change. "Psychology of course is not the answer to all social problems. . . . But again and again it is clear that the reason for a lack of progress with some problems of society is that we do not understand the mental processes of the persons involved" (Hebb 1968, 1). We do not know or understand all of the origins and manifestations of mental illness and deviant behavior that occur in our society, or for that matter the role and impact of society and culture on forming and regulating positive (appropriate) and negative (inappropriate) behaviors. Coaches and athletes comprise a team which represents a structured miniature model or microcosm of society with all its attendant behaviors and outcomes. An understanding of collective behavior via sociology and group dynamics as it affects human performance and the variables that impact and control the collective behavior of a team is another area of applied sport psychology that can benefit both coach and athlete.

SOCIOLOGY OF SPORT

Among the various entities which comprise the area of sport science (sports medicine), the interests and application of psychology and sociology appear to overlap from time to time. It is not unusual for gray areas to exist where psychology and sociology are both investigating the same topic or several similar areas. In order to provide a frame of reference and present the scope of psychology in more definitive terms, it is appropriate to briefly present the interest and scope of sociology.

"As a scientific endeavor, sociology commences with two basic facts: (1) human beings are social animals, and (2) human behavior exhibits repetitive and recurrent patterns" (Leonard 1984, 42). Sociologists believe that the concept of social organization is vital in explaining and understanding the repetitive and recurrent patterns of human behavior as a function of humans as social animals. Social organization refers to the ways in which human conduct or behavior is regulated and organized as a result of the social conditions in which people are encapsulated rather than their physiological or psychological characteristics. Athletic teams are social organizations.

SOCIAL PSYCHOLOGY

Sociology, like psychology, studies human behavior. However, where psychology as primarily a biological science studies behavior from biologic origin and application, sociology studies human behavior as a result of the social conditions in which people operate. The gray area in terms of interest, scope, and application in which psychology and sociology overlap is identified as social psychology. Whereas the sociology of sport can benefit the coach in terms of understanding individual human behavior and team behavior in terms of social organization and cultural values (importance) associated with sport participation, social psychology of sport can offer yet more information to the coach.

Social psychology is defined by Cratty (1981, 2) as ". . . the attempt to understand how people affect each other. It is the study of conditions among people, as well as within them, that influence the totality of their relationship, their ability to work together toward some common goal, and their possible pleasure and displeasure with one another. Thus, such topics as group cohesion, attitude formation, dissension, aggression, group motivation, and interpersonal communication are respectable subtopics in social psychology." It is readily apparent that many of the subtopics of social psychology are of significant benefit to coaches as a way of understanding, predicting, communicating, and controlling both individual and collective behavior so as to fashion the optimum mental and organizational environment for practice and competition. The social psychology of women athletes in addition to the study of women's athletic teams in terms of social organization regarding perceived and attained goals is an area of research that has yet to be fully explored.

BRIEF OVERVIEW OF PSYCHOLOGY

The discipline and practice of psychology can trace its origin and initial affiliation and orientation to that most time honored course of study in the academe, philosophy. Within the traditional scope of academic orientation and scholarship, psychology as an academic discipline is approximately one hundred years old. Yet, in our society the impact and utilization of psychological theory, tools, techniques, research, and practice are extensive. New areas of psychology continue to emerge, such as sport psychology and the psychology of space travel and astronauts; both involve human performance in precision, stress-oriented environments.

Psychology is categorized as a behavioral science. The study of the many and various ways people behave has been the traditional focus of psychology. Although the field of psychology appears to have taken quantum leaps in a scant one hundred years, an understanding of the basic concepts of psychology is necessary if one is to appreciate and utilize applied sport psychology. Theories and orientations are part and parcel of psychology. As a behavioral science, psychology seeks to understand why people as individuals or as members of a group behave the way they do. Environmental settings such as home-field advantage, hostile stadium crowds, and quality of facilities can have a significant impact upon the way athletes perform.

We all recognize that behavior can be labeled as good, bad, or indifferent. In addition, we know that the cause of a wide variety of behavior can be a result of physiologic considerations or biological origin. For example, lack of sleep, clinically referred to as sleep deprivation, can affect the mental process and behavior patterns. Mental stress due to a divorce, death of a loved one, broken personal relationships, or significant change in employment or status can also affect our physical well-being and, consequently, our behavior is likely to change. However, when behavioral changes occur as a result of biological factors, such as a chemical imbalance within the body, specifically the brain, a physician who specializes in psychiatry can provide a valuable and necessary service. Thus, behavior can have both physiologic and biological (chemical) origins, or a combination of both—psychophysiologic.

The direction or thrust of contemporary twentieth-century psychology in general terms is perceived to be twofold. Academic psychology, a form of what is considered to be "pure science," is the attempt to learn more, to better understand the human mind and behavior. Applied psychology, the second area, actually puts theory into practice; it is the attempt to put what has been learned to practical use (Hebb 1968). Recognizing the fact that traditional academic psychology is to be credited with the very existence and source of psychological tools, techniques, and applications, the theme and content of this book will focus on applied psychology of sport and its attendant areas as they pertain to women athletes. However, it is imperative that the coach, athlete, trainer, and the various people who seek to utilize sport psychology have a general understanding of the theoretical principals and constructs that comprise the domain of academic psychology. After all, how often has it been said that a little bit of knowledge can be a dangerous thing? Coaches and athletes who receive limited exposure to several hours of sport psychology education during a clinic or meeting and then assume they know enough about applied sport psychology to practice psychological technique will in all probability find themselves in a very volatile and uncomfortable situation when attempting to incorporate limited applied psychology; there is an enormous difference between "knowing about" and "knowing how." The reader is urged to consult the many introductory psychology textbooks available in addition to enrolling in relevant course work in order to refresh the memory and expand the base of knowledge.

During the past two decades, there has been a significant amount of research generated in the area of human performance as it pertains to sports. Research in the multidimensional physical education departments in the leading universities around the country has produced meaningful results. Vital and perhaps seemingly esoteric areas of research within human performance are oriented, but not limited, to the following:

1. Exercise Physiology
2. Biomechanics and Kinesiology
3. Anthropometric Measurement
4. Sport Sociology
5. Biochemistry of Performance
6. Nutrition
7. Sport Psychology
8. Motor Behavior
9. Motor Control
10. Social Psychology of Sport

With the exception of sport sociology, social psychology of sport, and sport psychology, the majority of research undertaken in physical education and the medical community is focused on the physiologic areas of human performance. However, how many times has it been suggested, and will no doubt continue to be said by coaches, that competition is 10 percent physical and 90 percent mental? More importantly, what does this statement actually mean? What coaches and athletes are actually attempting to represent by this statement is that, within a competitive situation, the probability is that both teams and individual athletes possess nearly the same physical skills and fitness levels. Beyond that the winner is determined by mental preparation. Understanding, explaining, predicting, and controlling behavior of athletes and coaches as it is formed and exhibited in the athletic arena is part of the purpose of sport psychology. If we seek to learn and understand the theoretical framework and constructs of academic psychology in general terms, the principles, tools, techniques, and application of applied psychology as it relates to sport will be better understood, appreciated, and applied by coaches and athletes.

The general opinion within the competitive athletic community is that the vast majority of all athletes, trainers, and coaches utilize and practice from the same knowledge base relative to training routines and biomechanical and kinesiological application and techniques (blocking, tackling, throwing, jumping, swimming, hitting, etc.). As a result, the state of the art relative to the physiological parameters of human performance is known and utilized by most successful coaches, athletes, and trainers. Yet, they are all constantly searching for an "edge" or "equalizer" that will enhance the performance of an athlete or team just enough to help provide a margin of victory or success. The study and effective application of applied sport psychology and mental preparation can help to provide that very "edge."

Recent increased interest in the area of applied sport psychology demonstrates the importance of how much greater the applied value of psychology will be when theoretical understanding is further developed. The scientific process has often been described as a way of thinking as opposed to the collection of facts. Among the various rules and regulations that govern scientific research and inquiry, perhaps the most revealing and yet absolute creed is that science "offers no difference to anyone or anything, with no respect for existing ideas if there is any prospect in improving on them and no respect at all for common sense or traditional ideas" (Hebb 1968, 2). In regard to psychology, the mental preparation of women athletes is subject to change based upon the availability of sound scientific research. The psychological preparation of women athletes is not limited to gender-specific preparation but also androgyny and, to an extent, feminist psychology. However, the mental preparation of athletes in general appears to remain culturally oriented toward gender-specific practices, although the androgynous approach is also practiced.

Research psychologists can utilize a comparative research model that seeks to compare one subject with another in much the same fashion that coaches evaluate athletic talent (e.g., compare the skill and potential of one athlete against another). Most people equate psychology with the brain in much the same manner that they equate dentists with drills. Psychology is indeed concerned and interested in the function of the human brain. In order to understand and effectively utilize the tools, techniques, and principles of applied sport psychology, a basic understanding of how the brain is constructed and how it operates in terms of directing and controlling behavior will help expand the efforts of coaches and athletes. Again, the reader is urged to consult basic psychological texts for this important information.

Knowledge of the operational terminology utilized in psychology is necessary for the reader to understand a stimulus-response situation, sometimes referred to as cause and effect, and how to incorporate the application of tools and techniques developed by psychologists to enhance human performance. The following terminology will enable coaches and athletes to understand basic psychological content.

Psychology	Scientific study and analysis of behavior
Mind or mental	Processes that occur within the brain that determine organization and behavior
Objective evidence	Information that is scientific and quantifiable in terms of established origin and application
Subjective evidence	Information that can be internal in origin; not subjected to scientific evaluation or proof
Personality	The complete and total makeup of a person—cognitive, social, and gender in origin—that distinguishes one person from another.

Behavior and its attendant areas of interest and origin can be thought of as the primary foundation of psychology. The factors involved that produce an *observable behavior* contain the following characteristics (Bourne and Ekstrand 1973, 22):

1. The organism (species, biological structure, capacity)
2. Motivation (intentions, wants, needs, drive)
3. Cognition (perception, learning, memory, knowledge)
4. Competence (know-how, skills)
5. Performance (movement, activity)
6. Achievement (outcome, results, feedback, reinforcement)

What the six factors represent is that any *real behavior* that is carried on by humans or any biological organism is motivated, based on known facts and skills, and includes performance by the organism and a resulting achievement. These six factors should not be taken as the origins or "causes" of behavior, although these factors do reflect the behavioral process.

Behaviors originating from an athlete or coach are a result of a complex series of actions which are inherently personal. However, it is important to understand that conditions of the organism (athlete) can limit his or her behavior. A tired or preoccupied athlete will generally not perform to expectations, nor will a coach who is ill or on certain medications teach at the expected standard of excellence he or she has previously demonstrated. Thus, conditions that are both internal (biologic and physiologic) *and* external (societal and cultural) can affect behavior and, as a result, athletic performance.

Coaches and athletes are forever trying to understand *why* a team, athlete, or coach "did something" that was counterproductive to the collective goal, or "didn't do anything, just stood there," which was equally as aggravating. In any attempt to describe and explain behavior, it is essential that the coach have a basic understanding of the biological characteristics of human beings. If you are able to describe and explain the behavior of athletes and coaches, you can then begin to predict change, control (manipulate) behavior, and, presumably at the same time, elicit the behaviors that will enhance performance and possibly provide the "edge."

Psychological Research: Theory into Practice

The purpose of psychological inquiry and research is based on the premise that "the focus of any psychological study is basic knowledge or a practical application" (Bourne and Ekstrand 1973, 10). It is not the intent of this book to present, explain, and analyze in depth the numerous theoretical constructs that provide the foundation and operational basis of contemporary, orthodox psychology and feminist psychology. There is, however, a point of clarification that needs to be presented relative to the seemingly pointless experimental procedures and projects that many people outside the realm of psychology fail to understand. The general public tends to view psychologists as "rat runners," scientists who perform behavioral studies with animals such as running rats through a maze or having monkeys push certain levers as a result of a specific stimulus (cause and effect). The casual observer would have to wonder about the importance or value of such seemingly pointless "scientific research" for humans.

Bourne and Ekstrand (1973, 10) state that "studies like these seem too far removed from human behavior to be of any importance, and yet psychologists continue to do them and for good reason. Studies of this sort are often the simplest way to get at fundamental behavioral principles. By piecing together the results of such studies a scientist may be able to confirm an existing theory, deny an existing theory, or propose and construct a new theory. Thus, a theory is a way of representing, organizing, and summarizing facts, and of understanding why and how certain things [behavior] occur." As coaches and athletes, we all have "theories" about certain offenses and defenses. Invariably each year, after years of study and trial and error, a new offensive or defensive system is introduced that promises to revolutionize the game—e.g., basketball, volleyball, field hockey—due to experimentation, research, and analysis. The studies that are conducted result in more information that will provide sound operational theory by which we can refine our ability to describe, explain, predict, and control behavior. Because of the ethical nature of science in general and the dignity of the individual as represented in our human rights beliefs and protection, the necessity of animal studies relative to the construction and operation of theoretical constructs as applied to humans is a very deliberate, purposeful, and methodical process. The application of the knowledge gained in psychological and medical research on the basis of animal experiments can often be transferred, with modifications, to human subjects with positive benefits for all of us. Thus, while it may at first appear that the rat and monkey experiments have no direct bearing on the health of the human race, the great majority of animal experiments in psychology and medical science are indeed initiated, in almost all cases, for the eventual betterment of us all.

As was previously stated, the focus of traditional orthodox psychology can be looked at as being twofold: the development and acquisition of basic knowledge *and* practical application as applied psychology. Within the latter focus lies the content of applied sport psychology. In the same fashion that a teacher or educational psychologist developing a curriculum should be able to analyze and understand, through reliable research, which topics should be taught and in what order (Bourne and Ekstrand 1972, 11), the coach who has the familiarity and expertise in applied sport psychology should utilize similar concepts as they apply in the sport. An example is the position, again based on theory, that psychologists who adhere to the school of Behaviorism as pioneered by B. F. Skinner agree that human behavior is a product of environment. Theoretically, if a coach who is a Behaviorist can manipulate the environment correctly, behavior of an athlete or team could be manipulated or changed for the better. Workers will produce more products and a better quality product when the work place (environment) is pleasant and supportive of their activities; this same type of procedure can be just as effective with coaches and athletes. As a coach, construct an environment (locker room, practice area, etc.) that will serve to produce and reinforce those behaviors—attitudes that you want to instill in your athletes.

INTERESTS AND DIMENSIONS IN SPORT PSYCHOLOGY

What are the various research areas that comprise the academic discipline and subsequent research areas of sport psychology? The following topics are representative of the scope of sport psychology, but by no means represent a complete content analysis. However, the areas identified appear to be of primary interest to athletes and coaches.

1. Personality and sport performance
2. Motivation in sports
3. Arousal and sport performance
4. Anxiety and sport performance
5. Aggression and sport performance
6. Leadership and coaching behavior
7. Audience effects
8. Team cohesion
9. Intervention strategies, e.g., mental rehearsal, goal-setting, etc.
10. Youth sports and adolescent psychology
11. Communication between coach and athlete, athlete and athlete
12. Group (team) dynamics
13. Deviant behavior: athletes, coaches, hostile environments
14. Positive and negative reinforcement
15. Hypnosis
16. Behavior modification

At this point in time it would appear that the title of sport psychologist could be used by almost anyone. However, most states prohibit the use of the term psychologist by anyone not licensed as a psychologist. Definitive standards in conjunction with the physical education profession and American Psychological Association are being developed by the United States Olympic Committee to establish a certification process that will provide both integrity and control over sport psychology practitioners. As discussed earlier, the content of sport psychology can encompass the disciplines of physical education, psychology, sociology, and social psychology. Thus, the multidisciplinary approach and application of sport psychology might be at home within several different academic specialties. The activities that take place in physical education and sport act as a laboratory for the discipline of psychology, which helped to foster, encourage, and nourish the field of sport psychology. In terms of a positive and productive relationship, the disciplines of physical education and psychology have the ability and opportunity to form a very dynamic and important bond. Physical educators should utilize, not practice, psychology to provide insight into athletic performance and physical education. Within the same context, psychologists should utilize, not practice, physical education and sport to provide insight into psychology, e.g., sport psychology.

Perhaps the most formidable problem or obstacle that is continually encountered in the often-ambiguous area of sport psychology is the acceptance and application of "theory into practice." It is not unusual to hear coaches say that research in psychology cannot help them work with their teams. This "obstacle" is further complicated by the "academic curtain" that continues to separate the scholarly community—Ph.D.'s in psychology and physical education—from the coaching fraternity. The perennial argument or position that select members of the coaching fraternity use is that a big difference exists between "knowing about" and "knowing how." In other words, how is a clinical psychologist or experimental psychologist who is not completely absorbed in the competitive environment on a daily basis able to relate and make a significant contribution to success (i.e., win-loss record)? Conversely, psychologists and physical education professors agree that for anything positive to occur within the realm of sport psychology, principles, methods, and application of the technique associated with sport psychology must be based upon selected psychological principles. Psychologists don't "coach" and coaches are not psychologists. Herein lies the problem and related obstacles.

Another area of discussion and contention among coaches is how to prepare athletes psychologically for competition, and whether the methods can be or should be varied with respect to gender. The question of whether psychological preparation for competition should be adjusted or varied based on gender is further complicated by those who maintain that an androgynous approach is mandated because there are more similarities than differences. Athletic success based upon gender, socioeconomic background, personality traits, and personality dynamics has undergone intense investigation relative to the effect and importance of gender, socioeconomic background, etc., upon success.

The study of personality traits as a predictor and determinant of success in athletic competition is an interesting, although inconclusive, area of research in sport psychology. Numerous psychometric tools have been utilized in an attempt to measure a specific personality trait that may distinguish athletes and athletic potential from nonathletes. Personality studies are conducted on athletes, male and female, in team sports and individual sports. Football, swimming, basketball, track and field, volleyball, soccer, and baseball are investigated in an effort to determine the "personality type" that specific sports seem to attract or produce, and the subsequent differences in the degree to which specific personality traits manifest themselves differentially in successful athletes and unsuccessful athletes. Can winners and losers be identified on the basis of personality inventories? Not at the present time. Some sport psychologists (sport scientists) may actually ignore or become oblivious to the fact that athletic ability and not specific personality types as determined by psychological inventories is primarily responsible for athletic success.

Morgan et al. have done extensive work in the area of personality structure of athletes and have attempted to develop personality profiles that could assist in predicting success in sports. Morgan (1974, 374–90) was able to identify five psychological concepts that can be used in the daily work of sports medicine physicians, coaches, trainers, and physical educators:

1. Athletes from various sports differ in a variety of psychological states and traits.
2. High-level performers in athletics are characterized by psychological profiles that generally distinguish them from lower level performers.
3. Attempts to elevate anxiety ("psych up") and reduce tension states should be used cautiously and employed on a personalized basis.
4. Mental health plays an important role in athletic success, and it is quite likely that "emotional first aid" following competition is just as important as physical first aid.
5. There is frequently a lack of congruence between the athlete's conscious and unconscious motives.

Fisher (1976, 316) states that "if it could be shown that mere participation in sport actually influences the personality of the participant, then perhaps various claims could be made for participation. . . . Such claims have long been made . . . but without seriously considering the evidence." Although personality investigations on athletic performance are many and varied, the actual definition of "personality" is also multivaried in form and substance (theoretical positions). Although past research efforts in "personality" continue to be an interesting area in sport psychology, limited research is currently being conducted by sport psychology professionals. According to Fisher (1976, 317), "Physical educators seldom have a sound theoretical framework behind the questions they ask and this is especially true in the assessment of athletes. The result is often a rather self-contradictory position—for example, assessing personality change as a function of athletic participation by methods based on assuming that personality is static and rather unchanging after early childhood." This rather limited and superficial analysis of the cognitive preparation of physical educators, although perhaps credible in part, would appear to accomplish very little in promoting a bond between physical education and psychology. Then again, scientists take nothing for granted.

SOCIAL AFFILIATION AND COACTION

For years, coaches and athletes alike have adhered to the belief that they have an edge on the majority of their opponents whenever they compete "at home." The positive or negative effect that spectators and audiences provide athletes relative to performance potential has been documented by Cox et al. According to Cox (1985, 244), "Perhaps no social-psychological effect is more important to athletic performance and outcome than the audience or spectator effect." The presence of a supportive audience can have a significant positive impact for the home team and, conversely, be perceived as an additional opponent (hostile?) by the visiting team. There are numerous arenas and stadiums around the country commonly referred to as "snake pits" because of the nature of the hometown fans—supportive for the home team and quite often obnoxious and contemptuous toward the visitor.

The effect of crowds upon athletic performance has long been a concern of both coaches and athletes. Some athletes and coaches are oblivious to crowd behavior at home or away; others are significantly affected in terms of their behavior and subsequent performance depending upon where they compete, at home or away. In an effort to analyze the cause and effect crowds have on performance, psychologists focus on an area of research known as social facilitation. Although the paradigm of social facilitation may initially appear somewhat vague, research in this area holds a great deal of promise in terms of application for both coach and athlete. Social facilitation research focuses on the effects an audience can have upon performance. Cox (1985, 244) states that social facilitation "is reserved for that area of research dealing with the noninteractive effect of an audience upon performance."

Noninteractive audience refers to a situation where the audience does not articulate or interact with athletes but is "merely present." In this area of research, the goal is to learn via observation the effect the presence of a passive or active audience will have upon performance. To achieve this environment, the researcher must eliminate all of the interactive variables to isolate and thus observe the singular effect the presence of spectators will have upon the performer(s).

Another interesting thrust of social facilitation focuses on the cause and effect that coactive participation can have upon performance. An example would be a group of archers (coactors) who are in the process of independently shooting arrows at their respective targets in close proximity to each other. These archers would be classified as a noninteractive coactive group; i.e., they do not interact.

The effects that an audience can have upon performance and the effect athletes as opponents have upon each other is an ever-expanding focus of sport psychology. In terms of the research, what is significant is that, whether performing alone or in front of an audience, women are not affected any more than men are (Murray 1983 as cited in Cox 1985). However, it has been observed that pre-adolescent boys will perform better when the spectators are male adults as opposed to female adults (Fouts 1968 as cited in Cox 1985). According to Cox (1985, 263), "it appears that if the audience or coactors are of the opposite sex, the potential for an audience effect increases."

Both coach and athlete should be aware that a leveling effect will occur when athletes of varying ability compete against each other. Research in regard to the leveling effect created when competitive coactors of varying ability compete against each other can be revealing. As cited by Cox (1985), this type of research has been done by Triplett (1897), Moede (1914), Carment (1970), and Hunt and Hillery (1973). Their research and subsequent findings enabled the leveling effect concept to arise. This concept, according to Cox (1985, 263), means that ". . . when coactors of unequal ability compete against each other, there is a tendency for the performance level of the coactors to become more alike. The performance of the less skilled subject improves, while the performance of the more skilled subject declines. Thus, rivalry does not always result in enhanced performance. However, if coactors are of equal ability, competition should enhance motivation. . . ."

The psychological investigations written on the effects of various forms of social facilitation, even with extensive analysis, appear to remain inconsistent and conflicting in terms of results and application. Although the findings are perplexing, Kozar (1973) maintains that because of the methodology of physical education relative to content and method, learning and performance out of necessity and purpose have to occur in the presence of others. Thus, the content, form, and application of methods and procedures inherent in physical education and sport necessitate the understanding of social facilitation.

Can the mere presence of a crowd create a "cause and effect" situation whereby a passive audience can enhance and facilitate learning and/or performance? Kozar states that, although the presence of a crowd can be a source of arousal and drive, it may be perceived by the athlete that the crowd is collectively an evaluative group which could place the facilitation component within the performer and not the crowd.

MOTIVATION

Motivation of athletes more often than not represents the major topic in sport psychology that is first and foremost in the minds of coaches. Questions that are frequently asked by coaches include:

1. How can I motivate my team on a collective basis?
2. How can I motivate athletes on an individual basis?
3. What types of "things" are counterproductive in motivating individual athletes and teams?
4. What type of reward system, if any, will act as an agent for motivation?
5. Can "pep talks" actually motivate my team?

As perhaps the most competitive society in the world, Americans recognize and reward "first place." Perhaps Lee Iacocca, chairman of Chrysler Corporation, summed up the competitive character of America as well as anybody when referring to the mission of his company: "We just want to be the best; what else is there?" With the enormous number of competitive athletes engaged in sports, it is both reasonable and logical that the quest and subsequent motivation "to be the best" is manifested in both America's sporting heritage and in general societal values and expectations.

It would seem reasonable to assume that the vast majority of coaches and athletes have little interest or need for lethargic or weakly motivated teammates. Adapting this position, the understanding of the concept as put forth by Fisher (1976), who researches the dynamics of motivational behavior as a variant connected to the types of stimuli, should provide insight and applicability for coach and athlete, e.g., can motivated athletes actually "feed" their teammates?

Are emotions and arousal important elements in the motivational process, especially when athletes are often typecast as "playing with emotions, displaying no emotion—win or lose, lacking emotion"? Emotion is not an easily defined term. Emotion is a cognitive label we use to explain physiological processes in certain situations. Within the parameters of emotion, the following descriptive states most often occur: joy, love, pride, fun, anger, jealousy, fear, grief, shame, depression.

Emotion is often both organizing—making behavior more specific and thus effective—and disorganizing; i.e., it is both energizing and debilitating. For example, peaking of the athlete or team in the optimum manner or peaking beyond the most productive-optimum level tends to create a highly emotional situation that can often be chaotic and counterproductive.

Arousal and the degree to which an individual athlete or team is aroused can have a definite effect upon performance. Within the arousal framework, Hebb (1968, 235) categorized anger as a "temporary heightening of arousal accompanied by a tendency to attack, and at the other end of the continuum is fear which is a temporary heightening of arousal accompanied by a tendency to withdraw or flee." Within the competitive arena of athletics, the motivational constructs of anger and fear have manifested their respective "products" for centuries. In this same vein, fear is the origin of yet another emotion that can be counterproductive in sports. Hebb (1968, 235) describes the negative side of fear: "When fear is chronic because the threat is inescapable, or when no external threat exists and the fear is due to some disorder within, it is called anxiety."

The relationship between emotion and motivation is very significant. In general terms, emotion is closely related to arousal. As arousal increases, emotion also tends to increase (Hebb 1968, 236). This concept is depicted in the inverted-U curve of arousal in Graph 1.

Athletes and coaches must realize that research in psychology has demonstrated that although motivation rises initially with an increase in arousal (see Graph 1), per-

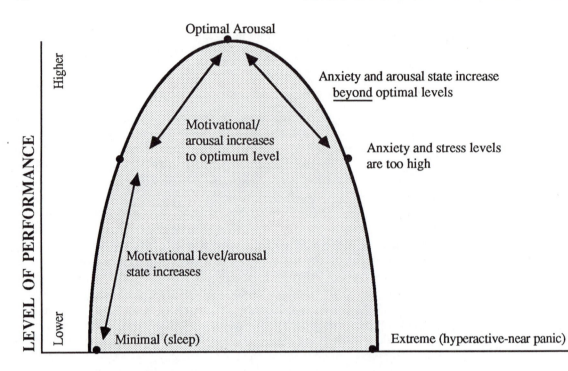

Graph 1: Relation of the effectiveness with which stimuli guide behavior (cues) to the level of arousal, varying from deep sleep to disorganizing states of emotion, with maximal (optimal) behavioral efficiency at an intermediate level of arousal (Hebb 1968, 235).

formance tends to reach a peak not at the highest level of arousal, but rather at a midpoint and perhaps several degrees beyond the arousal continuum. The research indicates that motivation may actually start to diminish as arousal significantly increases beyond the "peak point" and may disappear altogether at the highest level of arousal due to the athletes' becoming too responsive and attempting to mentally process too many things at once. When this emotional level is reached, the athletes may panic, lose their concentration and choke. Hebb (1968, 236) says, "Though we ordinarily think of emotional excitement as a cause of vigorous effective response—that is, we think of it as motivating—there is well authenticated evidence showing not only that it can impair behavior [performance] but also that it can reduce the effectiveness of response to zero . . . a loss of motivation."

Motivation is thought to be the source for psychological momentum in athletic competition. Research conducted by Iso-Ahola, Seppo, and Mobily (1980, 391–401) sought to theoretically define "psychological momentum" and empirically validate its influence in competitive sports. Psychological momentum was defined in that research as "an added or gained psychological power that changes interpersonal perceptions and influences an individual's mental and physical performance."

High levels of arousal are part of the emotional spectrum; however, high arousal can actually reduce motivation and, as a possible result, performance. How often has the term "overmotivated" been used in competition to explain defeat, or that highly emotional "pep talk" actually proved to be counterproductive depending upon the arousal state of the athlete or team?

Some athletes and coaches are very comfortable while working in a situation that seeks to promote and produce significant degrees of emotion. These people are often categorized as highly emotional athletes and coaches who appear to need and utilize emotion to coach or compete. More often than not, they tend to become frustrated with the athlete or coach who does not display emotion or, if at all, in very limited and controlled circumstances. This situation does not necessarily mean that emotional athletes and coaches are highly intelligent and that complex and unemotional athletes and coaches are dull. The reason, states Hebb (1968, 246), may be cultural in origin: "The structure of "civilization" is such as to cushion the adult's sensitivities, to protect [them] from the causes of fear, anger and disgust. . . . The lack of emotional outbursts in the civilized adult is evidence . . . of the effectiveness of the social cocoon in which we live."

The evolutionary process of human development, among other things, has led to the growth and development of a large cerebral cortex, which appears to have greatly enhanced our ability to learn and solve problems. However, the development of the larger cortex has also increased our emotional sensitivity. To reiterate a statement by Hebb (1968, 254), "Emotional susceptibility is correlated with intelligence in the growing animal, so it is the older rather than the younger subject that is most easily disturbed. . . . Our emotional sensitivities have led us to organize social patterns that reduce the frequency of emotional stimulation, allowing us to categorize our behavior as unexcitable.

This chapter has attempted to illustrate that the interdisciplinary and interprofessional scope of sport psychology has made a significant contribution and provided considerable insight into the biological and social nature of athletic performance. Historically, conformity to societal values and traditional expectations has provided a comfortable professional basis for both psychology and physical education, which could perhaps explain the lack of sport psychology research addressing the female athlete as opposed to the abundance of research on male athletes. Within the domain of sport science (sports medicine), sport psychology is one of the premier areas of study in terms of immediate and future potential contributions. The psychological preparation of female athletes is seemingly at the leading edge of contemporary sport psychology; much will be learned and applied. It is logical that, for a coach and athlete who desire to remain "current" and competitive, the study of sport psychology should comprise an essential element of the continuing educational process.

chapter 2

Research in Sport Psychology: An Historical Overview

As a social and biological science, psychology is considered the new school or discipline on the block primarily because a century of scholarship is not significant when compared to the disciplines of philosophy, chemistry, mathematics, and astronomy, which have existed for centuries. While noted scholars such as Socrates, Plato, Descartes, Michelangelo, Galileo, Newton, and Copernicus can trace their affiliation and contributions to scientific disciplines that have existed for centuries, the reputations of noted scholars in psychology and sport psychology are equally deserving. Sigmund Freud, B. F. Skinner, James Watson, Carl Rogers, and Eric Erickson are recognized names in the world of psychology; these psychologists made a tremendous contribution to the application and scientific study of behavior.

While psychology as the parent discipline can identify with scholars who, at the very mention of their name, elicit admiration and respect, sport psychology has a proud and still-emerging history that is representative of outstanding scholars who have dedicated their professional lives to the area. Landers, Bird, Harris, Martens, Gould, Kozar, Lord, Miller, Cratty, Kroll, Fisher, Singer, Griffith, Morgan, Nideffer, and Tutko and Ogilvie in their early work are recognized for both their significant teaching and research in sport psychology, basic and applied.

Where did it all begin and what has shaped the content of sport psychology? The intent of this section is to provide a brief historical overview of sport psychology in the United States. The rationale for this limiting geographical representation is not ethnocentric or provincial in nature but rather one of expediency and relevancy. It should be understood by the reader that within the parameters of international athletic competition between the world's superpowers, America's nemesis, the Soviet Union, has been extensively involved in the research, study, and application of psychology of sport in human performance since before the Russian Revolution of 1917. The German Democratic Republic (DDR), Poland, and Bulgaria as well as Great Britain, Canada, Cuba, Italy, and France have demonstrated considerable research accomplishments in sport psychology. These countries receive research funding from government sources as well as generate research in their respective colleges and universities. It is important to note that within the American scientific community there is general consensus that a gap exists between the acquisition of new theoretical knowledge and the time that theory is put into practice. Most of the leading scientific communities in other nations do not have as wide a gap as exists in the United States. However, stringent government control in the United States relative to the use of human subject research could account for the scientific gap between theory and practice. Although information from the Soviet Union and other Eastern bloc countries in regard to sport psychology is very limited, the reader is encouraged to examine the following, but by no means comprehensive, sources for current basic and applied research in sport psychology: *Journal of Sport Behavior; Perceptual and Motor Skills; Journal of Sport Psychology; Yessis Review of Soviet Literature; International Journal of Sport Psychology; Sex Roles; Dissertation Abstracts International;* and *Completed Research in Health, Physical Education, and Recreation.*

COLEMAN R. GRIFFITH

Although the first psychological research specific to sport in the United States was conducted by Triplett in 1897, the honor of being America's first sport psychologist belongs to Professor Coleman R. Griffith (Kroll and Lewis 1970). As the first American to intensively investigate the formal study of the psychological aspects of sport, Professor Griffith began his investigation in 1918 at the University of Illinois. His research efforts, initially directed to some of the psychological factors involved in basketball and football, attracted the attention of the director of athletics, George Huff. It is evident that Huff was somewhat of a visionary in regard to recognizing the enormous impact sport psychology would eventually have.

Professor Griffith was a prolific scholar. After receiving his Ph.D. from the University of Illinois in 1920, he stayed at the University until his retirement in 1953. In 1938 his athletic research laboratory was closed; from 1944 to 1953 Professor Griffith was provost of the university.

In one of Griffith's first experiments, he utilized a Sanborn Reaction Timer to measure the reaction time of football players at the Illinois Athletic Field (Griffith 1930, 35). According to Griffith:

Some attempt was made to divide men into groups according to their "quickness," but the formal measurements were liberally interpreted and modified by what the coaches already knew of the physical and mental traits of the men under examination. The one fact that appeared independent of these "interpretations" came during the second year, when a rather significant difference in the reaction time of the men's two squads seemed to be correlated with pronounced difference in the success [athletic] attained during the two seasons. That is, the squad of men with the shorter reaction times seemed to be more successful than the squad with the longer reaction times. Further studies and observations were made in vision and attention, the former with a view to helping . . . to make a more skillful use of the whole field of vision in sizing up a situation or play, and the latter in selecting those types of formations and shifts which offered to the opposing team the most confusing spread of apprehension or span of attention.

It seems rather ironic that Griffith's work and interest in studying and analyzing the field of vision in relation to constructing shifts and formations in order to *confuse* and exasperate the opposition over a half century ago is remarkably similar in design and purpose to the multiple and complex shifts and formations utilized by the National Football League's Dallas Cowboys. It is of interest to note that several national football league teams have utilized, for quite some time, sport psychology and psychometrics.

Dr. Griffith taught a special section of that traditional and most often required "Introduction to Psychology" course that almost all students take; however, this special section was reserved strictly for athletes. In the fall of 1923, this course was specifically modified and changed into a new course titled "Psychology of Athletics" (Griffith 1930, 35). The approach of "Psychology of Athletics" was to examine and analyze psychological data and theories by specifically utilizing the athletic environment rather than general society. The content of "Psychology of Athletics" included attention span, emotion, vision, reaction time, and reviewing current literature that was relative to the psychology of sport.

From a pedagogical position, Dr. Griffith believed it necessary to present and analyze various problems and methods that coaches deal with on a regular basis. An example provided by Griffith (1930, 39) relative to coaching methods of the day addressed the "effect of fear and of related emotional conditions upon the rate of learning and upon the retention of habits." The end result was a book titled *Psychology of Coaching,* a series of observations on what the various coaches at the University of Illinois did to prepare their teams.

In 1925, George Huff approached Professor Griffith with a plan for establishing an athletic research laboratory which "would devote itself to problems in psychology and physiology of athletic activity quite independently of any attempt to create bigger and better athletic teams" (Griffith 1930, 36). The laboratory was established in 1925 and located in the newly completed men's gymnasium. According to Griffith, "so far as we have been able to determine, the Illinois laboratory is the second psychological laboratory devoted wholly to problems in athletics. There is, at the Coaching school in Berlin, Germany, a psychological laboratory in connection with a half dozen other laboratories and clinics. . . . " Griffith's laboratory consisted of one room (550 square feet) specifically designed for use as a workshop, animal laboratory, and physiology lab. A rat colony from the Wistar Institute was used by Griffith for learning experiments, exercise effects, and similar research studies.

THEORY DEVELOPMENT

Physical education is a unique and important academic discipline in terms of methodology and mission; as a scholarly area of research and presentation, physical education is both interdisciplinary and intradisciplinary. In the same mode that exercise physiology utilizes the research methods of the parent discipline of physiology, sport psychology appears to have embraced the parent discipline of psychology as opposed to finding a permanent home in physical education. Professionals in both academic areas, physical education and psychology, have chosen sport psychology as their primary research and teaching interest. One of the results of this multipronged approach to the investigation of sport psychology, in historical terms, is the development of appropriate methodologies with which to actually study and research the area and the construction and application of a sound theoretical basis. Are both physical education and psychological theories equally utilized? Psychological theory has been the dominant force primarily because of theory development. Theories and methodologies have changed over the years, as reflected in the different thrusts that sport psychology has undertaken. It should be noted that upon the demise of Professor Griffith's athletic research laboratory in 1938, interest and research in sport psychology in the United States became dormant for a number of years.

Bird and Ross (1984) and Landers (1982) provide an analysis of the theory building and development in sport psychology. According to Landers, the development of a theoretical basis for sport psychology, commonly referred to as theory testing, can be divided into three periods. During the period between 1950 and 1965, the majority of research was oriented toward developing an empirical approach in order to assess personality types. In regard to this initial thrust, Bird and Ross (1984, 1, 2) state that "typical comparisons were those made between groups such as athletes and nonathletes or elite and beginning participants in the same sport. The assessment instruments employed were generally standardized tests of a multivariate nature. The basis of test selection was availability rather than theoretically based." The information deduced from this type of data collection method was at best inconclusive, and personality testing remains an intriguing but still inconclusive area for sport psychologists. Because of the unsatisfactory results of personality testing and the recognized lack of theoretical approach, the majority of sport psychology research deviated from personality testing between the mid 1960s and mid 1970s and proceeded to move toward one of two major research thrusts—theory testing and Interactionism.

Landers (1982) as reported by Bird and Ross (1984, 1, 2) states, "Theory testing, as it was conceived at the time, generally involved attempts at testing existing theories from the parent discipline [Psychology] to determine their value and in providing a theoretical basis for sport psychology and motor performance. One of the premises being that once workable theories from the parent discipline were determined appropriate for basic research in sport psychology and motor behavior, the application of the findings would become part of the tools and techniques of applied sport psychology. The primary examples of such theory borrowing were drive theory and allied studies which tested the social facilitation effects as they were thought to affect motor skill acquisition. The overall results generated on the basis of such endeavors were rather discouraging. . . . As a result, similar to the empirical atheoretical framework which preceded it, the laboratory oriented, theory based approach also fell out of scientific favor."

During this same period, Landers (1982) identified Interactionism as the other, and still continuing, form of research. After examination, analysis, and operational research efforts in atheoretical personality testing and the subsequent but brief interest in theory borrowing, sport psychology researchers turned "their attention to the task of attempting to select and test one or two psychological factors which seemed to be systematically related to . . . performance" (Bird and Ross 1984, 2). Interactionism attempts to study and determine the extent, if any, that one or two psychological factors such as anxiety or self-concept have upon performance in a specific setting. Settings and all their attendant environmental contents are thought to have a direct influence on the performance of an individual relative to the psychological state of the individual. For instance, a great basketball player with constant high anxiety and low self-esteem who is about to compete for the league title on a neutral court or hostile court could be a research topic in Interactionism (person vs. situation). What is the perceived value of the results and intent of Interactionism relative to sport psychology or motor behavior? According to Bird and Ross (1984, 2), "Much worthwhile evidence is still being conducted from the interactionist point of view. However, the results of the vast majority of those studies have allowed for neither descriptions of motor performance effects or greater insights into individuals' relevant perceptions of situations. They [Interactionist researchers] have not allowed us to explain what it is that anxiety does within the person [athlete] that causes differential performance as a function of identifiable levels of anxiety."

From 1977 to the present (Bird and Ross, 1984; Landers 1982), theoretical research in sport psychology has been minimal. In its place are a pronounced interest and emphasis in the applied area of sport psychology in terms of establishing communication, goal-setting, intervention strategies, mental rehearsal, etc. Martens (1979, 56) expresses his concerns about the relevance of sterile controlled laboratory research in sport psychology in regard to application to important problems in sport:

> . . . I have doubts about the snapshot model of linear causation so fundamental to laboratory experimentation, doubts indeed that the categories of ANOVA with its neatly isolated independent and dependent variables can provide a useful model of what goes on in the personal and social world of sport. I have misgivings about the use and deception, and more generally with the manipulations used in laboratory studies. In fact, I have grave doubts about the utility of laboratory research for most of sport psychology.

In concert with the recent shift from the theoretical to the applied has been "the tendency to disfavor the laboratory in favor of the field and an associated decrease in attempts at theory building specific to motor skill performance" (Bird and Ross 1984, 2). In tune with the times, Professor John Silva at the University of North Carolina has formed the Association for the Advancement of Applied Social Psychology, which holds promise for both the researcher and the practitioner.

PROSPECTS FOR THE FUTURE

When analyzing the historical evolution of sport psychology, one could conclude that the research and applied nature of the discipline has, and may well continue to be, multidirectional and multidimensional. Some may feel that, because of the various directions in terms of methodology and theory that have been tried and disregarded over the years, sport psychology is fragmented and in a state of chaos, while others will undoubtedly view this situation as intellectually healthy and stimulating. However, it would appear unlikely that the professionals (athletes, coaches, professors, teachers, researchers) interested in and involved with sport psychology as a field of study would ever say the historical evolution and future prospects are severely limited. An innovative and yet seemingly obvious proposal is the construction of a new and potentially dynamic paradigm in sport psychology that was presented by Bird and Ross (1984), who proposed that physical educators develop theories indigenous to their own discipline and interest and not borrow from the parent discipline (psychology). From both a pure research and applied perspective, their proposal is timely. Some psychologists engaged in research in human performance appear to have little tolerance or respect for physical education professionals regarding their knowledge base of psychology in general and human behavior in particular and, again, there may be merit in their assessment. On the other side of the coin, there are coaches, athletes, and other physical education professionals who seem to be uncomfortable with psychologists in terms of what psychologists claim they can do to enhance athletic performance; there is an enormous difference between "knowing about" and "knowing how." For the most part, coaches and athletes may not be too receptive to a clinical psychologist (sport psychologist) who arrives on the field and insists he or she can help both coaches and athletes especially if the sport psychologist does not have a background in competitive athletics. Then again, a psychologist who has a case load of patients who are in the midst of and adjusting to divorce doesn't necessarily have to have gone through a divorce in order to help his or her patients.

The relationship between the parent discipline of psychology and the physical education profession/discipline has been rather tenuous and rocky. There is a solid historical relationship between psychology and physical education when viewed through the compatible and related areas of sport psychology and motor learning. Although the parent discipline of psychology has supplied the initial theoretical constructs and research designs, physical education may soon develop and utilize sport psychology theory indigenous to physical education in general and sports in particular. As a result, basic research and application of sport psychology techniques and tools could originate from several sources independently as well as collectively. This concept represents the possibility of a tremendous expansion and development of the field with enormous potential for increasing both the body of knowledge, coaching expertise, and athletic performance.

The practice of sport psychology is an important area in sports medicine as reflected by the extensive utilization of sport psychologists by virtually every United States Olympic team and many professional athletes. The United States Olympic Committee has established categories for three different types of sport psychologists—clinical, educational, and research—which reinforces the importance of and scholarly preparation that is necessary for an effective professional sport psychologist. Although the historical distance between Professor Coleman Griffith's sport psychology laboratory and the "state of the art" as practiced by today's sport psychology professionals is brief (fifty years), the interest and progress have been exceptional. Youth sports, interscholastic athletics, and intercollegiate sports are just beginning to utilize, understand, and appreciate what applied sport psychology can offer.

chapter *3*

Sociology of Women Athletes: Social Status and Societal Expectations

Based on participant intensity, fan interest, technical sophistication, logistical support, financial expenditure, and level of athletic competition (amateur and professional), America is generally considered the premier sporting nation in the world. However, in terms of gender participation in sport specific to societal acceptance, encouragement, recognition, and overall program of support, a number of sport sociologists may be hard pressed to rank the United States in the top five regarding opportunity, acceptance, and equality of women athletes.

The status of women in the United States has centered around the male-developed concept of an appropriate female; women are perceived as the weaker sex, and, as a result, societal expectations (constructed by males) are in line with this traditional societal norm. General societal views as expressed and reinforced in school, church, home, mass media, books, political orientation, and social engagements act as a powerful stimulus as well as a deterrent to prescribing appropriate behavior and accepted pursuits. Although the women's movement, as represented by the National Organization for Women (NOW), and other feminist action groups have raised the public consciousness of inequality, major changes in society are slow in coming.

A significant amount of social upheaval and resulting change in America has occurred during the past twenty-five years. At one time, not so long ago, it was unusual to find a career woman executive and, if so, it was indeed rare that she was married. However, due in part to Affirmative Action, women's rights organizations, and perhaps the social revolution of the 1960s and early 1970s, the career woman executive (married and unmarried) has become symbolic in our society, as evidenced by the "Yuppie Movement." Societal norms and expectations continue to undergo significant change as reflected in societal viewpoints regarding appropriate behavior and role expectation.

WHO WILL COACH WOMEN ATHLETES?

Fifteen years ago a male coach who wanted to establish himself as a respected coach among his peers would in all probability have opted to coach males instead of females. However, how many male coaches are coaching girls' high school sports and women's intercollegiate sports today? How many women express a preference to be coached by a man? Fifteen years ago a male coach who chose to coach women in college or high school would in most cases have been under close scrutiny by the community and school. It must be remembered that, according to many feminists, males set up these seemingly appropriate societal norms. In a short fifteen years these societal values and norms relative to the idea and peer acceptance of male coaches of female athletes have undergone a 180-degree change; male coaches of female athletes have been bestowed "most favored status" by the male coaching fraternity. In the 14 October 1985 edition of *The NCAA News* appeared an article headlined "Women's Coaching Opportunities Dwindling, Report Says." The report, which originated from DePauw University, stated that male coaches are moving into coaching jobs that were once held by women. The report indicated that basketball is perhaps the most visible. The author of the article, Judith Jenkins George, associate professor of health, physical education, and recreation at DePauw, presented the following significant findings:

1. Despite the growing numbers of team sports for women, there is a noticeable erosion of opportunities for women coaches.
2. Ten years ago, only 5 percent of Indiana's high school women's basketball teams were coached by men. A year ago, that number had reached 68 percent. Male coaches had also taken over in golf, cross country and swimming, and it was about 50–50 in softball.
3. In 1977–78, 21 percent of the women's basketball teams at the college level nationally were coached by men. That figure was up to 35 percent by 1983–84, with increasing male roles in at least six other sports.
4. In the Big Ten Conference, men coached 40 percent or more of at least five women's sports.
5. Nearly 87 percent of all coed colleges and universities have their women's athletic programs directed by males. Almost 40 percent of all schools have no females involved in their women's programs, e.g. administration.
6. The study also showed that men attributed the decline in female coaches to a perceived lack of qualified women coaches and the unwillingness of women to recruit and travel. Women, on the other hand, felt they were being overlooked because of the strength of 'the old-boys' club network and the absence or weakness of an old-girls club or network [*The NCAA News*, 14 October 1985, p. 3].

Professor George states that "administrators may have become gender blind to the large pool of skilled women in the job market" (1985, 3). Perhaps one of the more distressing scenarios based upon the declining number of women in the coaching ranks is the absence of female role models. According to Professor George (1985, 3), ". . . it is important to have women coaching women because women need to have other women as role models. Girls and women should have experiences in not just being the followers of male leaders. They need to be inspired by female leaders as well." Just as male coaches have served as role models for young boys and men, female athletes need to identify with women coaches as positive role models.

Why is it almost unheard of for a woman to be a head coach of male athletes?

For a long time, sport was considered a male bastion for the exclusive socialization of males into society and as a medium for the education of the male in terms of maintaining the traditional social order. With few exceptions, female athletes were shunned and presented as atypical. According to Leonard (1980, 192), "The traditional role of women in sport is not that of a competitor. Rather, women have been forced off to the sideline to fill some kind of supportive-affective role. This parallels the societal expectations of females. . . ."

One premise that continues to be presented relative to achieving equality and parity in sport, specific to gender, is that when equal numbers of women and men play sport, sport equality will have been obtained. This premise is very simplistic and superficial. Bryson (1983, 8) disagrees with this premise and goes on to state that sport contributes to male dominance in general. According to Bryson, "It is suggested that sport serves to ritually support an aura of male competence and superiority in publicly acclaimed skills, and a male monopoly of aggression and violence. A corollary of this is an inferiorization of women and their skills, and their isolation from their ultimate basis of power—physical force. These effects act to support patriarchal ideology and are usefully seen as occurring through a traditional process. . . ."

SOCIAL STATUS AND ROLE OF WOMEN ATHLETES

Leonard (1980, 192) states, "Females . . . seemingly have to go through a whole process of social-psychological redefinition to participate in sport. In a sense they are forced to prove their femininity, which illustrates that femininity is not a characteristic inherent in womanhood, but rather a function of social and psychological definition."

The impact and influence of significant others* (SO's) in terms of encouragement, discouragement, and indifference relative to athletic participation in general, and female athletic participation in particular, falls within the area of sociology known as role conflict. The appropriate and inappropriate behavior of males and females is based upon what is considered socially and culturally acceptable; e.g., women who want to compete in wrestling would likely experience "role conflict" since wrestling is an activity that is socially acceptable for males but not yet entirely appropriate for women. Weiss and Knoppers's sport-specific and gender-specific study titled "The Influence of Socializing Agents on Female Collegiate Volleyball Players" (1982) examines the role of significant others and the socialization of female volleyball players. The investigators administered a sport socialization questionnaire to ninety-five athletes during the 1979 Big Ten Volleyball Championship. The questionnaire was designed to measure the degree of influence of socializing agents on active sport involvement. According to the researchers, the statistical finding of the study indicated that the athletes were surrounded by SO's who strongly supported and encouraged their participation throughout their lives. An important outcome of this study may have a direct impact upon the early years of an aspiring young female athlete. As presented by Weiss and Knoppers (1982, 267–79):

*Significant others can be fathers, mothers, sisters, brothers, coaches, teachers.

"Multiple-regression analysis revealed that of the SO's who supported participation, parents, peers, and physical education teachers/coaches collectively had a significant influence on sport involvement only during the athlete's childhood. Brothers were significant agents of sport socialization during the athlete's childhood and college years; no other agents reached significance for any of the life cycle stages."

This study would suggest that, given the interest and support of the athlete and SO's, the channeling of the young aspiring female athlete into socially acceptable sport activity may occur during this time of the life cycle and is significantly affected by people (SO's) who are perceived as close and thus influential.

Societal logic (logic being a relative term) as a culturally defined sanction has designated certain sports as acceptable in terms of competition between female athletes. Tennis, field hockey, golf, figure skating, gymnastics, and swimming have received the societal seal of approval in America. Overtly or covertly, these culturally approved sports and their appropriate attire apparently continue to reinforce and promote the traditional image and socially correct concept of femininity; tennis, golf, figure skating, and field hockey utilize skirts while swimming and gymnastics rely on functional Lycra suits and leotards and convey feminine qualities. "According to cultural norms [Leonard 1980, 193], however, there are certain activities which, historically, have not been acceptable for females. These include bodily contact (basketball), application of body force to some heavy object (discus, shotput), projection of the body into or through space for long distances (track and field events—although springboard diving is considered acceptable), and cooperative face-to-face opposition in situations in which some bodily contact may occur (soccer, softball, basketball)." Volleyball could be considered as an appropriate sport for women although the aggressive nature of spiking, bodily contact with the floor, and the ability to jump has raised questions of appropriateness apparently based upon traditional ill-founded societal logic. It is an absolute necessity for a coach to be both aware of and sensitive to societal and culturally prescribed norms, values, and expectations and how they can influence and impact the future of young athletes especially when coaching in the junior high and high school ranks.

Snyder and Spreitzer (1983) analyzed the findings of five surveys that were conducted over the past decade specific to social acceptance of female athletes. Their findings showed "a clear pattern of differential attitudes depending on the type of sport." According to Snyder and Spreitzer, the general public will favorably accept female athletes in tennis, swimming, and gymnastics. Reservations were expressed concerning females who participated in basketball, softball, and track and field. However, the evidence suggests that the attitude of the general public has become more favorable toward female athletes during the last ten years. Parity and acceptance have yet to be achieved.

Social status in America, for various reasons, has a significant impact upon the way we perceive people and our behavior toward and within certain social groups. While social and cultural norms, values, and expectations support the aspirations of those of us who want to become doctors, lawyers, professors, scientists, and corporate tycoons, these same factors can easily discourage athletic competition for girls and women. Although more women than ever are serious joggers, soccer players, tennis players, golfers, etc., and again recognizing that these norms, values, and expectations are socially changing for the benefit of everybody, there will continue to be societal restraints that adversely impact the status and support of women athletes.

As the proverbial melting pot of the world, America has a rich heritage of cultural diversification. Many of the ethnic groups in this country still continue to abide by culturally defined values which traditionally relegate the status and role of women to a secondary position. Many families who are immigrants as well as first- and second-generation citizens from Asia, the Middle East, Africa, and some Latin American nations may be surprised at the interest and importance we attach as a society to sports competition and the encouragement and support we provide for our athletes. The intensity and expectations we now have toward our female athletes may well be very uncomfortable to many new arrivals in the United States based upon the cultural position and status of women in their country of origin, e.g., Middle Eastern countries. It is not unusual to discover a young woman athlete with a lot of potential in a junior high school or high school physical education class who is discouraged by her family from trying out for a team. Coaches are often torn between respecting the beliefs of the family and attempting to open the doors of access to sports for the young girl against the wishes of the family. However, when a young woman from a different cultural background or one who hails from what many may refer to as a "traditional patriarchal American family" expresses her intent to "try out," the coach should be aware that in all probability (perhaps depending upon the selected sport) she had to gain the approval of the family and this approval may have been very difficult to finally attain. The psychological state that the young athlete arrives with, in addition to having a biological nature, is also molded and directed by both societal and/or cultural values and norms. For the immediate future, not only might she be walking on "cultural eggshells," she will be sensitive to her social status among her peers as both athlete, student, and social being. How those people important to her and her own peer group perceive the status of being a female athlete will most likely have a major impact upon her future athletic success and her immediate and future growth as a person. This seems to be especially true in high school, where social status tends to dominate reason.

Role conflict, an area that involves appropriate and expected roles that members of a society are expected to adhere to but instead deviate from, is a dynamic and important area of investigation in sport sociology. In Anthrop and Allison's study (1983), titled "Role Conflict and the High School Female Athlete," 133 female high school varsity athletes completed a thirty-three item questionnaire designed to determine perceived and experienced role conflicts of female athletes based upon their socioeconomic background, and instances of encouragement or discouragement from significant others during their athletic careers. The findings of this study are particularly interesting and quite relevant for coaches: 32 percent of the female athletes said that they perceived little or no problem with role conflict and 50 percent had experienced little or no role conflict. Seventeen percent said perceived role conflict was a great or very great problem with 11 percent actually experiencing role conflict to the same degree—great or very great. The athletes indicated that they actually perceived greater role conflict than they experienced. However, female athletes who chose to participate simultaneously in both socially approved sports (swimming, gymnastics, etc.) and nonsocially approved sports (basketball, track and field, etc.) experienced more role conflict than athletes electing to compete in only one sport, whether socially approved or disapproved. Although role conflict can manifest itself in many forms and from many sources, the results of this study would suggest that coaches may well expect the possibility that female athletes who elect to compete in more than one sport may experience role conflict (perceived or expected) more so than athletes who choose to participate in one sport only.

Salisbury and Passer (1982, 413–426) conducted additional research on role conflict, gender-role attitudes, and female athletes. They examined the relationship between women's gender-role attitudes and their participation in what they considered stereotypical feminine and unfeminine sports competition. The gender-role attitudes of 189 female athletes (aged 19-65 years) and 184 high school female athletes (14-18 years) were sampled from seven sports: basketball, soccer, volleyball, track and field, tennis, softball, and rugby. "The gender-role attitudes were assessed using a short form of the Attitudes Toward Women Scale. The perceived stereotypic femininity of each sport was determined by questionnaire ratings completed by a subsample of 126 athletes." The results of the study are of significant interest to coaches and athletes alike in terms of expectations and trends that have been scientifically evaluated. According to Salisbury and Passer (1982, 486–93), "Findings from the adult athletes support the prediction that women who participated in traditionally unfeminine sports would have more liberal gender-role attitudes than women who competed in feminine sports. No relationship was obtained for the high school athletes. Overall, the findings provide little support for the notion that women participating in traditionally unfeminine sports use general sex role attitudes to compensate for gender-inappropriate behavior."

It could be inferred that women athletes at the collegiate level and perhaps beyond who compete in traditionally unfeminine sports may shun appropriate sex role attitudes in order to confirm the fact that they are female after competing in gender-inappropriate sport. With reference to the position that, in general terms, males are socialized into society via sport and women are socialized away from sport, Leonard (1980, 198) notes that "the experience of black women in sport seems to be an exception to the general socialization of females away from sport. Some authors believe it might be easier for the black female to be accepted in the world of sport." According to Hart (1971) as cited in Leonard (1980), "There is a startling contrast between the black and white female athlete. In the Black Community it seems that a woman can be strong and competent in sport and still not deny her womanliness. She can even win respect and high status. . . ." Leonard (1980, 199) calls attention to the "scarcity of empirical data regarding female socialization via sport. Most of the information isn't the result of vigorously conducted scientific investigation but, instead, speculation. Time and opportunity will tell if women become more dominant and aggressive as a result of sport participation."

In terms of women who participate in sport as members of a voluntary support group, it has long been thought that voluntary membership in such an association (sport and nonsport) is linked with increased personal satisfaction. Based upon this premise, it could be suggested that mothers and female SO's who voluntarily elect to help out in numerous ways at athletic competitions enjoy positive enhancement of their own socioemotional well-being. It could also be expected that because of the SO's' perceived socioemotional well-being via sport association, this situation could provide positive support for young female athletes.

Rosenberg and Chelete (1980) criticized empirically based studies that cite socioemotional well-being as a product of voluntary sports association on the basis of the small population sample, narrow age range of the subjects, and the lack of a representative geographical sample. As a result, Rosenberg and Chelete conducted a study utilizing two cross-sectional samples of the American adult population consisting of 3,020 respondents for the purpose of testing the relationship of the type of voluntary association (sport vs. nonsport) with avowed happiness. The results contradicted the researchers' earlier studies. According to Rosenberg and Chelete (1980, 263–275), "Membership in a sport [vs. nonsport] voluntary association did not lead to substantively higher levels of life satisfaction. For women, the relationship between membership in a sport voluntary association and avowed happiness was negative."

Based upon their findings, it would appear that coaches who work with booster clubs and other organizations of this type should be sensitive to the distinct possibility that the women involved may not be receiving the positive socialization and emotional benefits that a coach may wish to believe occur as a result of association. In addition, a coach should not automatically expect that, just because a young female athlete's mother or other female SO's are involved in a voluntary sport association, a specific amount of participant reinforcement support, encouragement, etc. is to be expected. How much positive reinforcement for both male and female athletic participation should a coach expect the majority of volunteer women to provide if there is, as the investigators claim, a negative return on avowed happiness? The studies are conflicting and therefore coaches should take nothing for granted in this area. Promote your program with respect to the positive effects your athletes will receive. This may serve to increase avowed happiness on the part of volunteers with the possibility of a corresponding level of encouragement and support for the athlete or the home front. This should have a positive effect on the athlete and enhance motivation on the part of all participants, coaches, athletes, parents, and volunteers.

SOCIETAL EXPECTATIONS AND NORMS

The need to achieve is both intrinsic and extrinsic and often provides the impetus for deciding to become an athlete. Achievement motivation is a term that initially would appear to comprise psychological rather than sociological parameters (Leonard 1980, 199). Achievement motivation has a high degree of relevance with reference to the participation and involvement of women athletes. Birrell (1978, 153–171) presents two general myths concerning women:

1. They do not have a high need to achieve.
2. Achievement motivations are developed solely as a result of early childhood training and that level is irreversibly fixed at an early age.

Definitive conclusions based on the relationship between achievement motivation and subsequent gravitation to sport, regardless of gender, have yet to be determined. The reasons which influence both men and women to become athletes are numerous; however, many reasons still exist that discourage girls and women from competing in athletics. Men are expected to become involved in and identified with sports, while females may have access to sports but lack complete acceptance.

There are still a number of widely held, although scientifically inaccurate, beliefs that many parents continue to accept as compelling reasons for discouraging their daughters from athletic competition. Although their reasons appear primarily subjective rather than objective, the fact that their rationale represents societal dogma and cultural values and norms can make the coaches' job quite difficult in terms of educating students, athletes, and parents about the positive outcomes of athletic participation. The concerns include:

1. Sports competition is physically dangerous; strenuous physical activity will harm the delicate female reproduction system.
2. Women athletes are genetic and cultural physical freaks.
3. It is abnormal for girls to be interested in sports.
4. Females who compete in sports eventually lose their femininity and become masculine.
5. Girls and women were not meant to become athletes.
6. Girls and women should be oriented toward the traditional role of becoming a wife and parent, not an athlete.

As ironic as it may seem, Victorian women physical educational professionals did as much to discourage and suppress the desire for serious athletic competition for females as did society in general. "The early sport magazines, under the control of female physical educators, reinforced the traditional images of women as weak and inferior to men physically and emotionally. Their editorials urged a de-emphasis of collegiate sport for women. A study of advertisements showing women participating in sport from 1900 to 1968 in the *Ladies Home Journal* revealed that in no year did the total exceed 20 out of an average total of 1,400 advertisements" (Leonard 1980, 200).

Considerable debate has occurred about the appropriate societal role of women and men as determined by their biological differences. Consequently, for centuries women have been categorized by society as the weaker sex, emotionally inclined to behave irrationally, and athletically inferior to men. The question should be raised, are males and females different (other than secondary sex characteristics)? Males and females differ very little, if at all, in terms of learning and motivation. Wyrick (1971, 21–30) described how sex differences between males and females affect the research in physical education. Wyrick confirmed the idea ". . . that there are many variables in which men and women have been found to be statistically different, and suggested . . . that it is important to determine whether the environment is actually creating differences that do not exist biologically."

Miller (1974, 24) provides an analysis of the difference between male and female athletes specific to the coaching of men and women as follows: "Perhaps the significance of these reports is simply that, for whatever reasons, cultural or otherwise, women are different than men, and the same generalization regarding the psychology of coaching cannot be applied to both." There are differences; however, are the differences due to biologic origins, sociocultural influences, or both?

Sage (1980) administered a questionnaire to 268 female and 497 male varsity intercollegiate athletes representing eleven sports that focused on previous and present participation in sports and orientation toward sport and demographic data. The study yielded significant differences in the response profiles of male and female athletes. "Males expressed a stronger orientation toward skill and victory than did females. In general, neither group endorsed an extreme 'play fair' nor an extreme 'quest for victory' orientation. Both groups emphasized the skill dimension of the sport, stressing playing as well as one is able" (Sage 1980, 44). Bird and Williams (1980) investigated attributions made by 192 males and 192 females in four age groups: 7–9, 10–12, 13–15, and 16–18 years old. The purpose of the study was to investigate the attributions regarding identical sport outcomes achieved by a male or a female subject who either had success or failure in three sports. The results of their study indicate that "differential patterns of attributions did occur for male and female outcomes as a function of the age of the evaluator. By age 13 and continuing through age 18, male performance was explained on the basis of effort, whereas by age 16 female outcomes were explained in terms of luck" (Bird and Williams 1980, 319–22).

Societal role expectation and appropriate gender behavior and inappropriate gender behavior relative to female athletes will seemingly forever remain a timely and often-discussed topic within coaching, sport sociology, sport psychology, and the social psychology of sport. The continuing investigation and discussion focusing on the similarities and differences between male and female athletes in athletic performance and the correct method of psychological preparation of women athletes is not one-dimensional. The concept of androgyny as a basis for preparing athletes for competition psychologically is gaining in terms of interest and will be presented in the next chapter.

chapter *4*

Psychology of Women Athletes: Trends and Issues

Criticism of gender-specific training regarding the mental preparation of athletes is supported by some coaches, researchers, and athletes who lean toward the concept and practice of an androgynous approach to physical training and mental preparation. The primary premise of the androgynous concept of competition has psychological and biological bases. Androgyny from a psychological perspective has little, if anything, to do with biology, but is based upon the traditional societal nature of appropriate sex role orientation versus a holistic, gender-neutral androgynous perspective which, in general terms, does not recognize sex role differentiation based upon gender. The biological position indicates that there are more biological similarities than differences between men and women. However, because that may be the case, recognition of the sociological forces suggests that significant differences do exist that may preclude the use of psychological androgyny as a universal model for the training and preparation of athletes. It would appear that many coaches and athletes, male and female, remain uncomfortable with androgyny and do not fully understand its use in sport.

What is it that specifically differentiates between masculine and feminine characteristics and behaviors and thus promotes a different psychological and sociocultural system based on gender? More importantly, how is the distinction between sex and gender represented? Biological differences between male and female are obvious. Basic anatomy, physiology, and casual observation will establish the fact that internal and external reproductive organs are different, as are chromosome structure and hormone distribution. These biological characteristics determine the sex of a person, but do not determine gender. The concept and development of gender is presented succinctly by Murphy (1984, 187–210) when analyzing the biological formation of sex and the social process of gender construction: "The sociologist, however, is more concerned with the analysis of gender: the social meanings that are given to these biological differences. Members of societies attribute certain characteristics to the individuals of the different sexes; we assign tasks and ascribe behavior and attitudes. This social construction of roles, norms, and values make up what we call the social organization of gender in society."

The composition or makeup of a particular athlete will be derived from that person's sex, gender construction, and psychological state in addition to athletic ability. The assessment of psychological and psychosociological characteristics of women and men specific to the attainment of optimal athletic performance in terms of the coaching process is an area of investigation and practice that continues to hold promise. Dickason (1977, 79) states that "recent scholarship has widely investigated the legal, economic, and religious status of women in various societies and current research is exploring the biological and psychological characteristics of women and men to see if there are any innately feminine and masculine traits. But it is obvious from the level of current debate that final answers are not yet available on this question. There is, in fact, much contradictory evidence."

Dickason's statement still holds true today.

Many theories exist in an attempt to explain and maintain "gender behavior." Two major theories that attempt to explain this supposed difference between men and women are Accidentalist theory and Essentialist theory. "Accidentalists believe that all masculine and feminine qualities are non-essential properties of what it means to be a man or a woman. They argue that both men and women are primarily shaped by the surrounding culture, and that neither sex is formed with any sex linked psychological characteristics" (Dickason 1977, 79). Accidental theorists and proponents of psychological androgyny are compatible since both assume that the influence and impact of the surrounding culture rather than some innate tendency produce gender differences. According to Dickason (1977, 80): "Essentialists take the counter position, and believe in definite, universal masculine and feminine characteristics. They cite studies that link the presence of male sex hormones to increased aggressive behavior (Hutt 1972), and they emphasize the agreement among cultures on feminine and masculine identification. . . . Psychosexual neutrality at birth is a misconception; the concepts of feminine and masculine contain specific qualities that are independent of cultural differences." Essentialist theory states that there are innate psychological differences between males and females that are *further* defined by the dominant culture.

Upon initial observation, the majority of veteran male coaches appears to identify with the Essentialists' belief as opposed to the Accidentalist-Androgynous model. Some coaches may be divided between Essentialist theory and Accidentalist-Androgynous theory when psychologically preparing athletes.

The idea that sex roles, characteristics, and gender are linked is an area of research that is applicable and significant in terms of articulation and practice in physical education. Many males and females, however, are attempting to remain comfortable with their respective traditional gender roles and expectations based on sex and would seemingly be opposed to an androgynous society in general and the training of women athletes in particular. Androgyny is a model that will provide some select female athletes with a successful system of physiological and psychological training. These select women athletes are perceived as being sociologically and psychologically comfortable with their perceived role, status, and sexuality when placed in a competitive environment that incorporates both masculine and feminine characteristics. In addition, it would be expected that these select women athletes, as well as their male colleagues, be physiologically capable of serious training and performance expectations. Although androgynous training and coaching experiences are not yet considered the norm, it would appear that over a period of years androgynous preparation in sport may very well become state of the art. The concept and acceptance of androgyny in sport and culture is still too recent an arrival to categorically state that this method of training and coaching is better than other systems. However, some select women athletes may find an athletically androgynous training and coaching environment to be of more help and support than other traditional methods based primarily on gender roles.

PSYCHOLOGICAL AND SOCIOLOGICAL CONSIDERATIONS

Research on sex and gender roles suggests that the justification for maintaining the status quo is subject to serious question. By no means should the results of studies that support the traditional status quo of gender-specific psychological training or androgyny be accepted as conclusive. Research on the psychological preparation of women athletes from the position of both traditional, orthodox psychology and from the androgynous approach, which makes no distinction regarding psychological preparation based on gender, still needs to be conducted. However, it is absolutely crucial for coaches to understand that they cannot psychologically prepare all women athletes nor all male athletes the same way, androgynously or based on gender-sex role expectations. Although some female athletes will be comfortable with androgynous preparation, it can be assumed for a variety of reasons that many female athletes continue to prefer traditional training and coaching experiences and may not respond favorably to androgyny. A significant number of women athletes, for personal and/or societal reasons, elect to live via the traditional feminine gender roles regarding image and behavior and cannot be expected to be trained in an androgynous method.

In order to present androgyny as a concept, it will be useful to refer to work in this area (cited by Cox 1985) done by Helmreich and Spence, who in 1977 constructed a test, the Personal Attributes Questionnaire (PAQ), which was designed to classify people according to their own perceived sex roles. The PAQ was based upon several theoretical concepts developed by Bakan (1966) and cited by Cox (1985). According to Bakan, all humans are characterized as possessing two fundamental qualities, agency and communion. Agency reflects an awareness of self and is linked to masculinity; it is manifested in "self-assertion, self-protection, and self-expansion." In contrast to agency, communion is linked to femininity and feminine principles. Communion traits are identified as selflessness and a concern for others.

As a result, masculinity and femininity become separate and distinct characteristics. However, possession of one does not necessarily eliminate the other. Cox (1985, 163) states that "individuals may possess factors associated with either or both of these dimensions of masculinity and femininity." The guiding principles for development of the PAQ were:

1. Masculine attributes are those characteristics considered to be socially desirable to both sexes, but found in greater abundance in males.
2. Feminine attributes are those characteristics considered to be socially desirable to both sexes, but found in greater abundance in females.

The PAQ developed by Helmreich and Spence is composed of twenty-four items. Each item is measured by using a five-point/five-response selection format, with very submissive represented by A and very dominant represented by E, e.g. A, B, C, D, & E.

Based upon the subject's response to each of the twenty-four items, three scores are arrived at: femininity, masculinity, and sex-specific. The subject's score regarding masculinity, femininity, or sex-specific is dependent upon how *high* a score or rating the subject has chosen on the scale. However, "the sex-specific scale (masculine-feminine) is derived from questions that are considered to polarize the responses at either masculine or feminine. A high score on the sex-specific scale implies masculinity" (Cox 1985, 163). The next step was to develop a classification system that would permit the researchers to analyze their results and present their findings.

In 1977, Helmreich and Spence constructed a simple classification system for the masculine and feminine scores obtained from the PAQ. As described by Cox (1985, 163, 164):

> Subjects are first pooled according to their scores on the feminine and masculine scales. Next, the median for each pool is established and the subjects are classified as high or low according to the median split. Female subjects classified as high in femininity and low in masculinity would be categorized as feminine. Women low in femininity but high in masculinity would be categorized as masculine. High scores in both masculinity and femininity indicate androgyny. Since the items in both the feminine and masculine scales are considered socially desirable for both sexes, the androgynous classification should be very desirable for both men and women. Finally, subjects scoring low on both the feminine and masculine scales are classified as undifferentiated, since they are high in neither dimension.

The idea and basis of androgyny could well become a major component in sport as well as society. Androgyny is a measured human situation or condition in which an individual male or female achieves high ratings in both masculine and feminine characteristics as opposed to a purely masculine rating, which indicates high masculine traits, and low, if any, feminine traits. A purely feminine rating would indicate strong feminine traits but low, if any, masculine traits. Although the PAQ is utilized here as an aid to present the idea and concept of androgyny, it is by no means the only available tool to assess perceived sex roles. Bem (1974) developed an instrument, the Bem Sex Role Inventory (BSRI), a tool for measuring psychological androgyny. Cox (1985, 165) states that:

> The BSRI asks people to indicate on a seven-point scale how well each of sixty masculine, feminine, and neutral items describe them. On the basis of these responses, the subjects receive a femininity, masculinity, and androgyny rating. The masculinity and femininity scores indicate the extent to which a person endorses

masculine and feminine personality characteristics. The androgyny score indicates the degree to which the individual has both masculine and feminine characteristics.

From continuing discussions with colleagues and others in the field, the majority of male coaches and athletes view androgyny as a coaching tool and process of physical and mental preparation specific to females. It should be clear that androgyny is not restricted to females but can apply to males as well.

Sex role orientation (SRO) and sport selection with reference to the degree of psychological masculinity and/or femininity associated with specific sports have undergone investigation on several levels. A review of the research yields varied conclusions as illustrated by the following. Edwards et al. (1984) administered the Bem Sex Role Inventory (BSRI) to eighty-four female gymnasts. The results were compared with previously published studies on the SRO of female athletes and nonathletes in order to examine the relationship between female sex role orientation and status as an athlete in, in this case, eighty-four female gymnasts. The reader is cautioned not to draw concrete conclusions on a single study that utilized eighty-four subjects. However, suggestions and inferences may be drawn from studies of this nature. The data obtained from this study showed that the sex role orientation of the gymnasts was significantly different from that of the normative sample of college students and previously published sex role orientations of track and field athletes. The conclusions of this study support the hypothesis that sex role orientation may be a major factor and determinant in the selection of some, but not all, women's sports. Some of the gymnasts who were more masculine and less feminine in orientation suggested that strength and power attributes took priority in their decision to become competitive athletes.

Coaches may infer from this study that women gymnasts may have more masculine or androgynous characteristics than previously thought. The findings of this particular study were obtained from champion gymnasts (NCAA), not high school or junior college gymnasts, which, as always, should preclude an across-the-board generalization in regard to psychological preparation. Blucker and Hershberger (1983, 14) found that female athletes who are rated highly androgynous may possess higher self-esteem than female athletes who are considered to be more masculine or more feminine. A coach who is able to determine that the athletes on the team reflect feminine, masculine, or androgynous, gender roles, or a combination of the three should seriously consider, from a motivational and communicative standpoint, a multipsychological approach and technique when preparing athletes psychologically for competition.

A study on anxiety as influenced by feminine and masculine characteristics was conducted by Owie (1981). The BSRI was administered to forty-three female and thirty-four male undergraduate students in order to identify the subjects as possessing feminine or masculine orientations. A comparable number of subjects not identified in the study as either masculine or feminine as determined by the BSRI were given the Sport Competition Anxiety Test (SCAT). The results of this study indicated that males with masculine characteristics as a group are less susceptible to sport competition anxiety than females who are characterized by femininity. This study would seem to suggest that women athletes who regard themselves as feminine as opposed to androgynous are more likely to experience anxiety before and during competition. Based upon these findings, the coach should work on reducing anxiety in athletes individually as well as the team on a collective basis.

Colker and Windom (1980, 38) conducted research investigating self-esteem, psychological masculinity and femininity, and attitudes that female athletes have toward women. The study was done to examine the validity of various stereotypes. Their findings signaled a departure from similar studies and results. Seventy-one women college athletes who participated in crew, basketball, squash, and swimming were compared with a random group of 185 women from the same college. According to the results, female athletes were significantly less feminine than their college peers but not more masculine. Highly committed athletes, according to the study, were both more masculine and more feminine, as well as more profeminist.

Of historical interest, Berkey (1972, 51) stated that "the number of investigations designed to measure the specific effects of high-level athletic competition upon personality have been abundant. However, when questions referring to the female competition are posed, there is little literature available. . . ." One decade later this paucity of research has not changed significantly. Morgan (1972) and Williams (1978, 353–359) appear to support Berkey by referring to the fact that the number of investigations designed to obtain information that will enable us to understand the personality of the female athlete is minimal. This is further reinforced by Balazs (1975), who noted that psychological research directed to the study of high achievement on the part of women athletes is extremely limited. An examination of the sport psychology literature contained in *Psychological Abstracts* and *Dissertation Abstracts International* from 1980 to June 1985 oriented toward the general area of psychology and female athletes revealed that many of the studies appeared to be of similar interest and orientation, which could suggest a high instance of replication. It would appear that significant research investigations and advancement in the research area of the psychological preparation of women athletes have not yet been as fruitful as expected.

From a sociological basis it has long been recognized that, in general terms, our culture takes more interest in supporting the activities of male athletes than female athletes. This would help to explain the disproportionately high number of sport psychology research studies focusing on male athletes as opposed to female athletes. However, the most obvious fact is that, until recently, the number of women athletes engaged in serious competition has been minimal at best when compared to the number of males competing in sports. Researchers did not have access to a significant population of female athletes in order to conduct investigations. Although America is traditionally described as a cultural melting pot, our society appears to be trying to come to grips with the idea that women who elect to compete in athletics can have their femininity remain intact. As was presented earlier, centuries of reinforced role and behavior expectation based on gender have been continually reinforced. As a result, it can be expected that cultural attitudes toward female role expectation will often be different from attitudes and values the dominant culture imposes on males.

Berkey (1972), in one of the earliest articles focusing on sport psychology and women titled "Psychology of Women Who Compete," did not appear to endorse the androgynous position of some coaches and athletes. She provided the following response when asked why it is important for a coach to be aware of the personality difference of the competitor and if it will affect her play, especially during the important contest:

"Yes, I believe it will. It is also important to realize women are different than men as people and will be different than men as athletes. They will not test the same, I believe, due to the nature of our culture. So I do not think it is possible to pick up one of the latest books on Psychology of Coaching and really know how to apply the material to female athletes" (Berkey 1972, 4). Williams (1978, 353–359) provides further insight into the psychological preparation of the female athlete: "When questions referring to the female competitor are posed, there are relatively few answers available. We cannot generalize the findings on the male athlete to the female athlete unless we believe there are no sex differences in personality. Females have the same needs as males, and females will respond the same way to sport and coaching as males. Such assumptions remain to be proven."

It would seem logical to conclude that, with the absence of significant research (when compared to males) in the psychological and sociopsychological area of women and sport, the position that women athletes can be universally psychologically prepared for competition from an androgynous approach remains inconclusive. There are simply not enough data from research efforts that will answer the question conclusively. At this point in time, there is limited research to provide answers to all the questions about the psychology of competition as it applies to women. This dearth of research, however, is changing due to the emergence of serious athletic competition for women.

In reference to appropriate role behaviors and their influence in sport competition, Harris (1973, 197) states:

> the accepted pattern has been that sport involvement is male territory, that competitive athletics and participation in vigorous sport are prerogatives only of the male. . . . All too often it has been difficult for the skilled, athletic female to stay "feminine" and still gratify her need for high-level participation. If she desires to be successful in athletic competition, she must become more aggressive, dominant, achievement oriented; she must demonstrate tough-mindedness and endurance and be less afraid to take risks. These are the characteristics that are most often used to describe masculinity in American Society. . . . These traits are not the traditional ones revered in the female.

If athletes and coaches agree with Harris et al. that to achieve athletic success females must recognize, accept, and develop the traditional male traits of aggressiveness, dominance, achievement orientation, endurance, tough-mindedness, and a capacity for risks (traits which are culturally imposed on males by our society), it would appear to support the position of an androgynous orientation where male and female characteristics in each athlete are valued. However, will coaches ignore or dismiss significant factors affecting prescribed societal and cultural behavioral patterns that remain operational? Harris states that "until society recognizes that the female shares the same joys and satisfactions in sports as the male, and until society allows her to pursue these without questioning why she might wish to do so, the female will continue to evidence psychological responses which distinguish her from the male." Harris's statement presents the position that, due to our societal and cultural norms, values, beliefs, and institutions, there does not exist an identical sociopsychological growth and development process between male and female but a marked difference between the psychosocial characteristics of male and female. How then is it possible for some coaches to maintain that the psychological preparation of male and female athletes for competition is identical regardless of motivation level, gender, maturity, and role identification? The questions that arise from the research in sport psychology and sport sociology remain inconclusive, since the research pertains to a definitive promotion of one specific method of psychologically preparing athletes for competition over another. However, it appears that the mental preparation of athletes for competition by coaches currently tends to be more gender-specific than androgynous.

Uguccioni and Ballantyne (1980) administered the BSRI and Attitudes Toward Women Scale to 333 undergraduate women. Eighty-three were varsity athletes (swimming and basketball), 192 participated in a limited competitive athletic program, and 58 did not participate in athletics. Results of the study indicate that the sex role orientations, but not values, were significantly different among the three groups of women. A greater number of the athletes were masculine and androgynous. The researchers' findings seem consistent with those of Colker and Windom (1980), who found that female athletes were less feminine than their college peers. An earlier study by Landers (1970) showed that college women who major in physical education have lower femininity scores than other women education majors. This could suggest that a bias toward androgyny by women coaches with physical education degrees may be present, which would influence how they psychologically prepare their athletes for competition and relate to them as individuals.

Psychological traits that are thought by coaches to be established and/or enhanced through athletic competition are many, although several of these "outcomes" seem to originate as fact from sources of "folklore coaching psychology." Leadership, competitiveness, ambition, and aggressiveness are character traits that are supposed to be manifested within the process of athletic development; it should come as no surprise that these four character traits are categorized as strong male traits in society. Coaches should understand that although development of these traits in women athletes is considered necessary for competition, especially in the more physical sports such as basketball, field hockey, and volleyball, some women may take longer to accept and develop these traits than others because of perceived role expectations.

Parental control and influence regarding sports participation specifically from the perspective of the mother, which is further compounded by the vast (and still growing) number of single parents, will continue to have considerable impact upon the type and level of sports involvement. While signs exist that seem to indicate traditional gender roles relative to sports involvement are in the process of diversifying, the traditional values, norms, expectations, methods, and avenues—while not as firmly entrenched as they once were—will apparently be slow to change as they impact upon female athletic participation and development. The sociological parameters as they currently exist most definitely have an impact and influence upon the psychological preparation of athletes, both men and women. To ignore or dismiss the obvious at this point in time would appear to be less than optimal for athletes as a whole. Neal (1975), in her book, *Coaching Methods for Women*, provides a brief but sound summation regarding the sociological and psychological considerations of the female in sports: "We still don't know everything there is to know about women and competition. . . . The area of sociological and psychological factors is a relatively unexplored one, in which we definitely need more research." It would appear that the concern voiced by Neal over a decade ago relative to limited research and subsequent information on the psychological preparation of women athletes continues to remain a valid and important concern today. Traditional academic psychology has investigated the area of psychology of sport performance as it relates to males, females, and androgyny. However, the arrival of feminist psychology may promote intensive investigation in this area. The potential impact that feminist psychology could have upon applied sport psychology is considerable.

THE PSYCHOLOGY OF WOMEN: A FEMINIST VIEWPOINT

The origin, development, and theoretical foundation and practice of psychology is based, according to feminists, on a male interpretation. An important consideration and cause for reflection by coaches who utilize sport psychology in general and, more specifically, incorporate traditionally accepted psychological tools and techniques as they apply to the female athlete is, who correctly interprets psychological constructs and resulting practices? Historically, the originators of socially acceptable behavior and societal cultural roles have been, and apparently continue for the present to be, primarily men. From a feminist viewpoint, socially constructed gender parameters have had, and will continue to have, an enormous impact on the acceptance and progress of women's sports and are rooted in an interesting and apparently questionable foundation regarding the social position and thus psychological nature of women. Low and Hubbard (1983) state:

> In reality, Western industrial societies are highly structured and stratified, with a few people—mostly upper-middle and upper class white men—holding power and privilege at the top, and the large majority of people hierarchically arranged below them. . . . For the people near the top, the attractions of a belief in meritocracy should be obvious. It is in their interests not only to believe in it, but to convince those lower down of its validity. . . . Once the meritocratic model is accepted, it is easy to believe that a particular group does badly because its members are less able or have less of what it takes for success than those higher up. Discussions and analysis of social hierarchy become limited to examining differences in the relative abilities of individuals or groups and to searching for the biological origins of these differences.

> Those who do research on sex, race, or class differences or who popularize research in the media usually are not advocates of major social change. Not surprisingly then, theories that root sex, race, or class differences in biology receive a great deal of publicity. To someone who really believes that this unequal social system is based on equal opportunity, a belief in biological determinism is almost inevitable. And for someone who opposes social change, it is convenient to believe that social inequality is rooted in biology.

This "cause and effect" feminist perspective of the deliberate and continuing subordination of women in our society as presented by Lowe and Hubbard et al. provides a most illuminating and controversial picture. The constraints, attitudes, and enormous barriers that women athletes continue to negotiate even today seem quite compatible with many feminist positions as they relate to equality, access, and source of the obstacles. The psychological nature of women as examined and analyzed by feminist psychology will deviate from the traditional focus and foundation of psychology. At this point in time, limited research by feminist psychology professionals relative to sport psychology has been initiated. It is important to note that although feminist psychologists have thus far not focused on applied sport psychology, women physical education professionals tend to be profeminist and for many years have been interested in applied sport psychology research at it applies to women.

The psychology of women in general and women athletes in particular can be approached and studied from different orientations—traditional scientifically based orthodox experimental psychology and scientifically based feminist psychology. Both directions have the ability to expand and enhance our understanding of human behavior, although only traditional orthodox experimental psychology has a track record of note regarding applied sport psychology and women athletes. However, the questions and challenges posed by feminist psychology may yet alter the general thinking of the psychology community. In *Female Psychology, The Emerging Self*, author Sue Cox (1981, 3) provides a feminist interpretation of the psychology of women that focuses on the social and political bases of women's behavior as opposed to the traditional biological origins of behavior. With reference to the basis of female psychology, Cox states:

> While valuing the objectivity and analytical abilities intrinsic to scientific work, academic feminists tend to be aware of limitations inherent in the extremes of these and feminist scholarship tends to be more interdisciplinary and aware of ethnic and class differences among women (and men). There is more of an emphasis on the sociopolitical context of the psychology of women combined with an explicit awareness and concern with values in their own work and the work of others. As feminists value women and female experience, feminist scholars value cooperation and interdependency in contrast to the more competitive individualistic style of the male experience and value system.

It may be plausible that, to a degree, feminist psychology may not have expressed an intense interest in sport psychology because of the competitive, winning-is-all-important goal of serious sports competition, which is masculine in origin and is perceived as a primary cause of the subordination of women. In regard to feminist conceptions of the subordination and status of women, Cox states that "such differences in values create a 'female' and a 'male' culture with male values and culture having higher status and being the dominant culture" (1981, 4). If one substitutes the word "sport" for "culture" in the preceding quote, the impact becomes further clarified. There are two methods by which to study the psychology of women. With reference to orthodox science, Cox (1981, 17) claims that "questions regarding the biological and cultural bases of psychology of women remain unanswered by traditional science. . . . Male bias has persuaded both content and process of scientific activity. . . . Both the methods of science and the content of what is studied reflect the narrowness and rigidity of masculinity."

However, until feminist psychologists (not just some women physical educators) elect to actively and significantly initiate research in sport psychology regardless of approach, traditional orthodox psychology and physical education will provide the theories, subjects, and expertise utilized in applied sport psychology. The trends and issues in sport psychology as they pertain to women athletes are both multidimensional and remain somewhat controversial. With the continued increase in the number of males who are coaching female athletes, it remains to be seen what psychological system, if any, will eventually reign and what effect traditional male perceptions and expectations as manifested in male coaches will ultimately have upon the psychological makeup and preparation of female athletes under their direction. Psychological androgyny as a component of applied sport psychology is based upon the premise that there are more similarities than differences between male and female; women coaches seem to be much more comfortable with an androgynous model than are male coaches. In the event that the number of male coaches of women athletes continues to increase, the immediate and long-term future of psychological androgyny as a tool and technique of applied sport psychology will be a topic of considerable interest.

chapter 5

Motivation and Performance

How often have you heard the expression "She came ready to play" or "She has a lot of heart"? What actually draws coaches and athletes alike into sports? What motivates them to put in countless hours in formal practice sessions, and yet more hours practicing and preparing on their own? Why do some coaches simply "go through the motions" year after year in what would appear to promote a less-than-ideal competitive environment while other coaches devote their personal and professional lives to coaching? Is there an avenue in which assistant coaches or head coaches can effect an overall change? As a coach, how can I motivate my athletes and coaching staff to aspire to be champions and "pay the price to be champions"?

In order to construct an environment and concurrent operational process that will be dynamic and alive in terms of process, interest, and enthusiasm for both athletes and coaches, it will be useful to examine the motivational process and how it impacts upon learning and performance. Within the context of athletic performance by athletes and the ability to "coach well" exist two fundamental factors—physical and mental maturity.

Physical and mental maturity are the two components that successful coaches and researchers continue to stress as key areas of importance. Emotional arousal may or may not be identified as a positive asset (too much emotional arousal can produce extremely high levels of anxiety that can cause athletes and coaches to lose control of a situation and "choke"). However, Oxendine (1984, 222) states that "in fact, probably no type of human activity is as vividly affected by emotional arousal and general motivation as is performance in motor skills."

Emotion and arousal are a necessary part of the motivational process, which is essential to success as both an athlete and coach.

SOCIAL AFFILIATION AND PARTICIPATION

For a coach, the ability to identify and encourage sport interest (subject interest) as reflected in terms of enthusiasm and participation level displayed by both current and future athletes acts as a strong motivational tool for positive reinforcement just as a child with a particular interest in a specific subject (music, art, physical education, chemistry, etc.) in school can be similarly encouraged by an astute teacher and can develop a desire to learn and excel. However, teachers and coaches alike must contend with individuals whose presence in the classroom or gymnasium results in behavior that is not productive but disruptive. Some of these individuals warrant your attention because of what they can evolve into as a result of athletic participation.

A classroom teacher may have problem students who may not be motivated to perform up to standard and may disrupt the learning process on occasion. Just as teachers have problem students, coaches will also have to contend with problem athletes who may be quite gifted athletically but may not possess a good attitude and are not motivated to conform. Besides thoroughly enjoying competition, a reason for deciding to join a team is social affiliation. The coach will have to make a decision whether or not to keep the athletes who are participating only for reasons of camaraderie and social affiliation. These athletes may become quite disruptive because their perceived purpose for sports participation is not for the activity and resulting competition. Their motivation for trying out for the team is usually entirely different from that of the coaches or positively motivated athletes who are primarily involved because they want to learn and compete in *addition* to belonging to a team.

A young girl may try out for sports for several reasons—the insistence of her parents, peer pressure, family traditions—reasons that are other than her own. Although most young girls continue to be socialized and directed into appropriate feminine sports, it is not unusual for a coach to discover that the impetus for their participation stems from a parent(s) who, for a variety of reasons, wants his/her daughter to be an athlete. There may be situations where the young girl is directed by "significant others" to participate in an athletic activity that does not fall within the traditional realm of socially acceptable feminine sports, which may present a formidable conflict for the aspiring athlete and her coach. This athlete is probably not motivated for reasons of social affiliation, but is externally pushed into a situation she neither wants nor can comfortably back down from. A coach must be sensitive to these situations because each type of athlete will not necessarily, in most circumstances, make a positive contribution to the team initially but may eventually experience personal growth. These sensitive situations can usually lend themselves to positive solutions. The conduct of the coach during these sensitive situations will be observed by the rest of the team and staff. Judgments will be made by all involved parties. A professional attitude, kindness, tact, and discretion by all coaches will have a positive effect and provide a solid role model for both athletes and assistant coaches.

A coach needs to make every effort to leave the dismissed athlete feeling good about herself and the coach feeling good about his/her actions. In some cases, this single exposure to organize athletics will be the only experience she has with highly structured and serious athletic competition.

Her self-esteem and social position among peers can remain intact or be severely damaged, depending upon the tact and actions of the coach. The mental health of the team can be adversely affected by a coach who is insensitive and cruel. In the case of a young girl who is thrust into organized athletic competition via an external agent such as a parent, the coach may want to consider contacting the parents by letter or phone to explain an alternative experience or to suggest why their daughter may not find the sport of her choice rewarding for various reasons. This tact may well serve to give both parents and athlete a graceful way out. At the same time, the athletic program and coach will be perceived in a positive light.

Coaching is both a rewarding and demanding occupation. The ability to motivate and direct the activities of athletes is a crucial component of success. It is not reasonable to expect coaches to act as interim parents or tolerate inappropriate behavior although more than once coaches may feel like surrogate mothers or fathers. Athletes and would-be athletes who, for one reason or another, present significant problems to the team should be carefully evaluated by the coach prior to allowing the athlete(s) in question the opportunity and privilege of becoming a member of the team.

An additional consideration in regard to the motivation behind athletic participation is the fact that, because of a situation that is prevalent at home, it is quite possible that an aspiring athlete will avoid coming home directly after school because the environment at home is anything but positive and athletic participation may be the most acceptable recourse. Athletes from broken homes, economically depressed areas and ghettos, or without much to come home to often will discover that athletic participation represents a rewarding and enjoyable world for several hours a day.

The motivation for deciding to become an athlete may originate from several collective sources or be restricted to one. Miller (1974, 84) states that ". . . performance may be said to be skill multiplied by motivation." Oxendine (1984, 222) describes motivations as ". . . the process whereby needs are created within the individual, forcing him to seek particular goals to satisfy those needs. Motivation refers to one's internal state, which may be initiated from within the person, as in the case of a biological need or from the outside, as in the case of a social need."

MOTIVATION

The origin of motivation is external and/or internal. Motivation in the biological sense (to eat, drink, sleep, etc.) is internal in origin. Motivation derived from social needs, as in the athlete's quest for recognition through awards, need for social affiliation, or avenue for possible material success, is external. Many coaches comment that they would prefer to coach athletes who are motivated internally as opposed to those who are motivated externally. It would appear that many excellent athletes experience a combination of internal and external motivation. According to Miller (1974, 88):

Perhaps more than any other endeavor, sports call forth unusual emotions. The pressures of competition, the crowd and its behavior, the importance of winning, the influence of the coach, parents, and friends, all these and more are among the conditions that set into motion such responses as self confidence, poise, expectancy, and the like, as well as fear, hate, anxiety, anger, frustration, despair, grief, feelings of guilt, resentment, indignation, and similar emotions. . . . Motivation is a complex mixture of many things, and emotions is part of that mixture.

Although it may appear that behavioral scientists attempt to explain human behavior and its attendant motivational process in biological terms as opposed to the more subjective social process, they do not ignore the latter. To limit the contents or makeup of people as merely biological in terms of operation severely restricts the scope of human nature. Internal and external conditions relative to individual and social factors significantly affect behavior that, to a large extent, will determine the degree and intensity of motivation that may be inherent in athletes.

There are various ways in which both athletes and coaches may become motivated. The agent that acts as the stimulus or the condition that, because of personal or social appeal, creates the interest will be based in general terms on motivation that is either internal or external in origin. The *task* or *actual process* may be the primary reason for participation, which can relegate the perceived goal(s) (acclaim, material rewards, peer approval, etc.) to secondary status. Many athletes look forward to and enjoy practice. They may be identified as task oriented, meaning their motivation is probably significantly internal.

How often have veteran and new coaches wondered what a particular athlete or group of athletes was doing, toiling away long, hard hours in practice when they had but limited athletic ability at best? Task motivation is a type of intrinsic motivation. Task motivation, according to Oxendine (1984, 225), is "the interest or pleasure created by the participation in the activity itself. Sometimes such motivation occurs with the mere anticipation of an event or activity, while at other times it results from such participation itself." Ausubel (1968, 365, 366) puts forth support for recognizing that, although it would be ideal if athletes and students were perpetually motivated, this situation is seldom a reality: "It is unnecessary to postpone learning activities until appropriate interests and motivations have been developed. Frequently, the best way of teaching the unmotivated student is to ignore his motivational state for the time being, and to concentrate on teaching him as effectively as possible. Some degree of learning will ensue in any case, despite the lack of motivation; and from the initial satisfaction he will hopefully develop the motivation to learn more."

The need to achieve, win, and excel is a trait all coaches would like to see athletes possess. Achievement motivation may be considered in terms of the fact that some people appear driven and even obsessed with a need to master any sport, task, or challenge that is presented (Oxendine 1984). The basis for this type of motivation would appear to be intrinsic. An example of achievement motivation is the mountain climber, who, after days of struggle and physical pain, reached the peak of one of the world's highest mountains and was asked why she did it. "Because it was there, and I liked the challenge" was her response.

Roberts and Duda (1984) conducted a study on motivation in sport. The purpose of their study was to determine the importance and significance of the relationship between how well an athlete thought she or he performed subjectively as compared with the actual results of performance. The study was limited to male and female racquetball players. Specific to gender similarities and differences, the evidence obtained supported the hypothesis that perceived athletic ability is an important cognitive factor with regard to success and failure. It is important to note that perception as a result of observing one's behavior does not necessarily result as a major factor that influences and affects success and failure but may very well originate as a *result* of success and failure.

However, the statistical evidence showed that, while the difference is not great, the demonstration of ability is more important to perceptions of success and failure for men than women. The *amount* of perceived athletic ability as perceived by athletes subjectively can have a direct bearing on success or failure. The coach and athlete are cautioned not to discount the importance of motivation regarding the acquisition of skill development and subsequent attainment of athletic ability.

The researchers also determined that male and female athletes will utilize different criteria in terms of determining their own perceived ability. Coaches who are involved with co-ed teams or who coach both male and female teams should take their findings into consideration when thinking about the relationship between the degree of motivation an athlete has and that athlete's perceived athletic ability. From a tactical perspective, the coach should monitor the psychological state of the athlete in terms of the athlete's perceived ability as a determinant of success or failure and attempt to ascertain how the opposition (individual or team) perceives their athletic ability in terms of motivation to succeed.

ATTRIBUTION THEORY

As internal and external in origin, motivation, as a force, is often researched as a component of Attribution theory. Attribution theory and achievement motivation go hand in hand in terms of a cause and effect relationship. Attributes can be considered as personalized internal explanations that in general establish reasons for success and failure in an individual athlete, team, or coach.

Some examples of attributes that people utilize as explanations or rationale for the success or failure of a performance are luck, talent, effort, lack of effort, opposition, weather, equipment, coaching, etc. One of the most important concepts that coaches should understand is the relationship between causal attribution, motivation, and resulting success and failure.

Many coaches and athletes will continue to reflect upon success or failure after the fact; that is, it is not unusual for coaches and athletes to discuss why they had success or why they didn't: "What can you *attribute* your success or failure to?" The explanations for performance are internal and/or environmental. Causal attributes are those factors which are determined to have a direct bearing on performance and are categorized as (1) internal, (2) external, (3) stable, or (4) unstable.

Attribution theory in sport attempts to study various attributes as manifested within individual athletes and teams prior to competition and after competition specific to their influence and impact as a motivational force and the athlete's and team's subsequent success and/or failure in competition.

The presence of attributes and their strength can be assessed by an instrument such as the Causal Dimension Scale (Russell 1982), or can be descriptive on the part of the athlete. However, a coach who elects to determine attributes specific to a particular athlete via description should take into account the athlete's ability to describe the emotions she experiences; education and vocabulary will in all probability impact upon the ability of athletes to provide an appropriate response.

In terms of causal attribution for failure, Weiner, et al. (1979) identified the following attributes (not a complete list) as explanations that have been provided by subjects: anger, depression, disappointment, disgust, fear, frustration, guilt, incompetence, mad, resignation, sadness, surprise, unhappiness, upset. It stands to reason that, should a coach detect any of these attributes present in the athlete(s) immediately prior to competition, steps should be taken, by communication and understanding, to reduce these attributional factors that often result in abnormal and/or inappropriate personal anxiety (a certain amount of anxiety and stress will always be present).

Each of these fourteen attributes can be categorized as stable, unstable, internal, or external by the coach and athlete and then dealt with. The fourteen listed attributes that explain failure are only a representative list; there are many more.

Attributes that explain success are coaching, talent, effort, motivation, goal attainment, fear of failure, revenge, etc. Attributes are more often subjective emotions than objective analysis when failure occurs, although the attribute of luck appears to be present in both victory and defeat. The coach can instill and reinforce positive attributes in athletes by modeling and the development of a positive mental attitude, which should have a positive effect on motivation and performance.

FEAR OF FAILURE AND FEAR OF SUCCESS

Success and failure in athletics on a personal level appear to be relative. A tennis player who comes up against a superior opponent may internalize numerous attributes prior to the match that will almost ensure a loss. Because of the anticipated outcome, motivation during a situation such as this is minimal at best. However, a coach who teaches the athlete to strive and establish personal goals that are not tied to the win-loss results can actually structure a positive experience. Perhaps the athlete will have a goal not to lose in straight sets like most players before her, or to win one match, or extend her superior opponent to the end. The athlete's goals, feelings, or attributes will have a positive result even when she is confronted with a loss. This same program of motivational encouragement can be applied to most athletes in all sports.

Psychologists and coaches alike are cognizant of the fact that the fear of failure provides incentive from both internal and external sources. Coaches and athletes who are driven to succeed apparently have an intrinsic need for success and, in all probability, have become workaholics and thrive on the process and results. At the same time, the resulting successes and victories have propelled these athletes and coaches into the public eye and now their public expects achievement and success and will not recognize or accept a mediocre performance.

Although it may first appear somewhat ironic, fear of success is a condition that affects both coach and athlete. Individuals who are prone to fear of success have apparently established a comfort zone that generates but a minimal amount of pressure and expectations. They enjoy the process, environment, and what would seem to be a non-crucial role during competition. They do not want to be thrust into a "do or die" situation.

Another aspect of fear of success is the feeling that "Suppose I win; everybody will expect me to do it again. What if I can't? Then perhaps people will say it was a fluke or I was just plain lucky." The comfort zone in this type of person may be caused just as much by a fear of success as by a fear of failure. The self-esteem or self-worth of athletes and coaches who appear to fall within this category may be changed for the better through clinical help by a psychologist and a coach who recognizes the condition and is patient, encouraging, and provides experiences and goals that are designed to provide positive reinforcement from internal and external sources. It is not unusual to find a very gifted athlete with enormous potential who is either prone to fear of success or fear of failure. These athletes lack self-confidence in their ability to perform. They may be constantly subjected to negative reinforcement at home or elsewhere.

MOTIVATION AND SPORT PERFORMANCE

Motivational theory in athletics seems to fall into one of two categories depending, in general terms, on the position from which one views athletics—that of the coach and athlete or the psychologist. While the behavioral scientists are able to generate information on cause and effect of motivation based upon scientific theories and procedures, coaches and athletes tend to generalize motivation in terms of subjective factors which are important in terms of what the athlete expects to achieve as a result of her personal goals and perceived ability of her opponent. All parties agree on the importance of motivation and on the need to be able to understand individuals and teams with regard to the motivational process. Singer (1977, 1–22) provides some basic assumptions in regard to sport performance and motivation:

1. "Performance at any one time = motivation (effect and expectancy) × capabilities (genetics and learning)."

Coaches will certainly find themselves in agreement with Singer's assumption and may indeed ask why it takes a Ph.D. in clinical psychology or physical education to reach this obvious conclusion. Singer states that "the athletes' actual performance is certainly dependent upon relevant hereditary characteristics that serve to predispose one for achievement. Heredity sets the boundaries or the framework of the human system. Yet there is always much room for improvement. Practice, quality practice that is, allows the athlete to more truly realize potential. Previous experiences influence the development of skills, abilities, knowledge, and tactics."

It is a pleasure to coach athletes who are physically and athletically gifted and are highly motivated either intrinsically, extrinsically, or a combination of both. One of the key concepts as stated by Singer and recognized by good coaches is that a *quality practice* will allow your athletes to realize their potential more so than a mediocre or boring practice. The practice and team environment, knowledge, people skills, fairness, and enthusiasm on the part of the coaching staff will certainly contribute to motivating athletes and helping to produce quality practices where optimum learning and athletic and personal development can occur.

2. "Degree of learning = performance level (when ideal motivation is present and normal body homeostatic conditions prevail)" (Singer 1977).

Again, the assumption as presented by Singer appears to validate fundamental beliefs (based on observation and experience) held by many coaches and athletes. Singer presents his assumption in a manner that is able to quantify and validate traditional athletic concepts about motivation. According to Singer: "The best and most widely used indicant of learning is performance. However, performance fluctuates for a variety of reasons, among which are health and nutrition factors, fatigue, and the influence of drugs. It also fluctuates with varying degrees of motivation. With reinforcement or rewards, expectations fulfilled, or other sources of motivation, performance is more apt to truly indicate learning level. With the absence of personal or externally-set incentives (performance) behavior is likely to be at its worst."

We can safely say that the degree of athletic performance as demonstrated by an athlete will, in general terms, depend on those factors that directly affect and thus control performance. How well or poorly an athlete eats, her health status (cold, flu, virus), how tired she is, and to what extent, if any, she has the use of drugs (prescription and illegal) are important in evaluating performance and performance potential.

The physiological factors may appear obvious relative to performance potential and end result. However, if the physiological factors are all in order and the athlete or team continues to perform in practice or competition at less than expected levels, the coach should perhaps review her practice of reinforcement, rewards, expectations (are they reasonable?), attitude of the coaching staff, credibility of the coach, communication with the team.

As presented in Chapter 1, the inverted-U hypothesis is one explanation of the relationship between motivation and athletic performance. According to Singer (1977), "With activities that involve complexity in sequential coordinated movements, controlled and perhaps flexible response patterns to changing and unpredictable situations, the inverted-U hypothesis is applicable. The 'best' motivation is a function of task characteristics." It is important that, in addition to the belief that optimal motivation (best) is a function of task characteristics, an individual athlete's "personal customary level of arousal" is also of prime consideration.
The inverted-U hypothesis addresses the problem area of overmotivation and optimal motivation/arousal levels for learning and performance.

An example of applying the inverted-U hypothesis would be the following situation. Your team's (basketball, gymnastics, volleyball, field hockey, softball, tennis, soccer, track and field) next opponent is very weak and not considered by players or anybody else to be a formidable challenge. The fact is that the next opponent is not very good (upsets occur every week) and, because of the nature of the situation, you and your team could overlook them because of a lack of interest and motivation. Applying the inverted-U hypothesis would suggest that you as a coach must strongly motivate your team and individual athletes throughout practice and conceivably during the actual game because a strong motivational and demanding coaching posture is necessary in order to produce the optimal level of motivation.

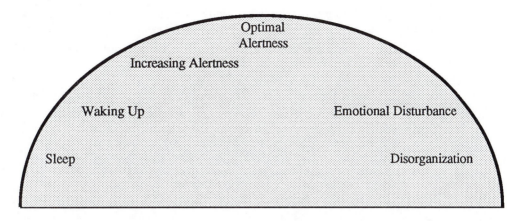

Low Arousal   **High Arousal**

On the other hand, all coaches have found themselves in the position of facing a formidable opponent or attempting to teach and peak a gifted athlete for a high-level competition. Rather than exhorting your underdog team to *win* through intense practices and high expectations if you haven't coached in this manner during the season, the inverted-U hypothesis states that the maximum level of motivation may be achieved by a coaching posture that is weak relative to the demands and expectations when the opponent is superior and seemingly unbeatable. Thus, the extrinsic motivational stimuli should be manipulated and varied depending upon the situation.

3. "Theoretical constructs can adequately describe performance at any one time as a function of motivational presence: Drive Theory vs. the Inverted-U Hypothesis" (Singer 1977).

The concepts of Drive theory and the inverted-U hypothesis when applied to sport psychology represent two interesting explanations of motivational presence. According to Singer, when the behavioristic school of thought was in its prime, and the noted psychologist Clark Hull shaped research efforts through his mathematical equations that attempted to quantify learning and behavioral potential, his concept of "drive" indicated the linear relationship of arousal (motivation) to performance. His concepts were geared to describe all types of learning. Contemporary researchers have tended to find fault with Drive theory as applied to motor behaviors. Instead they have tended to support the tenets of the inverted-U hypothesis as more applicable for an explanation of movement-oriented performances.

4. "Personal characteristics, situational variables, and task dimensions interact to suggest the optimal motivation to be imposed and/or generated" (Singer 1977).

According to Singer, the environment and the nature of the competitive situation itself may contain stimuli with arousal properties, as perceived by the athlete. The presence of spectators, the words of the coach, the contest conditions, and other variables are associated with potential arousal dynamics.

Training and performance are the primary foundation of coaching. Singer (1977, 1–22) provides eleven considerations for training which could be applied to most operational and philosophical beliefs:

1.   "Help athletes to set personally high but attainable and specific goals."

It is not unusual for coaches and athletes to confuse aspirations and expectations when setting personal goals and team goals. Goals should represent attainable targets that, with serious effort on the part of athlete and coach, will be attained. The forms of goals and expectations should be synonymous and *reasonable*. Goals as determined for each athlete as well as team goals should be based upon athletic talent (individual and collective), schedule, expertise and commitment of coaches, philosophy of athletics as stated by the school administration, length of season, maturity of athletes, probability of goal attainment. Goals can be thought of in terms of weekly goals, seasonal goals, or specific competition as represented by both the team and each athlete.

Aspirations as differentiated from expectations can be thought of as an ultimate reward, not necessarily stated as a goal. When seen through the eyes of a truly gifted athlete, aspirations could be thought of in terms of making the Olympic team, the national team, or becoming an All American. The fact that the level(s) of aspiration will be different for each athlete, based upon internal and external factors, is a crucial consideration for all coaches when attempting to determine and set individual and team goals. In terms of an average but dedicated athlete, aspirations may be listed as earning a starting spot during her senior year, being elected as one of the team captains, being selected as an alternate for an All Star team, or eventually making that special road trip. For many teams, a worthwhile team goal would be to finish in the first division of the conference and an aspiration would be making the play-offs or winning the conference title.

2.   "Supply appropriate reinforcement and feedback (knowledge of results) to athletes about their performance" (Singer 1977).

Win, lose, or draw, the coach should analyze the results in a manner that will provide valuable and insightful feedback to the athletes. After a victory, the coach can provide positive reinforcement about why, during practice, the athletes had to do specific drills, etc. that paid off in victory. Concentrate both on things they did well as well as things that still need work. Nobody feels good after a loss or tie; however, the coach should provide a comprehensive and objective examination on *what* happened and *why* it happened within twenty-four hours after competition. Do not dwell on the negative; there will be some areas that shine through on an otherwise bleak day or night. In the case of a loss, some coaches prefer to accept the loss as a coaching error, thus reducing the aggravation of the team.

3.   "Special strategies should be used to maximize motivation for training perseverance and to optimize pre-event motivation" (Singer 1977).

There are a number of ways that coaches can enhance motivation. A positive mental attitude (PMA) and a genuine, not superficial, belief on the part of the coach that this team can play with anybody (assuming skill levels are equal) will greatly enhance confidence and motivation. The use of mental imagery and the practice of concentration techniques will often provide an edge in performance when all else is equal.

4. "Practice situations should simulate contest situations when possible" (Singer 1977).

"You play as you practice" is a phrase often used in coaching. By all means, create in both intensity and demands the environment in which your team actually will have to compete. A practice environment that simulates actual competition can create a comfort zone for players and coaches. If the practice situation closely approximates the actual conditions and expectations of the contest, the athletes will feel at home during the actual game because they have been there before—several days per week. For a coach to soft-pedal a practice environment is an error of tragic consequences. Serious competition is serious pressure, which necessitates *in-kind* training of athletes and coach.

5. "Individual athletes should be understood and respected for their individual differences" (Singer 1977).

No two people are alike. As much as many coaches seek to impose conformity, athletes are going to differ behaviorally in a number of ways. Mutual respect between coach and athlete is absolutely essential for a common goal to be reached and should be developed early. Do not embarrass, humiliate, or destroy athletes privately or in front of their peers; it will be counterproductive and will destroy respect and team morale. Communication is an important avenue of understanding; a coach can still retain a professional attitude and objective distance from athletes while effectively talking with them at the appropriate time. They will know if you are sincere or if you are a "user" depending on how you as a coach treat and relate to them. Do you care about each of them as a person or are you concerned strictly with their ability to produce desired results, i.e., victories? The pressures and demands that young women must contend with on a daily basis are much more intense than they were ten years ago. An astute coach will recognize this fact in understanding the personal and athletic side of the athlete.

6. "The coach should do everything possible to help develop the self-confidence and self-concept of each athlete" (Singer 1977).

Athletes will react differently to praise and criticism. As a coach, one of your primary purposes is to provide the *means* whereby your athletes will achieve all that they are able to. Most people don't know to what degree they can actually excel in sports. After determining the extent of an athlete's limitation in terms of physical, mental, emotional, and maturation level, the coach should provide the means whereby each athlete will reach her maximum potential on a weekly, monthly, and yearly basis with respect to the situation. While some athletes will be motivated by highly critical comments from a coach and may actually perform better, many will be hurt, disappointed, and dejected, causing a further decline in performance. It is rare for an athlete who lacks self-confidence and has a low self-concept to perform well, especially if the coach continues to diminish her self-respect and self-confidence. Some athletes can take tough coaching and respond favorably while keeping their self-respect and self-confidence; many will react favorably with positive reinforcement.

7. "The Hawthorne effect or Placebo effect hold implications for training" (Singer 1977).

The Hawthorne effect refers to studies conducted from 1926 to 1939 relative to production and output by factory workers. The output of the workers increased when they perceived that a special interest by management was taken in trying to improve the work environment. The Placebo effect regarding behavior is different. An example would be a situation in which an individual claimed a certain pill to be a special mixture of vitamins and protein that would provide additional and expanded physical power when in reality the pill is composed of nothing more than dehydrated spinach or some other inactive substance. However, the psychological value of the pill to the user is real. According to Singer (1977), ". . . the interpretation of the word placebo has been expanded considerably to cover any contrived situation which the learner or the performer believes will be of some value in fulfilling objectives, but in fact should not. Deception can work if a person is truly deceived. The more the athlete is convinced of the value to be derived, the more possible the beneficial psychological effects will be noted."

8. "Leadership style should reflect the outstanding qualities of the coach, be compatible with the situation, and believed in by the athletes" (Singer 1977).

Among the many responsibilities and expectations that athletes and the public have come to expect from coaches are that they be legitimate authority figures. Leadership is a term and quality that has remained constant; a coach has it or doesn't have it. Confusion, indecisiveness, disorganization, disinterest, unpreparedness, and general inefficiency describe coaches who display limited or no leadership. Athletes, young or old, are very receptive to the quality and leadership ability of their coach(es).

Athletes will respect, honor, and for the most part obey the coach who *demonstrates*, not verbalizes, leadership quality of the highest order. The legendary basketball coach of UCLA, John Wooden, believed that his job was over when he could sit on the bench and assume the role of spectator, implying that his athletes had developed the necessary skill, basketball expertise, and leadership to take care of business.

However, there are times when your athletes will *look to you* for leadership that is dependent upon the situation, e.g., final minutes of a close game, sophisticated offense or defense by the opposition ("what do we do?"), race course strategy, and reinforcement.

9. "Training programs and practices should be meaningful to the athlete" (Singer 1977).

Just as practice should, whenever possible, simulate the actual environment of competition, training programs should relate directly or indirectly to the sport. In recent years, many coaches have thrown out the torture drills that are used to assess the "character or heart" of an athlete because, all too often, these torture drills do not directly or indirectly transfer to specific skills that the sport demands. Instead, they waste the time and energy of both coach and athlete that should be otherwise directed to productive teaching and learning.

There are still coaches, however, who run their track athletes over miles of sand (how often do they race on sand courses?) or volleyball coaches who demand that their players dive on concrete, asphalt, or other foreign surfaces to "make them tough and unafraid." These types of training programs are not meaningful to very many players and very little, if any, skill development will occur. Injuries can occur in this type of pointless training. Spend your time and the practice time of your athletes in sport-specific training.

10. "Intrinsic motivation is preferable to extrinsic motivation in most athletic activities" (Singer 1977).

A heavy dependence on rewards to influence the nature and type of athletic be-havior is not as desirable as behavior of intrinsic origin that is self-generated for personally rewarding reasons. Athletes participate in sports for a number of rea-sons. The most desirable athlete to coach is the one who is competing primarily because she personally likes the sport; she is intrinsically motivated. Tangible re-wards such as media coverage, trophies, and other forms of public recognition, although externally rewarding, are thought of as icing on the cake.

11. "The relationship of coactors and spectators to the performance of the athlete should be understood" (Singer 1977).

Social facilitation theory was formulated in an attempt to explain the observed effects of the presence of others on one's behavior. The situation, from an arousal or motivational point of view, may not be the same when performing alone versus performing with others or in front of others. Social facilitation suggests that spec-tators may dampen the performance of lowly skilled (beginning and veteran) ath-letes and raise the performance of the more highly skilled.

There are many considerations, both physiological and psychological, that successful coaches will examine and analyze before, during, and after the season. There is, how-ever, one dominant topic among coaches and athletes that must receive careful and deliberate thought before being put into operation. Goals must be reasonable and attain-able.

GOAL-SETTING

All of us have thought of certain goals and positions that we aspire to reach. It is not unusual to perhaps fantasize about being named to an All American team, coaching an All Star or Olympic team, or making the first round of the post-season play in high school. Goal-setting can provide a vehicle, an avenue of both motivation and operational order for coaches, athlete(s), and teams.

In general terms, coaches set goals as a staff and as individual coaches. The staff goals usually are not provided as public information. Goals for each individual athlete and team goals are the next step in identifying and implementing appropriate goals.

Goals should be analyzed and evaluated according to the expertise and ability of the coach(es), the level of competition, and the skill level of the athlete(s). These "do-mestic" considerations and evaluations are very important in determining appropriate goals. It is also important to evaluate the expertise and ability of the opposition in terms of their staff, facilities, and athletes as they will most certainly impact your goals as a staff and team.

McClements and Botterill (1980, 270) provide pertinent analysis in regard to goal-setting. "The goals must be more than just a wish or dream; they must be realistic. Specific factors must be considered in setting goals." Their four specific factors are listed below.

1. Performance.
The basic factors used in setting performance goals are the individual's long-term goal, the individual's current level, and the number of seasons available to achieve

the long-term goal. These are used to set a reasonable season or short-term goal as the intermediary step to achieving a long-term goal.

2. Commitment of the Individual.

A less obvious but crucial factor in planning goals is the commitment of the individual. This relates to the amount of time and the degree of effort that the individual is willing to dedicate to achieving . . . goals.

3. Opportunity.

It is also important to consider the effective opportunity that the individual has to achieve goals. The types of opportunities to be considered are: (a) practice time and facilities available, (b) the limits of coaches, (c) competitions available, (d) funds, and (e) climatic conditions.

4. Potential.

The last factor—the individual's potential—is the most difficult to assess. Coaches sometimes think that they "know" their athlete's potential; however, the certainty of this subjective evaluation is at best suspect. One clue of an athlete's potential may come from a review of the individual's rate of improvement, allowing for opportunity and effort. This necessitates that progress, opportunity, and effort be regularly recorded and evaluated. . . . If the short-term goal appears to be unreasonable when the coach and athlete are making the season plans, it is important to consider the feasibility of a long-term goal.

When discussing, analyzing, and developing motivational techniques and goal-setting strategy, an understanding of the concepts of and differences between aspiration and expectancy will prove helpful in clearly identifying and distinguishing motives and goals.

When establishing goals for both motivational purposes and formulating a systematic program to plan the progress of both athlete and staff, an operational understanding of *aspiration* and *expectancy* can help to crystallize the motivational opportunities and initially establish goals. Expectations are realistic; aspirations are ideal. Athletes who are progressing according to the planned expected goals are enjoying success, which will serve to increase their level of aspiration. However, from a motivational standpoint, the coach should expect and plan for an eventual failure, temporary setback, and the predictable decrease in aspiration on the part of the athlete or team.

Goals can be adjusted both for short-term and long-term results. If initial team and/or individual goals are too high and few, if any, are realized, to leave them intact is to invite frustration, anxiety, and perhaps repeated failure, which is not going to accomplish much of anything.

If, on the other hand, the coach's initial goals were projected as too low and the athletes are attaining their set goals with a minimum of effort and minimal increased skill development, the coach may be providing them with a false sense of security that will be quickly eroded when formidable competition occurs. A coach should, by all means, continually reevaluate the initial team and individual goals. Most athletes receive tremendous satisfaction when achieving goals that are attainable but require diligent work and coaching.

Operant conditioning as developed by B. F. Skinner has been applied to athletics. Although a minimum of literature is currently available on the application of Skinnerian psychology to sport, two informative sources are available that utilize Applied Behavior

Analysis in sport. The reader is referred to (1) *The Development and Control of Behavior in Sport and Physical Education* by Rushall and Siedentop (1972) and *Behavior Modification and Coaching in Principles, Procedures, and Research* by Martin and Hrycaiko (1983).

Applied Behavior Analysis operates on the basic operant conditioning paradigm with the expectation that behavior will be both determined and controlled by its consequences.

The reward systems as utilized by practitioners of Applied Behavior Analysis are scientific and systematic in their application. Motivation and goal-setting should be fundamental strategies and must receive significant consideration and attention by coaches and athletes. Diligent thought and the preparation of the proper goals will go a long way in helping to ensure success. The motivation process and desired outcomes as projected by the coach are primary ingredients in the realization of both intrinsic and extrinsic goals, aspirations, and expectancy.

chapter *6*

Tools and Techniques of Applied Sport Psychology

INSTRUCTION AND LEARNING

The quality and quantity of coaching instruction (cognitive and physical skill development) that coaches are capable of presenting to their athletes are multidimensional and seemingly deliberately calculated to ensure maximum performance. However, the ability of athletes to retain and process the instruction presented by coaches is a critical component of performance and should not be overlooked. Some athletes learn quickly while others require a longer period to understand what the coach wants them to do. How we learn and effective coaching and teaching strategies to promote learning should be of interest to all coaches. There are coaches who constantly talk, perhaps believing that their never-ending verbage is necessary to teach. Most athletes subjected to this type of coach will "tune out" the coach. At this point, an understanding and acceptance of the difference between learning and performance are useful. In behavioral terms, learning is usually defined as a process in which behavior is modified or, if you prefer, changed. As a process, learning should be distinguished from performance, which is a single act (Nixon and Jewett 1980). According to Nixon and Jewett (1980, 17), "Learning is inferred from a series of individual performances over a period of time during which the individual appears to change the performance significantly from what it was on the original attempt. Learning has taken place when the newly acquired behavior persists over time. Learned performances in sport and dance can be observed and in many cases be objectively measured."

How athletes learn and their ability to learn have a major impact upon their performance and your subsequent success, or failure, as a coach in terms of victories and defeats. Learning and performance can sometimes be objectively measured, which can provide a valuable data base to chart progress and plan the optimum learning environment that will help each coach and athlete to achieve their maximum performance capability. Klausmeier and Ripple (1971, 33) present six relevant and important steps that are essential if learning is to be purposeful. The learner (or athlete):

1. Becomes motivated; sets a goal.
2. Appraises situation; evaluates the means and goal relationship.
3. Tries to attain goal; engages in productive thinking and physical activity.
4. Confirms or rejects initial responses.
5. Reaches goals or does not reach goals.
6. Experiences satisfaction; remembers and applies learning, or modifies.

How we learn and the best methodology for instruction should be of great interest and concern to coaches. The motivation to learn should be of special interest for coaches who, unlike classroom teachers, must demand tremendous physical performance in addition to intensive mental concentration and processing. How to continually provide and nourish the optimum learning and performance conditions is vitally important if both coach and athlete expect to be consistently successful. Operant conditioning is a psychological tool that is gaining popularity among coaches in terms of teaching athletes specific reactions. Perhaps the most prolific psychologist of the twentieth century, B. F. Skinner is widely recognized as the father of operant conditioning.

Nixon and Jewett (1980, 9) explain the mechanics of operant conditioning as a situation in which "whenever appropriate responses occur, the subject is rewarded in some way. The person's individual response is instrumental (operant) in receiving a reward, hence the term instrumental or operant conditioning. . . . The reinforcing stimulus (reinforcer) is deliberately introduced soon after a subject has made the desirable response. . . ." Positive reinforcement in terms of verbal and nonverbal communication from coach to athlete(s) would be considered a reinforcing stimulus.

Through trial and error and what many in the coaching fraternity refer to as "common sense," it would certainly appear that coaches have *cued* the techniques and application of both classical and operant conditioning for decades. It may be hypothesized that many coaches have, over the years, made longitudinal observations of human behavior within the athletic environment and have either knowingly or unknowingly utilized basic principles of one of the best-known learning theories—operant conditioning. As a result, perhaps it would be plausible to assume that the serious study and practice of selected learning theories such as classical and operant conditioning could significantly enhance the expertise of coaches and the performance of their athletes. There is an important difference between observation and study. Observation implies that knowledge is generated from watching an activity and, as a result of visual input, impressions are arrived at based upon observation. Although very useful, observation without recording pertinent data over a period of time may not be as helpful as a study. *Conducting a study requires systematic data collection and analysis.* It would appear that most coaches casually observe, not study, behavior and from casual observation and intuition proceed to psychologically prepare their athletes. By learning how to scientifically study behavior, coaches can be trained in what to look for and then systematically utilize applied sport psychology methods.

One of the best-practiced coaching techniques is modeling. The initial exposure to the explanation and practice of modeling as a theoretical construct may elicit the response by many coaches of "this is certainly nothing new, I've been doing this for years." The premise of modeling is that the student and/or athlete will observe the model (coach or teacher) who is engaged in teaching a specific skill (task) and then, based upon the performance of the model, the student and/or athlete will emulate the tasks in the desired manner. Nixon and Jewett (1980, 20) state that:

> It is important that the real life model be prestigious, or highly regarded by the learners; it is also desirable that the model have the authority to bestow rewards on learners who improve through this process of imitation. . . . Two of the most effective rewards are positive reinforcement and self-satisfaction. . . . Finally, students from differing cultural and educational backgrounds must be provided with appropriate models with whom they empathize and associate; one model may not suffice for all members of a large, culturally diverse class of students.

While articles addressing modeling and the practice of mental imagery and mental rehearsal as applied to athletic performance are readily available, Dr. Russell Lord of Eastern Montana College and Dr. Bill Kozar of Texas Tech University are two sport psychologists and motor learning professors who provide an excellent source of applied sport psychology techniques in the following discussion titled "The Coach as a Modifier of Athletic Behavior."

At all levels of American sport, coaches face imposing if not impossible tasks. Our "sport-hungry" society (Singer 1972) recognizes coaches as socially legitimized authority figures who are expected to optimize their athletes' physical and mental development, save some kids from self-destructive behavior, provide other athletes with the motivation to escape from deprived living conditions, and accomplish a host of other equally difficult and ambiguous tasks. While striving for these and related goals, the coach is also expected to win.

In the microcosm of society that we call sport (Eitzen 1979), it is the coach who occupies the bureaucratic top rung; the buck stops with her. It is the coach who provides the primary point of contact and mediation between society's expectations and the athlete (Lord 1979).

Coaches are subject to demands from a very large public, a public that includes spectators, parents, booster club members, alumni, school boards and administrators, league officials, and employers. Such a diverse group of interested people brings a great variety of vested interests to bear upon the coach. While a parent may hope that sport participation will provide a means for his/her child to develop a more positive self-image, the president of the booster club that supplies the facilities and equipment that allow the team to exist may demand that only the most talented athletes play in order to increase the chances of winning.

A basic goal of sport participation seems to be the improvement of each participant's physical skill and performance; for that, after all, is an essential aspect of any sport activity. Another expectation shared by the participants and general public is a hope that participation in sports will have positive effects upon the psychosocial development of the involved athletes.

THE COACH'S TASK

If the coach is to successfully meet the diverse tasks which arise from the many expectations of the public, he must accomplish two goals. The first, and more obvious, goal
concerns the extent to which the coach produces changes in each athlete's performance
(i.e., acquires the skills of the sport). These changes in each athlete's behavior within
the sport activity must not only be observable and measurable, but must also be predictable and controllable. The second, and perhaps less obvious, goal concerns the
extent to which the desired behaviors and resultant athletic performance are brought
under each athlete's own self-control. For too long now, some coaches, athletes, and
others associated with sports have accepted the perspective reflected in a quotation from
a national gymnastics coach (Butt 1980, 78). When asked how he controlled the anxiety
of gymnasts facing a difficult vault, he replied, "I say, 'Look, you fool, you are not
making the vault, I am making it. Just do as I say.'" Such a perspective ignores not
only several important aspects of sport behavior and the respective roles of both coach
and athlete, but also neglects one of the major goals of sport participation. By definition,
it is always the athlete and never the coach who engages in the sport act. The athlete is
always the actor while the coach is, at most, the reactor. It is the athlete who copes,
adjusts, and performs on her own—independent of the coach during the activity itself.
While the coach can, in some sport situations, intervene by such means as time-out or
substitution, the coach never directly controls the sport performance athletes. The
coach's skill and wisdom can be useful only to the extent to which the athletes have
gained self-control over those behaviors which the coach desires. This fact was noted
by Wooden (1973) several years ago and recently paraphrased by Botterill (1980, 262)
when he emphasized that "it is important to remember that the preparation of an athlete
is complete when the coach isn't needed!" Botterill further cautions that preoccupation
with the athletes' physical preparation can easily lead to oversights in the area of psychological preparation. After making the point that "the coach really has no control
over spectators, the opposition, or the officials and how they might affect the athlete
(Botterill 1980, 262), the author goes on to cite personal growth and development as an
important goal of sports participation. He then discusses that goal in terms of cooperative planning and goal-setting rather than in terms of cognitive behavior modification
techniques and eventual self-control. Not only does self-control adequately address both
the athletes' and coaches' proper roles within the arena of sport, but it addresses the
goal or hope for personal growth and development through the vehicle of sport. In many
cultures, a major goal of personal growth and development is to become capable of
directing, maintaining, and coordinating one's behavior without reliance upon external
supervision, which is stated very succinctly by Thoresen and Mahoney (1974). "The
ability to control one's own actions in the absence of immediate external constraints—
to postpone or forego gratifications, to endure avoidable pain, to direct oneself—is typ-
ically thought to characterize an intelligent person. Self-control is often considered the
ultimate mark of socialization."

The primary purpose of this section will be to present several cognitive behavior
modification techniques which can be used by coaches who strive to (1) produce predictable and controllable charges in their athletes' sport behaviors, and (2) eventually
bring such behaviors under each athlete's self-control. The enhancement of athletic

performance and *not the solution of emotional problems* is an important limitation to this focus.

TECHNIQUES FOR THE COACH

The techniques which are presented share some common characteristics. Each of them is based upon a sequence which always involves (1) antecedent events which precede the behavior itself and serve as cues, (2) the behavior, which can be either observable or covert, and (3) consequences which are contingent upon the behavior. These techniques are also based upon the observed and well-documented importance which both antecedents and contingent consequences have in the prediction and control of behavior (Thoresen and Mahoney 1974). Vicarious means for behavior change, wherein observation and imitation can replicate the results of direct involvement, and covert behaviors such as thinking, self-talk, and imagery are included among these techniques. Each technique can, under proper conditions, be used by coaches and athletes at all levels of sport.

An example drawn from an actual situation illustrates several, though not all, of the basic principles upon which these techniques are based. Rainer Martens, a leader in sport psychology research, recounted the following incident from a peewee baseball game he was watching (Martens 1978, 279).

"My 8-year-old neighbor Kevin was playing in his very first game on a local peewee team. The first time he came to bat the much maturer pitcher of the opposing team threw three strikes past Kevin before he had time to get the bat off his shoulder. Kevin walked backed to the bench unperturbed by the outcome. The coach, seeing that Kevin was not unhappy with the outcome, concluded that he did not care and gave him a tongue lashing for not putting forth an effort to hit the ball."

"Now Kevin was sad. He sat on the bench with his head hanging low as he watched the older members of the team take their turn at the plate. What he saw was that when an older player struck out he threw his bat down, slammed his helmet to the ground, and stalked back to the bench to sulk. The coach would then yell to the players 'That's all right, hang in there. You'll get a hit next time."

The next time Kevin came to bat he struck out again, but this time he did swing at the third strike. Now when Kevin walked back to the bench he, too, threw his bat, slammed his helmet, stalked, and sulked. Sure enough, the coach yelled, "That's all right Kevin, you'll do better next time."

While the preceding example does not, for instance, specifically illustrate chaining, it does show the role of antecedents or cues, the role of vicarious observation and imitation in the modeling process, and the effects of contingent consequences, which in this case were the coach's expressions of approval and disapproval.

MODELING

For our purposes, modeling refers to the effects that observing the coach's behavior has upon the athlete's behavior. Referred to as vicarious or observational learning, modeling is an effective therapeutic strategy that can serve as an excellent motivational tool. This power is not, however, unlimited. As Bandura (1971a) has noted, factory workers would not continue their work too long if the only consequence was observing fellow workers receive paychecks instead of regularly receiving their own. Given such obvious limitations, however, modeling stands as one of the most impressive means for affecting behavior in predictable and controllable ways.

Modeling involves the acquisition of new skills and alteration of existing skills through observation of someone else (the coach) demonstrating those skills. From such modeling the athlete learns not only how to behave, but also what to expect as probable consequences of her behavior. Whether we talk about Kevin who wanted his peewee baseball coach's approval or the next Cheryl Miller or Mary Lou Retton—whomever and wherever she might be—the consequences, effects, or outcomes which occur as a result of a model's behavior have tremendous influence. Due to the nature of modeling and the social setting within which coaches and athletes interact, coaches serve as models, either knowingly or unknowingly. While Kevin's coach may have been unaware of how he was teaching his players to behave, Wooden made obvious and extensive use of modeling to teach physical skills (Tharp and Gallimore 1976); and the importance of modeling in teaching young athletes socially approved behavior patterns has been cited by Orlick (1972). By no means is modeling restricted to the clinical psychologist's office.

While modeling may be designated as group or individual, participant or vicarious, in vivo or symbolic, depending upon the circumstances, this discussion focuses upon the nature of the model as either a (1) coping or (2) mastery model (Meichenbaum 1971). The other aspects are not less important, but are often less determined by the coach and more determined by the situation or the task. For instance, you seldom if ever have the option of Chris Evert Lloyd giving a modeling session to one athlete at a time and waiting while that one athlete practices the modeled behavior. The coach can, however, decide whether to provide a coping or mastery model, and base the decision upon data rather than tradition.

A coping model is one who evidences some limitations and difficulties similar to the observer, but demonstrates steady improvement, which leads to successful accomplishment of the task. In contrast to a coping model, a mastery model evidences no incompetency or difficulty in task completion, but demonstrates control over the task and herself or himself from beginning to end. Early evidence indicated that perceived similarity between observer and model increased the likelihood of limitation (Bandura 1971 b). Subsequent research cited by Mahoney (1974) further documents the effectiveness of a coping model.

It would be a difficult task to determine how many coaches would prefer to offer themselves to their athletes as mastery rather than coping models, or to examine the reasons for whichever choice was preferred. Reasons might range from personal insecurity with admitting one's own struggles to the ambiguity of tradition. Regardless of the results of such a proposed study, some examples of how coaches can serve as coping models for their athletes are as follows.

1. The beleaguered parent who finally "volunteers" to coach the team rather than have no team at all can serve as a valuable coping model for many desirable

behaviors, among them, respect for authority. A coach cannot do this by meekly submitting to every decision made by every umpire nor by constantly resisting every decision. The coach should show efforts, successes, and failures at controlling honest emotional reactions to different umpires and their decisions. Of course, failures should be less frequent than successes, and become less and less frequent with time, but in any human there are shortcomings and mistakes. It is the improvement which is crucially important.

2. In teaching a physical skill, modeling has always been used, though sometimes called demonstration and without insight into the roles of contingent consequences and coping models. A coach teaching youngsters to shoot a basketball could offer a coping model by illustrating how he or she overcame some of the difficulties which every young basketball player encounters sooner or later. For instance, the coach's present skill level might never demonstrate taking off on the wrong foot when shooting a lay-up. The coach at some time, however, probably did—and probably overcame that difficulty. Instead of presenting athletes with only his or her current mastery of a task, a coach could model some of the steps involved in overcoming a difficulty—the process ultimately which led to a certain level of mastery.

IMAGERY

Coaches have referred to it as mental practice, researchers have studied it as covert rehearsal, and clinicians have labelled it as self-talk and symbolic self-stimulation. These are but a few of the names given to the phenomenon we refer to as imagery. Imagery refers to stimuli and responses produced internally by means such as imagination and internalized verbalizations which lead to physiological effects (Mahoney and Thoresen 1974). Several examples that many coaches and athletes could relate to might better illustrate the effects of imagery. For instance, many people have experienced the muscular tension which results when one vividly imagines oneself engaging in a very strenuous task or indulging in adult fantasies and erotic imagery.

Several accounts have recently been given of the use of imagery with elementary school athletes (Lane 1980), college athletes (Titley 1980), Olympic athletes (Suinn 1977, 1980), and professional athletes (Nicklaus 1974). In most of these accounts, imagery is coupled with one or more versions of progressive relaxation, quite often a modification of Jacobson's (1938) original work in progressive deep muscle relaxation procedures. While such relaxation may complement the use of imagery, our focus is upon the imagery rather than the techniques for relaxing, which is achieved by progressively tensing, then relaxing various muscle groups until a more relaxed state is attained. Imagery can by used by a coach at any level of sport, though present data indicate that more highly skilled athletes benefit more from the use of imagery than do novices (Singer 1975). Perhaps more thorough knowledge of the task to be performed enables the skilled athlete to experience more vivid imagery, though imagery vividness has not yet been correlated with greater behavioral change (Mahoney and Thoresen 1974).

The following examples of the use of imagery should be helpful and are meant to be representative rather than exhaustive.

1. A coach working with a young tennis player wants to make the maximum contribution to the youngster's improvement, but also wants to avoid overdoing it (with the physical and psychological effects they can have). The coach can use imagery to good advantage, to improve the youngster's forehand, for instance.

    The coach makes sure that the youngster knows what is involved in a correct forehand, and ensures that the setting in which imagery occurs is free of distractions and that the athlete is comfortable. The coach instructs the athlete to imagine herself on a familiar court, including the more vivid aspects of the situation such as the beautiful trees bordering the court or the smell of certain flowers. The athlete is then instructed to imagine hitting a perfect forehand—*not* watching herself hit one, but actually hitting it, including the feel in her hand, arm, legs, and the flight of the ball back over the net. Attention may be focused upon the overall stroke or a particular aspect such as foot position or knee bend as the coach selects. The imagery should progress to hitting forehands under various conditions, from different court positions, and so on. The athlete should be encouraged to experiment with use of imagery on her own, extending and expanding her use of it.

2. A coach confronted with an injured skier could assist that athlete in the use of imagery, following the example of Jean-Claude Killy, who reportedly experienced one of his best races when, because of an injury, his only preparation was mentally skiing in the course (Suinn 1980). Such imagery should involve as many aspects of the course as possible, going beyond watching oneself ski the course to feeling the nervousness in the starting gate and the wind in one's face during the race, experiencing the turns and moguls, even seeing a stopwatch timing the race.

3. The coach of a basketball player who experiences extreme anxiety at the free-throw line, often "choking" in such a situation, could help that athlete develop an imagery-based coping technique. Imagery could be used to both improve the skill (Lane 1980) and to deal more effectively with the situation-specific anxiety. Skill improvement would follow strategies similar to those outlined in the previous two examples. To deal with the anxiety, the athlete might use the feeling of tension as a cue to engage in imagery in which her own muscular tension is absorbed by the crowd around her (teammates at practice and spectators at a game)—so that the noisier the crowd, the less the tension. Such a procedure would have some commonalities with "stress inoculation" as explained and employed by Meichenbaum and Cameron (1974). The athlete might imagine a thin but strong line from the ball in her hand to the center of the basket, or even use imagery that involves the drainage of her tension into the floor—releasing the ball when the line is "right" or the tension gone.

SELF-CONTROL

The final technique presented for the coach's use—development of self-control in athletes—is not only a major goal of sport participation, but also exerts tremendous influence on the extent to which any coach can achieve stated goals. By self-control we refer to internal rather than external determination of the behaviors in which one will engage. The effects of both antecedents and consequences upon behavior are not ignored but are instead brought under the control of the person. Self-control consists of self-observation plus self-regulation and is effective in proportion to (1) the power of the techniques employed and (2) the consistency with which the individual applies them (Thoresen and Mahoney 1974). Both overt and covert behaviors are amenable to self-control, the development of which is analogous to the person becoming her own behavioral scientist—replacing unsystematic observation and control with systematic techniques. Most people make frequent use of both systematic techniques such as the use of an alarm clock and unsystematic techniques such as allowing themselves only one drink before dinner—unless dinner is slow in coming. Considerable support for the effectiveness of self-control techniques exists, including improved performance found when reinforcement and contingent consequences were self-determined, the motivational strength of personal choice, and the lack of difficulty in transferring behavioral control from in vitro (laboratory or controlled situation) to in vivo (real life) since self-control is always real life for the person involved (Thoresen and Mahoney 1974). In order to make a large and amorphous topic such as self-control manageable, focus will be directed toward some specific aspects: (1) thought-stopping, (2) self-talk, and (3) the interrelated techniques of self-observation and regulation.

THOUGHT-STOPPING AND SELF-TALK

Thought-stopping, as its name indicates, refers to interruption and cessation of certain thoughts. The athlete chastising herself to "get your mind back on the game" provides a readily identifiable example. As a technique for behavior change and self-control, thought-stopping involves the use of an interruption such as saying aloud to oneself, "STOP," as both a consequence of the undesired thinking and a cue for more desirable thoughts. A large number of case studies support the effectiveness of this technique, but well-conducted research data provide only meager support (Mahoney 1974). At the present time, combining thought-stopping with complementary techniques is probably the most advisable use of the technique. One such complementary technique is self-talk.

The therapeutic value and importance of private monologues, whether they are overtly spoken aloud or are covert inner talk, were recognized a long time before modern psychologists verified them (Mahoney and Thoresen 1974). Verbal self-instructions during an athletic performance play an observably important role in the performance of many athletes from Martina Navratilova to young Kevin in the earlier example. Some of the theorists in motor learning acknowledge the importance of the verbal component when they employ labels such as the verbal or motor stage (Adams 1971). Self-talk provides a crucially important complement to thought-stopping because it provides a desirable substitute to replace the unwanted process which was halted.

Self-talk can be implemented by using a progression which begins with initial modeling, moves to guided participation, and concludes with gradual shaping toward covert self-instruction. The following example illustrates how a coach could use thought-stopping and self-talk together.

The coach has a pitcher who becomes so anxious once runners get on base that she is no longer effective. To deal with this, the coach creates a practice situation duplicating the game situation and instructs the pitcher to engage in her usual anxiety-producing thoughts, nodding her head once she is thinking the undesirable thoughts. At this point the coach shouts "STOP" sharply enough to startle the pitcher and disrupt the thought pattern. The coach now points out that the distraction interrupted the undesired pattern of thinking, and together the coach and the athlete can decide to substitute a desirable monologue, such as "I'm in control out there" or "Take charge of things by staying calm." At this point, the coach can model the thought-stopping and desirable self-instruction aloud. The next step would involve the coach guiding the athlete through overt execution of both the thought-stopping and self-talk, followed by the athlete guiding herself through overt execution. The final step would involve fading out the external, out-loud process and gradually replacing it with less overt control until the entire self-instruction process was completely personal. Once personal self-talk was attained, practice conditions should ever more closely approximate actual game conditions in order to make success in games more likely.

SELF-OBSERVATION AND SELF-REGULATION

Development of self-control depends upon how adept the coach and athlete become at (1) detecting the cues and consequences surrounding a selected behavior, and (2) managing those cues and consequences. These respective aspects of self-observation and self-regulation form the basic skills required of the coach and athlete, who will become her own behavioral scientist.

Self-observation, in order to serve as the basis for self-control, must incorporate several important characteristics. The athlete must be capable of discriminating the selected behavior, along with its cues and consequences, from others. Systematically recording her observations is the next step toward self-control, and evaluation and analysis of the observations is the last stage in the athlete's self-observation process. Methods of self-observation vary widely, including such devices as wrist counters, note pads, and videotapes, and systems such as tallies of number of occurrences and "all-or-none" recording in which even one negative thought or act during the time period leads to a negative tally. All of these techniques, which are intended to lead toward self-control, share one common characteristic—systematic procedures. In self-observation, all aspects of self-control and systematic application are crucially important considerations, for without them, the cues and consequences that the person associates with the target behavior will be haphazard and unpredictable. Given such unpredictability, the behavior will not be brought under self-control, but will continue to occur haphazardly. Only when the relationship between the behavior and its cues and consequences is predictable and known can the behavior be brought under self-control. Imagine trying to treat an infection if no predictable antecedents preceded its onset, no consistent cues accompanied the illness, and treatment modalities were random rather than predictable in their effects on the illness. You would not have much chance of success.

Self-regulation includes both self-reward and self-punishment, each of which involves theoretical intricacies and nuances. However, the discussion of these theoretical issues is beyond the scope of this book. The primary concern focuses upon (1) the systematic application of the chosen technique, (2) selection of self-reward contingencies, and (3) whether the selected self-punishment involves administration of an aversive stimulus or removal of a pleasant stimulus as a contingent consequence.

Systematic application is no less critical in self-regulation than in self-observation and all other techniques for self-control. The chosen rewards and punishments must be used in a predictable manner, not necessarily after every observation, but systematically rather than haphazardly.

Self-reward involves the pairing of a pleasant consequence with the performance of a desired behavior. Direct self-administration may be the means for this pairing, such as a sprinter taking a water break only if her time is below a selected criterion time. Arrangement of contingencies can provide means, in which case our sprinter might have prearranged the presence or absence of a water bottle with the person timing her sprints. In either situation, the pleasant consequence *must* be contingent upon performance of the behavior which the athlete wishes to bring under self-control.

Self-punishment can occur by attaching an aversive stimulus to an undesirable behavior so that performance of the behavior leads to the aversive consequences, or by making the removal of a pleasant consequence contingent upon the performance of an undesirable behavior. For instance, a basketball player who wants to eliminate the missing of lay-ups could pinch her inner bicep or thigh very vigorously as an aversive consequence for missing the lay-up. Perhaps the removal of a pleasant stimulus could be imposed as the consequence of missing a lay-up, such as removing 5 percent from her predetermined amount of Saturday night spending money or deducting one minute of playing time from the next game for each missed lay-up, or, if warranted, removal from the immediate starting lineup.

The following examples provide a representative illustration of self-observation and self-regulation techniques applied to an athletic situation.

1. A golfer who experiences a recurring though not constant slice wishes to eliminate that particular problem. She can carry a note pad and pen for recording the details accompanying every slice which occurs, such as the hole on which it occurred, her stance and position (uphill or downhill from the ball), and the club used (3 wood, 4 iron, etc.). After each round the recorded data can be examined to detect the consistencies which are associated with hitting a slice, ranging from the golfer's hand position, foot placement, or a feeling of slowness in the hands during the swing to environmental variables such as the first or last three holes or just par fives. Such analysis should be used as a basis for future practice. After deciding upon the necessary changes, the golfer can then engage in self-regulation by using self-reward herself with a favorite beverage or food upon completion of a set number of holes without a slice. The reward might be as frequent as every hole or as infrequent as every eighteen holes, depending upon the reward. Self-punishment for slicing might involve giving a new golf ball of her own preferred brand to her playing partner or picking up and carrying her playing partner's golf bag for fifteen minutes. This self-punishment could become both expensive and tiresome.

2. A tennis player who wants to stop hitting overhead smashes which go long must use a recording technique different from that of the golfer, due to the reactive nature of the game. While a note pad and time to record foot and body position or game and set score would be impractical for the tennis player, other options exist. These options range from videotape to a piece of chalk with which to mark the sideline as an option. Have a friend or coach do the recording. If the athlete does the recording, she can devise a system in which the

recording interferes only minimally with the match. For example, if four aspects are of concern—head position, body control, foot position, and arm action—the athlete can devise a code so that four numbers or letters are chalked just outside the court where the error occurred. Easier and more extensive recording could be done by a friend or coach, or a videotape, but would not be absolutely essential. After analysis of the systematic recording of the behavior, and selection of the desired behavior changes, self-regulation would be used to establish new cues and consequences for the overhead smash, employing pleasant and aversive stimuli in ways similar to the example of the golfer.

The coach should assist athletes in their initial efforts to benefit from cognitive behavior modification techniques and develop self-control, giving different individuals differing amounts of assistance. External controls, guided and directed by the coach at the outset, should give way to internal controls as each athlete progresses toward self-control.

At every level of sport, the coach has the potential to be a facilitator rather than merely a manipulator or controller of athlete behavior—both within and outside of the athletic arena. When coaches go beyond performance enhancement to the establishment of behavioral control within the individual athlete instead of the coach himself or herself, perhaps sport participation can more often fulfill some of the long-term goals of personal psychosocial development that so many people hold for it.

COGNITIVE RESTRUCTURING

Coaches and athletes have often been overheard remarking about certain athletes who appear to possess incredible insight and intuition, which in sports require tactics and strategy (basketball, soccer, track, softball, tennis, field hockey) and are a tremendous asset. These athletes are often referred to as having a "sense of timing," "always being around the ball," and "making things happen." An understanding and appreciation of cognitive restructuring as a learning theory can enable both coach and athlete to assist in this area of performance enhancement.

The sophistication and technology that are operational in competitive sports have resulted in a very complex science of human performance, which seems to evolve into a more intricate and calculating endeavor each year. It is rare indeed that the stereotyped "dumb jock" or "neolithic era" coach will find success in sports on a formal, competitive level today. As described by Nixon and Jewett (1980, 20):

In complex learning situations the roles of perception and knowledge are crucial. Cognitive learning is the term applied to the phase of overall learning theory that concentrates on describing relationships and means. It suggests that learners develop a cognitive structure within their memory that organizes information for future retention and use. . . .Teachers should emphasize insightful learning rather than pure memorization or mechanical skills, and thus encourage problem solving behaviors. . . . Concepts, principles, generalizations, theories, facts, laws, and other forms of cognitive input are arranged in meaningful relationships that promote desirable learning results. The teacher assists the learner to recognize the relationship or choose other concepts or principals having the potential to solve a problem.

BEHAVIOR MODIFICATION

Cognitive theorists recognize and accept the concept and application of "insight," which does not enjoy the same respect or interest as operant conditioning espoused by B. F. Skinner. Insight as perceived by both adherents to cognitive restructuring and the vast majority of coaches is demonstrated by the athlete as a sudden revelation or solution to a problem which is immediate. Oxendine (1984, 83) states that: "This Ah, ha! phenomenon is usually followed by rapid progress or much improved performance. It is generally assumed that insight results from conscious or subconscious consideration of the problem. Insight often appears to be much faster than the usually slow and awkward trial-and-error process."

The operational environment in which the application of cognitive restructuring takes place is dependent upon signs, symbols, total stimuli, and structuring, according to Oxendine (1984). This operational scheme is quite similar to many practice plans traditionally developed by coaches, and the use of motivation as a tool for success is embraced by both coaches and cognitive theorists. As complementary as cognitive theory and cognitive restructuring may appear to be in terms of their application to sport, operant conditioning and the subsequent application and methodology of behavior modification have placed cognitive theory in a secondary position of interest. "The cognitive concept has not been as scientifically exact as the stimulus-response theory because cognitive theorists recognize a greater number of intangibles that cannot be precisely measured by available evaluative tools" (Oxendine 1984, 83).

In contrast, proponents of operant conditioning and behavior modification as developed by B. F. Skinner base their research and subsequent beliefs on absolute quantification of behavior. As a result of the methodology utilized by Skinner and his adherents, it is possible for psychology to "become almost perfect science" (Oxendine 1984, 82). As stated by Oxendine (1984, 82), Skinner

> . . . disagrees with the old axiom that "A horse can be led to water but cannot be made to drink." . . . He insists that the science of conditioning can be perfected to *assure* that the horse will drink. If the environment of . . . humans is controlled, behavior can be accurately predicted. . . . It naturally follows that the probability of man's responses can be predicted and his behavior controlled. Skinner's is a psychology of nationalistic determinism opposed to the philosophy of personal freedom. This determinism indicates that the behavior that results is the only behavior that could have occurred. Skinner has indicated that as the science of psychology develops, man will become more like a machine in that his behavior will be predictable.

Martin and Hrycaiko's (1983, 9–16) excellent book, *Behavior Modification and Coaching,* identifies six characteristics of effective coaching based upon behavioral modification principles developed by Skinner. The following list represents a limited introduction to their six characteristics; for a thorough analysis of applied behavior analysis and application, readers are directed to *The Development and Control of Behavior in Sport and Physical Education* by Rushall and Siedentop (Lea & Febiger, 1972).

1. An important characteristic of behavioral coaching is that it emphasizes specific, detailed, and frequent measurement of athletic performance and the use of these measures as the primary means for evaluating the effectiveness of specific coaching techniques. . . .

2. A second characteristic of effective behavioral coaching is that it recognizes the distinction between developing new behavior and maintaining existing behavior at acceptable rates, and it offers positive procedures for accomplishing both.

3. A third characteristic of behavioral coaching is that it encourages athletes to improve against their own previous performance.

4. A fourth characteristic of effective behavioral coaching is that it emphasizes specific, behavioral procedures for which effectiveness has been experimentally demonstrated—i.e., it views coaching more as a science rather than as an art.

5. The fifth characteristic of effective behavioral coaching focuses on the behavior of the coach. The first four characteristics recommend that coaches pinpoint behavior of beginning athletes, apply behavior modification techniques to change those behaviors in desirable directions, and rely on data to demonstrate and document behavioral change. The fifth characteristic suggests that this basic strategy can also be applied effectively to the behavior of the coach as well.

6. The final characteristic of effective behavioral coaching is one that has emerged as important in recent years. . . . This characteristic is referred to as social validation. In behavior modification in general, behavior modifiers are encouraged to validate what they do by constantly seeking answers to three questions: (a) to what extent are the target behaviors identified for treatment programs really the most important. . . ? (b) are the particular procedures used acceptable to the client, especially when alternative procedures might be available to accomplish approximately the same results? and (c) are the consumers of the program (athletes and coaches, clients-caretakers) satisfied with the results obtained?

Behavior modification as a component of sport psychology is a viable avenue for both athletes and coaches to consider.

Sport psychology or the psychology of coaching is an important and dynamic area within the realm of sports medicine, physical education, psychology, and parameters of human performance and athletic competition. Many coaches and athletes are weary of the methods and purpose of sport psychology, perhaps because these coaches and athletes don't understand or are intimidated by psychology in general. Then again, there are coaches and athletes who have enjoyed a great deal of success by relying on instinct or "flying by the seat of their pants." Kozar and Mechikoff (1983) for their book *Sport Psychology: The Coaches' Perspective* interviewed and collected data from numerous coaches, successful and not so successful, around the country. They found very successful and nationally prominent coaches who utilize the "scientific approach" of sport psychology and others who shun the concept and practice of scientific sport psychology in favor of their reliance as judges of human nature. It was revealed that those coaches who are very successful and do not embrace or rely on formal sport psychology theories and methods have, over many years of coaching, through trial and error and direct observation, come to employ many of the practices and beliefs of formal learning theories, although these coaches do it in a roundabout way. The primary reason for calling attention to this fairly typical pattern or process is that evidence would indicate that although some coaches and athletes do not yet hold the scientific principles of psychology and learning theories in high esteem, regarding their contribution to coaching, many others do. It would appear that the *successful* coaches seem to eventually employ many of the practices and fundamental tenets of contemporary psychology. The obvious and pragmatic approach is to avoid "putting the cart before the horse" and strive to become knowledgeable in the science and practice of the various areas of applied sport psychology.

section II

APPLIED PSYCHOLOGICAL
COACHING METHODS

INTRODUCTION

The Applied Psychological Coaching Methods section of this book is taken from twenty coaches' answers to fifteen different questions. The coaches' material follows the order of the questions. If a coach did not use a specific psychological technique, that area was not included in that coach's response.

The fifteen questions are as follows (the headings match the headings in the coaches' material):

Mental Preparation

1. What percentage (approximate) of your athletes' practice time is spent on mental preparation for the game or contest?
2. Do you utilize specific drills to develop mental concentration in your athletes and team?
3. Do you use imagery techniques in your coaching?
4. Do you use relaxation techniques in your coaching?

Motivation

5. How do you deal with overmotivation of your players?
6. How do you deal with undermotivation of your players?

Optimal Arousal

7. How do you help your athletes achieve optimal arousal for competition?

Emotional Differences

8. How do you or can you coach for emotional differences in your athletes?

Athlete or Team That Chokes

9. How do you coach the athlete and/or team that "chokes"?

Goal-setting

10. How do you use goal-setting (individual and team) in your coaching?

Extrinsic Rewards

11. Do your make use of extrinsic rewards?

Nonverbal Cues

12. Do you employ nonverbal cues to communicate to your athletes in practice and competition?

Sport Psychologist

13. Do you utilize the services of a sport psychologist (clinical psychologist)?

Psychological Methods

14. What general and specific psychological methods do you use to attempt an increase in learning, performance, and motivation in your athletes?

Mental Qualities of an Athlete Compatible with My Coaching Style

15. Discuss the mental qualities of current or past members of your team that you believe are highly compatible with your coaching style.

chapter 7

Basketball

ANDY LANDERS

Profile

Andy Landers is the head coach at the University of Georgia. After seven seasons there, his record is now 180–48 (.789). His teams have been to six consecutive post-season national tournaments, including five straight NCAA tourneys. Two of his past four teams reached the NCAA Final Four, the 1985 squad advancing to the championship game.

Landers' most recent team accomplished these notable landmarks: won thirty of thirty-two games; won the Southeastern Conference title, both regular-season and tournament crowns; ranked second in the final AP poll; produced two Kodak All America team members; and led the nation in field goal accuracy for much of the season.

The Lady Bulldogs have now enjoyed four straight seasons of twenty-five or more wins. And during his time at Georgia, Landers has coached seven All Americans and one United States Olympic team member.

Landers' overall coaching record in basketball is 262–69 (.792). He played basketball one year at Tennessee Tech, where he received both his B.S. and M.A. degrees. He also coached women's basketball for four years at Roane State (Tennessee) Community College.

Psychological Coaching Methods

Mental Preparation Individuals differ as to the amount of time they spend on mental preparation for a game or practice. The difference is due to the fact that each individual is very unique. Starters and first subs seem to take their preparation more seriously. Time spent in mental practice the day before the game and on game day is approximately 40 percent for individuals and 60 percent for the team.

Mental Concentration   All of our drills develop mental concentration. All of our drills are rapid quick-hitters which require players to understand the rotations, purposes, and skills of each rotation. Players must be ready to continue the continuity of the drill when their turns come around. Naturally, they are also required to talk and/or count repetitions so as to perform two or three things at once, thus increasing their mental capacity.

Related to concentration but what I consider to be also a form of relaxation is our approach to time between drills. Rather than move immediately from one drill to another, we try to take a few seconds to explain the criteria and purpose of the next drill as well as the proper execution procedure. I believe this relieves the anxiety of the athlete in that she has a clear picture of what is expected; thus there is little doubt or confusion.

Imagery Techniques   We use an imagery drill in each practice. I call it "ET Shooting Drill." Each day at the beginning of practice our players form an arc around the front of the basket. On command and without distraction the group will execute the proper fundamental involved in shooting the jump shot. No ball is used! We shoot twenty perfect jumpers, all of which we hit, in our minds.

Motivation/Optimal Arousal   When players are overmotivated or seem to be overanxious, I usually do one of two things. I deviate from my/our normal procedures so as to distract their thinking. The other approach is to plan the attack (game plan) so as to utilize energy over the entire floor (full court) early in the game.

My approach to the undermotivated player is through her pride. I believe any athlete who is truly a competitor has pride. Therefore, I make verbal or mental appeals to her pride or I challenge her pride with a physical challenge such as rebounding a certain number in the game. Finally, nothing hurts pride like sitting on the bench; it is a great motivator.

There are three approaches I use to help athletes achieve optimal arousal for competition. First, I appeal to team and individual pride. Second, I set **goals** to challenge the team and certain individuals for a particular game. And third, I verbally reinforce the importance of great effort and satisfaction derived from such output.

Emotional Differences   We do coach for individual differences because all people are not created equal. We consider each individual's background, past performances, etc., and approach that person at a halfway point—halfway between where she is coming from and where we would ideally like her to be. By using this method we are constantly raising her starting point; thus the halfway point becomes closer to the ideal result.

Athlete or Team That Chokes   I believe athletes and teams that have "choked" are those that were in high-pressure situations. Mentally, I try to remove the pressure from the team or individual. I also take the responsibility for everything that goes wrong.

The team and individual athletes are responsible for everything that goes right. This is my philosophy and I feel I do a good job of selling the athletes on this.

Goal-setting   The most important part of our program is goal-setting. We are very goal-oriented. We feel we must know which direction we are moving toward and why. Team goals are set with the sophomore, junior, and senior classes along with the coaches.

We strive for realistic but challenging goals. Goals must be measurable. We do not accept objectives such as "always play hard." Also we do not complicate the situation with too many goals. Three goals are generally the maximum number we set. Usually we select one or two as high objectives.

Extrinsic Rewards   We make use of extrinsic rewards. Perhaps the most common mistake a driving, intense coach makes is that of overlooking accomplishment. We use all kinds of rewards: no running, front of the meal line, Coca-Cola, etc. I do not feel the reward itself is as important as the recognition the athlete gets from her coach and peers. We have seen athletes compete as hard for a cup of water as they would for a T-shirt. I believe the extrinsic rewards work because of pride and recognition.

Nonverbal Cues   The nonverbal cue is evident in body language for both the athlete and the coach. Body language can reveal the degree of emotion both positive and negative that a person is feeling. First I look at the facial expressions. Second are the hands and arms; third is the body position or posture. The fourth area of communication is foot movements. There is also the combination of body language that gives me an idea of what the athlete is feeling and for her to know what I am expressing. A picture is worth a thousand words and a gesture is also.

Mental Qualities   The mental qualities that I desire in my athletes are present in my team. Our athletes are extremely determined. They have an incredible ability to prioritize things. They have self-discipline and are mature beyond their age. They deal well with the reality of life, winning, and losing. They are competitive and aggressive and they are people-oriented.

DARLENE MAY

Profile

Each year Darlene May continues to add to her impressive list of accomplishments. She has propelled the Broncos to success every year since she came to Cal Poly twelve years ago.

Her twelve-year record of 312–78 (.800) makes her the most winning coach in NCAA Division II history; with her 300th victory this past season she became the first Division II women's coach to attain the 300-win mark. A perennial national power, Coach May's Broncos have made four appearances in the five NCAA national championships held for women's basketball, finishing first three times and second once. After winning the Division II National Championship this season, the Broncos became the first team in Division II history to win back-to-back national crowns.

Coach May has guided the Broncos to ten consecutive conference championships; their league mark is 108–3. Since the California Collegiate Athletic Association (CCAA) was formed, Cal Poly has been 57–2.

May was named the national Coach of the Year for two consecutive years at the Wade Trophy Awards dinner in New York City; she was the only multiple recipient.

Besides her achievements as a coach, she has also earned the reputation of America's finest women's basketball referee. She was selected by the International Federation of Amateur Basketball (FIBA) to officiate in the 1984 Olympic Games in Los Angeles. This historic selection meant that May was the first woman to referee the Olympic Games women's basketball competition.

In addition to her impressive stint as Olympic Games referee, May has been selected to referee at the 1986 World Friendship Games in Moscow. She officiated international games at both the men's and women's levels in the World University Games in 1977. Later she refereed the Women's World Championships in Brazil in 1983 and South Korea in 1979. Another of her assignments was working the U.S. National Sports Festival in Syracuse, New York in 1981.

May's basketball career began at Fullerton College, where she played before transferring to Cal State Fullerton. At Fullerton College, she was an outstanding player, competing on teams that were among the best in their division levels in southern California. She earned both a bachelor's and master's degree from Cal State Fullerton.

After completing college, May signed on at Anaheim's Connelly High School, where she coached basketball, volleyball, and softball. At Connelly, her teams amassed records of 117–31, attracting the attention of collegiate programs.

A resident of Placentia, May enjoys boating and fishing in her spare time.

Psychological Coaching Methods

Mental Preparation   Very little time is spent in this area other than the use of game films, which we study, discuss, and use to rehearse our opponents' offenses and defenses.

Mental Concentration   All our drills are designed and utilized to develop mental concentration. I believe that athletes have to concentrate and learn as quickly as possible. They become better equipped to make specific game adjustments. As a result, I teach a drill—get them to run it as much as possible to perfection—then add other aspects to the drill.

Imagery Techniques   I do not use this technique.

Relaxation Techniques   I believe in this concept but do not use it at the current time. I think it depends a lot on your particular group of athletes. This group, 1986 National Champions, is very "loose," and I don't feel they would benefit from this concept that much.

Motivation I don't find overmotivation to be a problem! I love players who want to "go after it." What is "over"-motivated? If it means "hyper" or too aggressive, I'll try to harness all that energy by working hard in practice. I would think these types of players would rub off on the team and cause everyone to work harder and want to win more!

I do not *recruit* players who are undermotivated and not willing to work hard and who cannot "play for me." I tell them what to expect from practices and from me before they ever come to Cal Poly.

I think I tend to motivate players out of fear. I'm not easy to play for because I demand perfection. I have enough players presently on my team that have played for me that they give tremendous example to the other players, and I have very little problem with motivation. They either produce at practice or they don't play. It's also easy to motivate players when you have a winning reputation—they're expected to keep you on top.

Optimal Arousal We set goals for every game—especially on defense. We try to make them feel the pride of achieving the goals they set. Most of my players function better if they're relaxed and not "juiced up" for a game. We try to instill a solid game plan— one they have confidence in and that will work. Then they take the floor—ready to play and basically have fun. Ten years ago it was very different; athletes were different! There was a lot of rah-rah, cheering, getting excited before taking the floor. Not so now. I really believe that this is a more laid-back generation, but we still seem to be accomplishing the same results!

Emotional Differences I don't find this very difficult once you get to know each one of your players. It doesn't take long to find out which ones you can push harder than others, or which ones can take more verbal abuse than others.

Athlete or Team That Chokes I think you have to remain positive with them. They don't intentionally "choke!" In the past I have chewed them out at halftime only to find them even more tight second half and still unable to function. This past year we played USC and scored fifteen points the first half. At halftime we simply tried to let them know that we were still with them 100 percent; we tried to encourage them to *relax* and just play their game. The second half we scored forty-one points and at one time came back within twelve points! So I think it's important to not tense them up by "brutality"— screaming, etc.

Goal-setting We consistently talk about setting goals. I put up various charts, usually showing a staircase and a means of "climbing" to the top.

We talk to individual players about goals they would like to achieve. We write them down at the beginning of the season and remind them of their own goals and show them where they are in relation to achieving them. Usually things like field goal percentage, free-throw percentage, etc.

Extrinsic Rewards We give out "BRONCO" stickers for various achievements for a game. These small stickers can go on their shoes, for example, one sticker for any one of the following: *individual stats*—six assists; thirty points; fifteen rebounds; seven steals; 60 percent FG minimum of ten attempts; 80 percent FG minimum of five attempts. *Team stats*—fifteen turnovers; sixty rebounds; 80 percent FG minimum of fifteen attempts; 60 percent FG minimum of forty-five attempts; allowing forty-five points on defense. Each team member gets one for any of the above.

Nonverbal Cues   We use hand signals to indicate changes in our offenses and defenses, also when and when not to use the full-court press. Number 2 means a 2–1–2 zone. Pounding the fists together means to press. We use a lot of a different numbers to change offenses.

Sport Psychologist   We do not use a sport psychologist.

Psychological Methods   This is a difficult answer to put on paper. I talk a lot to my players in terms of the psychological aspects of sport and how you can get the edge on your opponents by being smarter and better prepared. A smart team can beat a physically better team many times—I believe that! I try to get my players to put the burden of beating us on opponents shoulders and not the burden of winning on our shoulder! We know what we can do, do it well, and let them worry about us.

Mental Qualities   Several of my current and former players are very compatible with my coaching theories. They are intense, competitive athletes. They are all good, intelligent students—players I have to tell to do something only once. Many of my former players in that group are now coaches—successful ones at that! These players are (and have been) leaders on the floor. They are like having another coach on the floor.

I like to be prepared for all situations. I am a very organized, precise type of person. Certain things *must* be accomplished during each practice session. I am very concerned about discipline and impose this on my players. I believe in *earning* respect between players and between myself and my players. I have a very hard time when players come to practice and don't put out 100 percent every day. I tend to "get down" on those players very quickly. It usually happens only once because I dismiss them from practice (usually not very politely or discreetly).

Despite the picture I've painted, I feel it's very important to be able to laugh with the players. I think I have a pretty good sense of humor and we can have as much fun in practice as we can have serious work. It's just important to keep it in perspective and to know *when to* and *when not to*!

JOYCE SAKE

Profile

Joyce Sake was named the South Coast Conference Coach of the Year in 1979. She was the Junior College/Community College Committee Chairman for the AIAW Regional Basketball Championships during the 1977 season. She is cofounder of the San Diego Summer Olympic Development League.

In 1983 she joined the University of Washington athletic staff as women's basketball coach and in a two-year period the team posted a 43–10 (.811) record. During the second year at Washington the team was 26–2, went undefeated in Northern Pacific Athletic Conference (Nor-Pac) play, won the post-season tournament, and received its first NCAA tournament bid. The team came from a national ranking of 77th in 1983 to 11th in the nation during the 1984–85 season. Sake received the Northern Pacific Athletic Conference Coach of the Year award in 1985 and the Converse-Region VIII Western States Coach of the Year award in 1985 at the Women's Basketball Association National Convention in Austin, Texas.

Joyce Sake is a 1961 graduate of Inglewood High School in Inglewood, California. She received her undergraduate degree in Physical Education in 1965 from San Diego State University after spending time at both El Camino Community College (1961–63) and the University of Redlands (1963–64). She earned her master's degree in Physical Education with an emphasis in exercise physiology in 1974 from SDSU.

While at El Camino Community College, Sake earned the outstanding athlete four-sport award for her participation on the basketball, volleyball, softball, and field hockey teams. She also played on the intercollegiate basketball, volleyball, and tennis teams at SDSU and played United States Volleyball Association (USVBA) volleyball, competing in three USVBA National tournaments.

She began her coaching career as a volleyball coach at Aragon High School in San Mateo, California in 1968, before moving on to Hawthorne High School from 1968 to 1972, where she coached volleyball and basketball. She joined the Grossmont College coaching and teaching staff in 1974 as women's basketball coach and physical education instructor. She directed the team to four conference titles, developing an overall community college coaching record of 151–52 (.744). Her conference coaching record was 97–25 (.795) during her nine-year reign.

Sake presently resides in San Diego, California, and is a full-time instructor in physical education at Grossmont College.

Psychological Coaching Methods

Mental Preparation   Leading up to game day we spend approximately one-quarter to one-third of the preceding practice on specific preparation for the opponent. Our scouting report is prepared to emphasize the opponent's defenses, offenses, special situations, and player match-ups. During the practice, we walk through these anticipated situations and scrimmage accordingly. During this time we key specific situations and look for tendencies in addition to specific opposing-player inclinations. Pregame talks (fifteen minutes) also comprise part of the mental preparation process.

At the end of practice, each athlete receives a written report to take with her in order to mentally prepare for the game.

Mental Concentration   Defensively, when the ball is picked up on the dribble, we have our players verbally shout "cover" in both drill and scrimmage situations. That reminds them to get to the offensive player as quickly as possible and smother their attempt at a shot or pass. Along with other-man defensive practices, such as "switching," "stay," and "help," we emphasize considerable verbal communication and incorporate these verbal cues into specific drill situations.

Imagery Techniques   My teaching style is one of incorporating analogies in the communication process. For example, if I want my players to react instinctively to certain situations, I may tell them that this process is like driving your car and having to go quickly from the gas pedal to the brake. There is no thinking, seemingly; it is a reaction, a stimulus-response perception.

Another example would be communicating to my rebounders the concept of aggressive, strength-oriented possession of the ball. The analogy utilized is the ball is in the air, four or five pairs of hands are going for the ball—similar to baby birds in a nest reaching up for the mother's food. I do not want to project or promote a "chirping, passive, democratic" attempt at ball possession but rather a *take charge*, *body-controlled*, *aggressive* attitude in conjunction with technically proper rebound measures of block-out, i.e., wide base of support, arms up, and quickness to the ball. An additional example is teaching the correct shooting technique. I have the players imagine they are inside a telephone booth with the top off. By using proper techniques in terms of legs, elbow, arm, and wrist, they would be able to shoot the ball out of the top. The majority of shooting problems originate from pushing (forward) with the arm instead of shooting the ball. I think this visualization helps them think in terms of body alignment and development of the proper touch on the ball.

Relaxation Techniques   I do not employ any consistent, sequential relaxation "lessons," although I believe this is definitely an area that is worth pursuing. I attempt to assess intuitively the tightness or pressure levels of different games and try to adjust my style of motivation to the perceived level. This takes many forms, from needing to psych up the players for games that I thought they were approaching with flat attitudes, to games that were pressure-packed and they needed toning down with humor to keep them loose and relaxed. This cannot be contrived behavior but rather a form of interacting that is natural in your personality.

Motivation   This is a very difficult area to address because it represents a two-part consideration—the social dynamics of group *(team) overmotivation* and the *individual* trying too hard and hence becoming *ineffective*. It helps to know your personnel very well individually and as a team. This comes through experience and observation over the course of a season. It is subtle and sometimes not valid, because individuals can react differently in similar situations. But there exist trends of continuity that can be knitted together to help the coach visualize the situations that can present themselves and plan accordingly. As much as possible, I try to reinforce with concrete images the job that must be done as a team effort and to build individual confidence in players that will serve to accommodate team goals.

With regard to undermotivation, the same information can be applied here. This area may necessitate a more extensive one-on-one confrontation or consultation or, in the case of the entire team, a team scolding—a clear clarification of purposes and goals of the season.

Optimal Arousal   I believe you build from the technical or strategic level to the personal or pride level of dedication. This starts from the onset with the creation of team goals. With each game the functional application of those goals is reinforced. Teams have to form an identity that says "We're going to play this kind of defense, we're going to get every loose ball in the gym, and we're going to rebound in this particular way." A *commitment* to *improvement* with *every game* that is played is *essential*. Winning is not the focus; it is the result. The emphasis should be on team and individual improvement and a dedication to specific standards of performance during the course of the season. Optimal arousal has to do with personally appealing to the team and individuals' competitive instincts and their will to play hard.

Emotional Differences   Based on observation, I believe that the best coaches have developed an intuitive ability to appeal to many different kinds of personalities. It is necessary to adhere to common standards and expectations for all athletes; however, you have to blend these with different personal methods for each individual. Because of the individual natures involved, some methods are effective with some and not with others. The coaches' ability to differentiate and to know their players is crucial to success. Each coach must find within his or her own personality the capacity to relate in the most appropriate way. This appears to be the difference in establishing effective communication. This is a tall order in coaching, but excellence and consistency depend upon it.

Athlete or Team That Chokes   I wish I had had the opportunity for more insight in this area; sport psychology work will no doubt lead to more answers than most coaches can find. It is a fascinating area of research because as a coach you feel that you are in touch with the variables operating, and then you have an experience that proves you quite wrong. I think, in part, it has to do with clarifying and demystifying the factors that can accommodate pressure and employing strategies (psychologically) to work with them. My past coaching experience has led me to believe that this area is somewhat like a changing true-false question: the more experience I have, the better I think I've become; and then there will be an experience that nullifies what I thought was my previous "learning." The bottom line may be the ability to acquire exquisite knowledge concerning set, setting, principles (players), and variables that are outside of our control. We may in fact have more control than we (or I) could imagine. Individual player confidence in players and team confidence in addition to on-the-floor leadership seem to be critical factors involved. If I were still actively coaching, I would develop more specific player communication techniques during games—something along the lines of a feedback system based on key performance expectations.

Goal-setting   I use goal-setting in pre-season, in season, and post-season preparation both with the team and with individuals. I believe it is essential to evaluate expectations as thoroughly as possible so that goals can be functional and applicable to the development of a team "identity" and improvement of each athlete.

Goals are maps that offer direction and guidance. They must be *specific* in nature and *measurable* in order to offer the developmental potential they contain. They can be used in every aspect of practices, games, conditioning, and pre- and post-season preparation. They should be used to motivate, inspire, and ensure that the team, as well as individual, is on track.

Extrinsic Rewards My use of extrinsic rewards is very minimal and applied to "fun," off-pace days. Free-throw awards during these days would break the monotony of in-season practice intensity. I did, however, make use of end-of-season awards for "Best Defensive Player," "Most Improved Player," and "Most Valuable Player" (MVP). Specifically the first two are ones that I think are useful and motivating to all team members. The MVP will take care of and define itself usually, but the other two can be very motivational in nature. In particular years, a coach may want to add a "Most Inspirational" award for outstanding leadership ability when applicable.

Nonverbal Cues The only ones that come to mind are (1) hands up on defense in game situations and (2) signaling of specific offensive sets with hand direction on offense.

Sport Psychologist I do not use a sport psychologist, although I have sought out specific resources (counselors, psychologists) for individual players' problems that may affect their performances and definitely affect their personal development.

Psychological Methods In general, the psychological methods I use are (a) construction of team goals; (b) application of goals to life experiences (school, relationships, future work); (c) motivational lectures on the importance of being a learner, improvement, self-assessment, commitment, and communication; (d) ongoing evaluation of team atmosphere and assessing specific team needs to address. Specifically, the psychological methods I use are (a) personal communication with players—all of them; (b) evaluation sheets for season and specific goal sheets for off-season development; (c) developing a sound rapport with players as developing *individuals*, not just athletes.

Mental Qualities The mental qualities I desire in athletes are (a) willingness to learn (open to *constructive* criticism); (b) competitiveness (strong will to win); (c) honesty (with themselves and teammates in assessing abilities and progress); (d) dedication (to skill improvement and development as persons); (e) sociability (ability to get along with teammates); (f) intellectualism (makes an effort to look at the game on many levels); (g) poise (ability to control emotions and to effectively communicate concerns); (h) sense of humor (recognizable by persons other than themselves). These qualities certainly transcend a purely "mental" interpretation.

LINDA SHARP

Profile

(Overall: 207-65) 9th year

General Information:
Years at University of Southern California: *completing 9th year* (began in 1977 as head coach)

College: *CS Fullerton* Major: *Physical Education*/Graduated—1973, B.S.
Birthdate: *3/14* Birthplace: *Okmulgee, Oklahoma*
Hometown: *Long Beach, CA.* Parents: *Juanita Thompson*

Coaching Chronology:

1977 to present—University of Southern California Head Coach (207-65 in 9 years)
1976 to 1977—University of Southern California Assistant Coach (under Marcie Cantrell)
1974 to 1977—Mater Dei High School (Santa Ana, CA) Head Coach (63–7 in 3 yrs.)

Coaching Honors:

1983—*Sporting News*/Coach of the Year
    Stayfree Women in Sports Program/Coach of the Year
    Western Collegiate Athletic Association Conference Coach of the Year
1981—American Basketball Association/USA Development Team Coach (Jones Cup)
1979—Western Collegiate Athletic Association Conference Coach of the Year
1977—Angelus League Coach of the Year

Committees:

1984 to present:
American Basketball Association/USA 1988 Olympic Games
National Collegiate Athletic Association Rules Committee
Women's Basketball Coaches' Association Kodak All-American

As a Player   1973 to 1974—Amateur Athletic Union Basketball
1970 to 1973—Cal State Fullerton Varsity Women's Basketball Team
1968 to 1970—Fullerton Junior College (Most Valuable Player sophomore year)

Coaching Record at USC:

Year	Overall W	L	Conference W	L	National Finish	Regional Finish	Conference Finish
1977–78	11	13	3	5	AIAW—	WAIAW*	WCAA—4th
1978–79	21	10	4	4	AIAW—	WAIAW—4th	WCAA—3rd
1979–80	22	12	9	3	AIAW—	WAIAW—2nd	WCAA—2nd
1980–81	26	8	9	3	AIAW—4th	WAIAW—1st	WCAA—2nd
1981–82	23	4	9	3	NCAA—	Mideast—2nd	WCAA—2nd
1982–83	31	2	13	1	NCAA—1st	West—1st	WCAA—1st
1983–84	29	4	13	1	NCAA—1st	West—1st	WCAA—1st
1984–85	21	9	10	4	---	West—3rd	WCAA—2nd (tie)
1985–86	31	5	8	0	NCAA—2nd	West—1st	PAC-West—1st
TOTAL	215	67	78	24	(9th year)		

*Western Regional Association of Intercollegiate Athletics for Women.

Psychological Coaching Methods

Mental Preparation   Practice time allocated to mental preparation for the upcoming game by *individual* is approximately 20 percent. Practice time allocated to mental preparation for the game by *team* is 20 percent. Mental preparation includes mental imagery through individual goals and game plans, resting on game day, going over information on opponents numerous times through chalk talks, handouts, etc.

Mental Concentration   Mental concentration is done by communication. I talk to the players prior to each practice session, going over our daily plan. I also give them chalk talks with plays, techniques, terminology, and visual aids (to see the play or player, etc.). I try to use the same methods on game day to establish a routine. A predictive pattern helps consistency. During the game, diagrams are used during time-outs, as in pre-game and practice sessions, to help the team members "see" the play, etc.

Imagery Techniques   Imagery techniques are used during quiet moments prior to practice. As team members have their eyes closed and are quiet, I talk them through a play, player, team, or opponents. Also, when the adrenaline is flowing during the game, I try to get them to calm down, close their eyes, and take deep breaths to relax as I talk them through a play or situation. I encourage them to practice this on game day as an individual preparation for the game.

Relaxation Techniques   I try to use my voice fluctuations and mannerisms to help relax the athletes. I have found if I show a nervousness in my voice or actions, they pick up on it and it can make them unsure.

Motivation   I try to get them to calm down, get back to basics, relax, close their eyes and take deep breaths. I raise my voice, use humor and films, read quotes by the opposition. I bring up things that will stimulate them. I give them a specific goal to reach, either as a team or as individuals. I read inspirational poems, etc.

Optimal Arousal   I use breathing techniques, relaxing, listen to music. I get into individual routines that help each person "see" herself being successful. I set up individual goals for a season, one particular game, or a particular opposition.

Emotional Differences   Emotional differences are controlled by the individual athlete. Being in an environment (basketball arena or stadium) will stimulate individual emotions; however, competitive emotions are controlled *only* by each individual athlete. Stimulating teammates to stimulate other individuals is an effective motivational tool. I challenge one individuals to stimulate her peers to play up to their ability when it becomes apparent that the team's overall performance is poor.

Athlete or Team That Chokes   This is done by the coach. First leadership then confidence, and confidence comes from the top.
     A coach who prepares the team and is confident will get an athlete or team through

those possible choking times.

If you know you have a "choker," substitute a confident athlete. This brings the team to another level. For the choker, I talk to them and put them in a successful situation. Example: Don't have the choker shoot or pass the basketball—have them screen for the shooter or rebound the miss. (Choker takes lesser responsibility.)

Goal-setting   At the beginning of pre-season, I hold individual conferences with each athlete and set academic and athletic goals (credits completed, points averaged, etc.). I set team goals after individual goals are set. Roles must be identified also. It is very important for individuals to see where they fit in with the team. Time must be given to each player to get accustomed to her role. I set goals on a daily as well as long-range basis: practice goals—no fouls on defense, no turnovers by individuals, ten free throws in a row; long-range goals—win conference, make play-offs, final four, national championship.

Extrinsic Rewards   None.

Nonverbal Cues   Hand signals are keys to change defense or offense. An example of body language is up off the bench with hands on hips means I'm not happy with the current situation, e.g. positive change must occur immediately.

Sport Psychologist   None.

Psychological Methods   I use communication. I ask individuals questions about themselves: How do they see themselves? What have they learned from experience? I try to get individuals to know and learn about themselves, keep things in perspective, review goals. I let the players see themselves on tapes.

Mental Qualities   Cheryl Miller is intense, enjoys playing, is motivated, hard working, competitive, goal-oriented. She plays to have fun; it's a game!

Rhonda Windham keeps cool. She is a heady player—doesn't show a lot of emotion but it's there inside.

The McGee twins always showed up to play. They exhibited high concentration, pride in play and appearance. They were always ladies and had a lot of class.

I believe that a truly successful coach is an educator, a person who cares about people, and is highly motivated to do well. Coaches need to keep calm and think about the next move. I like people to be happy and successful. I try to help my athletes be happy and successful because I am, and I wouldn't have it any other way. I find that in order to be happy and successful you must be willing to work at it.

TARA VANDERVEER

Profile

Tara VanDerveer, who has led the Ohio State women's basketball program to national prominence over the last five seasons, was named the new head women's basketball coach at Stanford University this past May 7 by Stanford Director of Athletics Andy Geiger.

VanDerveer becomes Stanford's third head women's basketball coach in history since the sport went varsity (1974–75). She replaces Dotty McCrea, who resigned shortly after the 1984–85 season.

VanDerveer comes to Stanford with extremely impressive credentials. A 1975 graduate of Indiana University, the 32-year-old Boston native has been named Big Ten Coach of the Year in each of the past two seasons. In her five years at Ohio State University, her teams won four Big Ten championships, compiled four consecutive 20-win seasons, put together three straight NCAA post-season appearances, and, last season, finished as the seventh-ranked team in the nation, runners-up in the NCAA East Regional to eventual national champion Old Dominion.

"We're thrilled to have one of the nation's finest join our staff," said Geiger of VanDerveer. "We're excited by her past achievements, and even more excited by her presentation and her intelligence. She seems to be a popular choice."

Ohio State has enjoyed remarkable success in its 20-year history of women's basketball — especially so under VanDerveer. Tara entered the scene at Columbus in 1980–81. Her first team there finished 17–15 and third in the last of the unofficial Big Ten tournaments. From there, however, it's been nothing but 20-win seasons; 20–7 in 1981–82, 23–5 in 1982–83, 22–7 in 1983–84, and an outstanding 28–3 in 1984–85. Overall at OSU, she went 110–37 for a very fine .748 winning percentage.

Following a 17–1 Big Ten record in 1983–84, VanDerveer was selected Big Ten Coach of the Year by her colleagues. She topped that with an 18–0 conference slate this past year, the first-ever perfect season in the three-year history of the league's double round-robin format, and her fellow coaches again named her Coach of the Year. In 1982–83, she was a finalist in the Stayfree Coach of the Year selections, and in both 1984 and 1985 she was a nominee for Converse Coach of the Year honors.

Ohio State had received some Top 20 recognition prior to the 1984–85 season (16th to 20th in most of the polls), but then burst onto the Top 10 plateau with wins over Penn State, UNLV, and Arizona State. From that point in the season through the rest of the way, Ohio State only moved up, reaching a Top 10 position in three polls for the last three weeks of the campaign. OSU made it to the final eight in the NCAA post-season tournament, losing by only four points to Old Dominion in the finals of the East Regionals—a game that was played on ODU's home court.

When VanDerveer accepted the OSU head coaching position, she was actually returning to Ohio State. She had spent two seasons with the Lady Buckeyes, one as coach of the junior varsity team (1976–77), and one as a varsity assistant to her predecessor, Debbie Wilson, while earning a master's degree (1978) in physical education.

This, however, is not VanDerveer's first coaching venture in the western part of the United States. Following two years of graduate school in Ohio State, she accepted the head coaching position at the University of Idaho in Moscow. In her two years there (1978–80), she brought unprecedented success to Vandal women's basketball. Her first Idaho squad set a record for single season wins with a 17–8 mark. That record was shattered in 1979–80 when her second and final Vandal team went 25–6. VanDerveer led that unit to the AIAW Northwest Regional title. The Northwest Empire League honored her as its Coach of the Year in 1979.

As mentioned, VanDerveer was a '75 graduate of the University of Indiana, where she was a Dean's List scholar for three years, majoring in sociology. As an athlete at Indiana, VanDerveer held one of the starting guard positions for three years on the women's basketball team. Her skills earned her invitations to the World Games (1972) and the Olympic Team (1974) tryout camps.

Since 1976, VanDerveer has served on the staff for the Cathy Rush (former Immaculata coach) Basketball Camp and the Pat Kennedy Camp. She has been a featured speaker at Kodak national clinics, and is a member of the advisory board for the Champion Athletic Equipment Company.

In addition to coaching, VanDerveer enjoys sailing. She was a crew member of the North American Lightning Sailing Championship in both 1975 and 1977.

VanDerveer will be assisted by a trio of Ohio State graduates, all of whom played for her while members of Lady Buckeye squads.

They include June Daugherty (Ohio State '78), Amy Tucker ('82), and Julie Plank ('83). All three will be involved in practice coaching, while Daugherty and Tucker will be active in recruiting. Daugherty will concentrate on the front-line players at Stanford, Tucker on the wing-players, and Plank on the guards. Plank's duties will also involve scouting and off-season conditioning, while Daugherty will be involved in promotions, and Tucker in clinics.

Year-by-Year with Tara VanDerveer

Year	School	Record	Pct.	Post-Season Tournament
1978-79	Idaho	17-8	.680	—
1979-80	Idaho	25-6	.806	AIAW
1980-81	Ohio State	17-15	.531	—
1981-82	Ohio State	20-7	.741	—
1982-83	Ohio State	23-5	.821	NCAA
1983-84	Ohio State	22-7	.759	NCAA
1984-85	Ohio State	28-3	.903	NCAA
Total	**7 years**	**152-51**	**.749**	**4 appearances**
at Idaho	(2 years)	42-14	.750	
at Ohio State	(5 years)	110-37	.748	

Year-by-Year—Women's Basketball at Stanford

Year	Head Coach	Record	Pct.	Post-Season Tournament
1974-75	Gay Coburn	8-3	.727	—
1975-76	Gay Coburn	11-6	—	
1976-77	Dotty McCrea	8-11	.421	—

1977-78	Dotty McCrea	17-12	.586	AIAW
1978-79	Dotty McCrea	19-7	.731	AIAW
1979-80	Dotty McCrea	17-14	.548	AIAW
1980-81	Dotty McCrea	15-16	.484	—
1981-82	Dotty McCrea	19-8	.704	NCAA
1982-83	Dotty McCrea	19-16	.543	—
1983-84	Dotty McCrea	5-23	.179	—
1984-85	Dotty McCrea	9-19	.321	—
1985-86	Tara VanDerveer	First year	13-15	
12 seasons		**147-135**	**.521**	**4 appearances**

Designated Coach of the "East Team" For the 1986 Olympic Sports Festival.

Psychological Coaching Methods

Mental Preparation   Over the course of a single practice, approximately fifteen minutes each day is devoted to mental preparation. The fifteen-minute allotment does not occur in a single block of time but rather is incorporated throughout each practice. Each athlete can thus expect to receive mental coaching in the form of specific concentration, imagery rehearsal, communication, etc. To complement the collective fifteen-minute individual mental development process, approximately forty-five minutes per week is allocated to the mental preparation of the team as a whole.

Mental Concentration   Specific concentration drills are designed and conducted by our team sport psychologist. In addition, almost every drill that the team does revolves around a running score or the clock so that, in order to be precise and effective on the court, each athlete must mentally process the two critical factors of time and score and then initiate the appropriate tactical strategy to win. Concentration drills can take the form of shooting ten free throws in a row (score and point reinforcement) or designating a specific group of athletes to play offense, and nothing but offense, until that team commits three turnovers (tactics and strategy). The mental concentration and development process that take place during concentration and physical drills of this nature are very helpful in both short-term and long-term development of the athlete. In addition, the environment in practice becomes "game-like," which provides a climate that is stressful and demanding but is controlled to allow the coach to coach and the athletes to learn and predict.

Imagery Techniques   Mental imagery is discussed in terms of predicting situations and then successfully completing specific tasks. For example, during selected drills, I stop the drill and each athlete is asked to visualize completion of specific assignments and/or tasks.

Relaxation Techniques   I utilize specific exercises that are designed to reduce stress. For instance, I conduct relaxation exercises whereby players focus in on letting all of the stress, both physical and mental, escape from head to toe. I believe that the tone of my voice and the verbal comments I make can significantly affect the level of tension in my athletes. As a result, I make a serious effort to be relaxed and confident, which reduces the actual stress our players feel.

Motivation   I individually counsel each athlete in an attempt to identify areas and situations which can and do result in arousal and anxiety levels that are much too high and can lead to overmotivation and a resulting loss of concentration. When overmotivation manifests itself as a recurrent problem, I identify the specific cause and formulate plans that enable both me and the individual athlete to successfully resolve the problem. It is important to note that the methods I use when dealing with athletes who are undermotivated are quite similar to the methods I employ when athletes are overmotivated: both I and the athlete identify the cause of undermotivation and then formulate a series of steps specific to each athlete that is designed to eliminate and/or control the causes of undermotivation. Because both the presence of motivation and degree/intensity of motivation are difficult to evaluate, especially when attempting to determine the source of motivation (internal and external), my recruiting procedures include making a concentrated effort in terms of becoming knowledgeable about each potential athlete specific to understanding both their reasons and motivation to play basketball and to succeed academically at Stanford.

Optimal Arousal   I expect every athlete to look upon each game as a challenge to not only *play as well as possible* but to *improve* as an athlete during the course of every basketball game.

   The practice environment is as ''game-like'' as possible, the purpose being that the actual game is approached as an extension of practice. This approach is quite helpful in reducing high anxiety that many athletes feel prior to and during the game. At various times, teams collectively can develop a posture whereby they try too hard instead of relaxing and playing *their* game. Thus, designing the practice environment to reflect the conditions of the actual game in terms of the clock, stress, demands, and strategy provides an avenue of preparing the team physically and mentally.

Emotional Differences   Each athlete is encouraged to be in tune with herself and to individually prepare for the opposition. I take the time and interest to know and understand each player's emotional makeup. I believe this allows a coach to develop a sensitivity specific to the emotions and values that manifest themselves in each athlete.

Athlete or Team That Chokes   When this problem begins to surface, I utilize the same tools for both individual athletes and the team. I focus attention on the success they have achieved by having my players view and analyze videotape. We watch practices and games that show and reinforce our past and current successful efforts. I never use the word ''choke''; it isn't a concept that is talked about because our emphasis is on the positive.

Goal-setting   Each athlete is instructed to set her own goals. Then I schedule a conference with each athlete before the season begins, where the athlete's perceived goals are discussed, analyzed, and perhaps adjusted. During the course of the season, periodic conferences between me and each athlete are scheduled where her goals are reviewed and, if necessary, revised. Once the season ends, I meet with each athlete to evaluate the goals that were set before and during the recently finished season. Goals for the next season are then presented by the athlete and are evaluated in terms of appropriateness and, if need be, adjusted.

In addition to individual goals, I have fifteen goals I expect to achieve during each game (field goal percentage, free throw percentage, etc.). I also identify and evaluate daily practice goals. Goals can help a coach measure the progress/development of the team as a whole and of individual athletes as well. When established goals have been reached, goals are then adjusted upward, which is another indication of success.

Extrinsic Rewards   The reward that is used the most is *praise*. Gimmick rewards such as candy, etc., are not used.

Nonverbal Cues   Most of the communication I employ is nonverbal: hand-clapping, thumbs-up, high 5's, standing up to cheer, smiling, posture—especially when things are going well, exaggerated body movements, stomping feet.

Sport Psychologist   I utilize the services of a sport psychologist who attends both home and away games. The sport psychologist meets weekly with the team and, among other duties, teaches players different techniques of visualization and imagery. The sport psychologist is also available to each athlete on an individual basis. It is important to note that the sport psychologist for the Stanford basketball team is used to maximize the performance potential of both the team and each athlete; the sport psychologist is not simply confined to working out solutions in "problem areas."

Psychological Methods   I am very specific in the type of behavior I expect my athletes to project, and I am very specific in the type of feedback I give individual players and the team. I positively reinforce expected behavior and will give *appropriate* feedback when the actions and/or behavior of the athlete(s) are inappropriate. Our staff stresses the positive when teaching and correcting mistakes. As a staff, we work hard to develop a good rapport and positive chemistry with both individuals and the collective team.

Mental Qualities   The mental qualities I believe to be of importance in athletes are leadership; the desire and intensity to compete; discipline; personal commitment to persist and persevere; accepting being a "team player"; and, perhaps the most important, possessing an attitude that is mentally tough. I have observed that athletes who are well-conditioned and physically strong seem to possess a higher level of mental toughness. I do not condone being content with a marginal amount of physical strength and overall physical fitness.

The most accurate description of my "style" of coaching is a sincere and genuine concern for my athletes. I care for them as people during their career at Stanford as well as after they leave. Win or lose, I am always their coach. I am supportive of each individual. The players on my team are given both an opportunity and encouragement to develop a solid relationship based upon trust with me and my assistant coaches. I recruit and evaluate potential athletes on the basis of a variety of factors, but two of the most important are athletic ability and personal quality. In fact, I recruit/evaluate personal quality as much as athletic ability.

I believe I am strict but fair, confident, open and honest, caring, and continue to learn a lot from each experience and the people I meet as a result of basketball. My overall purpose is to work with each player on an individual basis and the team on a collective basis in order that *all* will aspire and reach their maximum potential.

chapter 8

Field Hockey

PAM HIXON

Profile

Pam Hixon is the head field hockey coach at the University of Massachusetts, Amherst. Hixon's teams have been very successful in both the Association for Intercollegiate Athletics for Women (AIAW) and the National Collegiate Athletic Association (NCAA). Hixon's teams have been in the final four five times in the eight years she has coached Massachusetts teams. She has also had eight All Americans during her tenure at Massachusetts. Members of her teams have gone on to make the United States Squad and the United States Olympic team.

Psychological Coaching Methods

Mental Preparation If communication is part of mental preparation, then we spend a great deal of time in mental preparation. Because field hockey is a team sport, eleven players have to work together to make it happen, so we work in every practice in almost every drill on communicating who is going to be doing what.

Mental Concentration Rather than tell the athletes we are going to work on concentration—a term I think is too nebulous—I have them focus their attention. This means they can zero in or narrow their attention on whatever they are working on to make it simple. We do a lot on doing things in sequential order in their minds. For

example, if we are going to do a give and go, first you have to field the ball; the second part is making the pass, and then someone receiving the pass. Instead of thinking the give and go all at once, they do each piece singularly in their minds. That gets them to focus exactly on what their jobs are and exactly what skills they are doing. My basic philosophy is to keep it as simple as possible.

In the development of concentration, our focus is on jobs. Prior to a game or practice, we list jobs. I tell them this is what they will do today and this is what we are trying to accomplish. They have specific jobs, such as who they are going to mark. This gets them thinking on what they as individuals have to do and what the team has to do as a group. We go through the same warm-up prior to every game, so they start to see the ball and get ready to do their jobs.

When team members feel prepared to do their jobs, they will perform better. We spend a lot of time on special situations such as one goal ahead with a lot of time remaining, with little time remaining, a goal behind with little time left, and with a lot of time left. They have very specific things to do in these situations and this gives them something to fall back on when they are in these situations during a game. They gain confidence in certain situations to try and make something happen. This helps them in game situations to focus their attention when they are under pressure. They know their jobs and they have to be able to execute their jobs in a pressure situation.

Imagery Techniques   We use imagery technique a little, not very much. The most important thing in our game is to field the ball; the players have to touch the ball to make something happen. To get them to focus on the ball, when the ball hits their stick we have them say ball. Not before or after, but at the same moment. What that does is get them to focus on that one little piece. If they have missed several balls in a game, they have something to fall back on. This is something they can go do themselves to help them field the ball.

Motivation   When I have players that are overmotivated, I do not want to bring them down; I want to channel their enthusiasm in a positive way. I go back to focusing their attention on their jobs. Usually players get overmotivated or crazy because they are thinking of everything at once and they are looking at the outcome of the contest, the end result, rather than how to get there. Even when we do drills, we talk about winning the moment, winning the one on one. We try to move from the broad picture to the individual pieces—back to the basics and fundamentals. This seems to bring things back into perspective for them.

Winning a game that should not be a problem can become a situation where we have an undermotivated player. For these games I put pressure on the players, so they feel they have to execute more than what we would do in a more competitive game. For example, we want to make the opposing goalkeeper have to touch the ball in field hockey. We play percentage field hockey—if you make the goalkeeper touch the ball ten times, you get one goal. In a game where we will be attacking a lot, our goal may be to have the goalie touch the ball twenty times.

If we want more than the norm, we work to motivate the players to do more. We may also give them a different responsibility in the game. Again we try to motivate them to realize that all games are important. We also play one game at a time, and we

must prepare for each game and not think ahead to the "bigger" games. Winning the games we should win also becomes part of our team goals. This gives each game importance.

Optimal Arousal Before we start to play, I review all our opponents, find the games that we should win, games that will be the fifty–fifty games, and those that are going to require us to play over our heads to win. With this knowledge we try to develop consistent play to win the games that we should win. For the fifty–fifty games we focus more on responsibilities. We do things differently to try to win those games. To help us try and win those contests, we will have different player match-ups; we may change our penalty corners or other set plays to adjust to their players. For those games where we have to play over our heads, we must use consistent play, do the match-up with their players, and then add some motivation gimmick. This motivational gimmick may be that team's ranking if we should do well against this team, what that will do for us—the underdog theory; or, if we are number one, stating that we are where we should be and getting the players superexcited to play above where they normally do. We cannot play over our heads all season long because we cannot sustain that level of play. But we can be consistent all season long. We will peak for those contests that are going to be true contests where you put yourself on the line. But there is an opportunity to recover.

Scheduling is helpful for the team to achieve optimal arousal. At the beginning of the season we will have some games that are tough just to know where we stand and how the athletes will respond. In the middle of the season we will go with some of the middle-of-the-roaders. At the end of the season or the last quarter of the season, we want to play our best hockey and this is when we will be playing our most difficult opponents.

Emotional Differences To coach for individual emotional differences, you have to know your athletes. You have to know what makes them go. You will not know all the time or be right 100 percent of the time, but if you know the athletes then you can deal with their emotional peaks and valleys throughout their college careers. Knowing your athletes and how they react every day is very important.

Some students you get to know immediately because they are very open; others are quiet and it takes longer to get to know them. I have individual conferences with each athlete to discuss their individual goals for themselves at the beginning of the season. I do a follow-up conference at the end of the season, so I get to know what they expect from themselves in field hockey and college. Also, if you see an athlete for three hours of practice every day you have a pretty good idea of what your athlete is about.

If there is a problem, then you have to deal with that athlete differently. This does not mean that you baby her but you do have to take into account that she is having problems. When there are sixteen to eighteen players on a roster you cannot treat them all the same way every day. Players understand different treatment as long as you are fair.

The more responsibility you can give the players, the better off they are going to be as they mature and become upper class women. They have their goals, and when

they move too far away from those goals, you remind them of what they want to accomplish and give them the responsibility to achieve.

Athlete or Team That Chokes   I am not sure, but I believe that choking is lack of confidence. If I have an athlete that is choking, we will go back and work on those things that she needs to work on so she will feel prepared to do what she has to do. You build confidence by knowing what your responsibilities are; you have practiced it, and you feel comfortable with the fact that you can do it. For example, a forward who should be scoring goals but is consistently over-running the ball kicks the ball or is just putting it past the posts nine times out of ten. We will work on those particular things in practice so she can break it down and have her work on these things in the field area where she needs help. Then we will give feedback—not just positive feedback but teaching feedback. I will give the players time to practice on their own without a coach saying "good one" or "bad one." It is a time-consuming practice but I believe it assures more consistent behavior.

The other thing that I do is go back and do things in sequence. The important step is doing one thing at a time before they get to the end product.

The feedback that I would give a team or individual who is choking during half-time of a game would be positive. They know when they are struggling and I would try and give them specific things to do. I would try to get them to focus their attention on whatever they are having problems with. Direction and teaching at this point is better than negative or even sometimes positive feedback.

I do not believe a team chokes; I think a team becomes tentative. When opponents see a weakness, they just come at you that much stronger. The best thing to do at that point is to go out and take risks. Specific directions as to how to take those risks is the best way to get the team back on track.

Goal-setting   Goal-setting is a good motivational tool not only for the individual but also for the team. It is important to discuss just where we can go in a season as a team. This gives everyone a common bond; they have common ground to work towards. There are all sorts of things one can work on as an individual but when you are playing a team game you have to take it one step further as to where the team is going. You can tie this into everything, even how the players conduct themselves on and off the field. If they want to be at a certain place at a certain time, they know what they have to do to get there. They can make decisions as to whether they want to be part of that group or not. Thus, you are focusing your athletes and weeding out those who do not really want to be part of the group.

Nonverbal Cues   The nonverbal cues that I use are to call a play. There are specific signals that I use for a specific play. The only set play we have in field hockey is the penalty corner. We have a certain sequence that we run on penalty corners: the first will give us an opportunity to score, the second will let me see what kind of defense the players are using in case they have made changes since scouting them, and the third gives the players exactly where they are to go to eliminate any confusion. If I sense that something will work better than anything else, I have a certain player I will give the signal to.

My style is to give more verbal cues than nonverbal cues. I do a lot of cheerleading on the sideline. The distance on the field also makes it very difficult to do nonverbal cues. My verbal comments let the players know that I am right there with them in the game.

Sport Psychologist I personally have worked with a sport psychologist to help me or teach me the best way to go about setting goals. I have not used one with the team per se. The sport psychologist has been a great deal of help for me in working on goal-setting.

Psychological Methods An approach that I use extensively is feedback—all kinds of feedback—negative, positive, and instructional. I think it is important for the athletes to know how I feel. If the athletes trust me, it is easier for them to accept what goes on.

A method that I use that has been beneficial is to have the team get together the night before a big game. Maybe we will have a spaghetti dinner. The purpose is to have some fun together, talk about the game, and start to prepare a little early. I believe this takes the edge off and gets them excited about the game the next day—not nervous but excited.

Mental Qualities Discounting skill, there are four things that I look for in an athlete. First, I very definitely want an achiever. I want someone who is highly motivated to be better. I want a competitor, a fighter, one who is willing to take risks, not one who always wants to play it safe. I also want an athlete who is disciplined and who can take it on herself to prepare for the season. Also, I like a mentally tough person, the athlete who can overcome adversity, the one who can miss the ball five times and then get herself back under control and stop the sixth ball and then ask for the next ball.

The basic ingredient that I look for is that athlete to be a competitor.

chapter 9

Gymnastics

JUDI AVENER

Profile

Judi Avener is head women's gymnastics coach at Pennsylvania State University. Avener started her collegiate coaching career at Penn State in 1973. She turned a losing program into a perennial national challenger, first in the Association of Intercollegiate Athletics for Women (AIAW) and later in the National Collegiate Athletic Association (NCAA). Her teams have won many regional titles and they have held the national title twice. In addition to coaching winning teams, many of Avener's gymnasts have achieved the status of All American and national champion.

Avener's own background is that of being a winner. Her gymnastics career dates back to the beginning of national collegiate championships for women when Springfield College was a perennial challenger for the number one position. She was captain of the Springfield College team, member of three national championship teams, and an All American.

Psychological Coaching Methods

Mental Preparation Penn State's gymnastics team spends approximately 5 percent of their practice time on individual mental preparation and 10 percent of their practice time on mental preparation as a team. Prior to each routine attempt, each gymnast must review her routine. Each athlete has a 3x5 card with cues for each routine listed in order of priority. It is this card that they must review prior to each routine attempt.

Imagery Techniques   We do not really use imagery techniques too much as a team. All athletes learn how to do it, then they decide for themselves what works best. On occasion I do work one on one with a gymnast using imagery techniques.

Relaxation Techniques   Individually I have some athletes who like to use relaxation techniques and some who do not. I simply provide exposure to the technique and allow athletes to choose if they want to utilize it. I do not force it.

In the past we have had a team psychologist work with the team on relaxation techniques. The psychologist taught the relaxation technique of deep breathing, and the team practiced it regularly as a group.

Motivation   When the gymnast cannot control herself or she is overmotivated, I talk one on one with her. I identify risks and disadvantages, then ask her to detail why they can be a problem. We then work together to find clues and solutions.

When the team is "hyper" or cannot settle down for a practice, I talk with the whole team. We identify the goals, determine if present behaviors will work toward those goals, and ask for suggestions. Basically I want to calm the team down, confront the group, and either (1) change the goals, (2) play a game, or (3) cancel practice.

With an undermotivated gymnast, I confront her individually. We talk about it but I usually do not take action. It is really her problem not mine.

If the team is undermotivated at practice, I sit them down as a group and ask them if they feel they are motivated. I define objectives and then give examples of what I feel is undermotivation: three people late, four people sitting, two horsing around, etc. I then tell them if they are not willing to work, I would like the day off. They must recognize the lack of motivation themselves. Many times I will turn the problem over to the captain or the seniors.

Optimal Arousal   I help the individual gymnasts achieve optimal arousal for competition by asking them what they want out of the competition. I help to point them in a specific direction and encourage them to believe in themselves. I help them prove to themselves that they are ready. I have them determine a test for themselves, then take the test. For example, "If I can do five side aerials in a row on the balance beam, then I am ready."

For the whole team to achieve optimal arousal for a meet, I use pep talks. I also devise tests similar to the ones for the individual gymnasts, so that they can base a positive arousal on scientific data. Again I have the team participate in devising the test.

Emotional Differences   To coach for individual emotional differences in the gymnasts is to get to know them. You must spend time with them, ask questions about everything, always trying to find out how they feel. Encourage them to share their hopes, feelings, fears, and dreams with you.

It is important that they trust you or they will not share with you. I try to invite them over to my house, go to parties with them, and encourage them to drop by my office so I can better learn about them personally out of the gym.

Athlete or Team That Chokes To coach the athlete that chokes, I talk with her and help identify fears. I try to get her to learn to concentrate on specific skills, not possibilities of failure. I do believe, however, that there are "terminal chokers," people who are just so insecure that a coach cannot do much to help. These gymnasts I send for professional help.

The method I use for the team that chokes is the same as for the individual gymnast. Sometimes when the team, as a group, is a "basket case," I try to make the players more afraid of me than of failing. This is a last resort because it has a temporary effect.

Goal-setting We use goal-setting for both the individual gymnast and the team. For individuals, we talk about it, write lists (to be carried around in their gym bags), and make charts for the gym bulletin board.

Goal-setting for the team I believe in probably above everything else. If you do not have goals, general or specific, then most of your life, gym career, etc., will be an accident. I try to probe athletes to be constantly searching for the point of things. The point may be why are they doing gymnastics to why do they want to do another routine right now?

Extrinsic Rewards We do not use extrinsic rewards to motivate the individual gymnast. At the team level we really do not use them either, but sometimes we play games with dumb prizes like bubble gum or old team leotards. We may do this two or three times per year.

Nonverbal Cues In general I do not use nonverbal cues to communicate with the gymnasts, although I do know some gymnasts well enough that I can just look at them a certain way and the point is obvious, i.e., satisfaction, disgust, or questioning. Sometimes I also just turn and walk away and they also know that I am not pleased.

Sport Psychologist We do utilize the services of a sport psychologist. For four years we have had a sport psychologist meet with the team every one to two weeks and take psychological inventories. The sport psychologist also teaches relaxation, practice imagery, etc.

Psychological Methods The general psychological approach that I use to increase overall performance and learning is for the individual. I figure if they love me, then I'll be able to guide them, so I encourage friendship. For the team, I learned a while ago that you can not make them do anything, so I encourage them to do their own thing.

Mental Qualities Mental qualities in individual gymnasts that I find compatible with my coaching style are questioning, the desire to have fun, criticism, sarcasm, aggressiveness, being goal-oriented, not being deadly serious but intense about certain things.

For the team I think that the more fun they are having the harder they will try, and it is easy for me to have fun with them.

GAIL GOODSPEED

Profile

Gail Goodspeed is head gymnastics coach at the University of New Hampshire (UNH). Under Goodspeed's coaching, UNH has been a perennial top team in the East. UNH won the Eastern Collegiate Athletic Conference Championship in 1984, 1985, and 1986 and, with Goodspeed as the coach, seven UNH athletes have been named to the All East team. UNH is a regular competitor in the National Collegiate Athletic Association (NCAA) regional meets, placing second twice.

Goodspeed competed in gymnastics at Springfield College, where she captained the team her senior year and was a member of two national championship teams.

Goodspeed brings a special perspective to the psychology of coaching as she has a doctorate in sport psychology from Boston University.

Psychological Coaching Methods

Mental Preparation The percent of an individual athlete's practice time spent on mental preparation varies anywhere from 5 to 20 percent depending upon the individual. It is difficult to determine the exact percent of time during physical practice that a gymnast spends on mental practice because during physical practice there is also a great deal of mental practice.

We have organized team practice for mental preparation .5 hour two days per week. That is almost 6 percent of our total practice time of 17.5 hours per week.

Mental Concentration We train for concentration during performance through focusing first on external factors and then on internal factors. Athletes are requested to achieve a relaxed state and then key in on some physical aspect of the equipment, for example, the beam's texture. They then attempt the skills while thinking of this particular physical aspect of the equipment. We then move to listening to some aspect of the event, looking at the apparatus from all angles, studying the facility from all views, mentally singing a song while performing, selecting words to express the quality of movement one wishes to achieve, keying in totally on breathing, and finally allowing the mind to be totally clear. A group session trying all the techniques while physically practicing is conducted. Throughout subsequent practices, each athlete attempts to use the preferred technique(s).

Imagery Techniques Athletes initially practice mental imagery of physical skills, then coping with competitive stress in a simulated situation, and finally coping with stress in a competitive situation. Group sessions for mental preparation include step-by-step directed mental imagery exercise from typical practice sessions and also typical details of a day of competition. An example of directed mental imagery exercise is "visualize your first tumbling pass, making your body feel the actions." Athletes are often requested to picture skills or corrections during practice prior to actually physically performing the skill or routine.

Relaxation Techniques   All team members have a home relaxation tape consisting of five different relaxation techniques. Athletes are requested to use the tape on a daily basis if at all possible. Probably one-fourth of the team members actually listen to the tape on a consistent basis. We have found that most mental preparation needs to be a consistent part of the practice session and not added-on practice time.

Group sessions for relaxation are conducted a minimum of two times per week throughout the year. Relaxation training provides the base for the mental preparation program. It is important to note that relaxation techniques are utilized to give athletes an awareness of different arousal levels so that they can distinguish between low and high levels. This will hopefully help the athletes to achieve the appropriate states.

Group sessions are held prior to competitions. Attendance is on a voluntary basis. Most team members have preferred relaxation techniques or motivation techniques prior to and during competition which are specific to the individual's needs.

Motivation   Dealing with overmotivation varies from individual to individual. The more experienced athletes have fewer problems with overmotivation. We therefore attempt to have gymnastic exhibitions and intersquad competition prior to the season. Our schedule has also been expanded to meet high-level teams during the season. Meeting the high-level teams helps with "over" motivation or possibly arousal levels which are too high for obtaining peak performance when we compete with high-level teams in the regional or conference meets. The comprehensive self-regulation training program we attempt to follow includes relaxation training, mental imagery training, self-confidence training, development of concentration skills, and cognitive intervention. This training is intended to assist our athletes in selecting the best coping techniques for each of them and for each situation. The preferred techniques vary greatly and the gymnast's degree of dedication to the training appears to be determined by her success rate when attempting to use the techniques.

Generally, we have found that mental imagery of future competitive situations assists with undermotivation. It is also important to keep a "fun" atmosphere in the daily practice session. Setting appropriate short- and long-term goals with each athlete and success in achieving these goals greatly helps make the sport fun. Stagnation and the same pattern every day of practice can lead to undermotivation. Variety and a good sense of humor from athletes and coaches can help to alleviate undermotivation problems.

Another key to motivation seems to be allowing the athlete as much input in the decision-making process as possible. Athletes are requested to complete a questionnaire regarding goals, and the coaching staff discusses the responses with the athlete. We may help redirect goals which are too low or too unrealistic or help in establishing time lines for specific steps to reach the goals. The next key to motivation seems to be success! Providing opponents of equal level throughout the season also appears to be very important.

Optimal Arousal Our comprehensive self-regulation training is again intended to present various coping techniques to our athletes and have each individual select the most appropriate technique(s) for the situation. It is important that they recognize the different "feelings" of different arousal levels. They then need to determine which state is "optimal" for each skill, event, environment, etc. We attempt to have each athlete evaluate these feelings during good performances and during poor performances to recognize the best state for peak performance. Individual interviews are held to discuss performances and determine successful techniques.

Group sessions are held prior to competitive events as well as the twice weekly practice sessions. The group sessions prior to competition are attended by team members on a voluntary basis. Generally, 80 to 90 percent of the team participates. Each athlete is requested to achieve a relaxed state as quickly as possible using her preferred technique. She then attempts to visualize the competitive environment and attempts to achieve the optimal arousal level for peak performance. Very little detail is presented at this time. Focus is directed toward obtaining the appropriate feeling and then allowing the mind and body to function on an automatic level.

Emotional Differences To coach for individual emotional differences, open communication between coaches and athletes, between athletes, and between coaches is essential. Hopefully a mutual respect for individual emotional differences can be established so that understanding exists.

However, negative emotion, both from coaches and athletes, during practice and competitive situations only tends to destroy the training environment. It is my contention that "problems" due to individual emotional differences should be discussed out of the practice environment. Sometimes a negative emotional outburst means that individual needs a day off. Another technique is to allow a time-out, possibly for two to five minutes. Have the athlete take this time out and see if a positive change can occur at the end of the time. The athlete continues practice if a change is made or takes a day off if no positive change occurs.

Athlete or Team That Chokes To coach the athlete or team that chokes, an organized comprehensive self-regulation training program needs to be followed with consistency. Relaxation training, mental imagery training, self-confidence training, development of concentration skills, and cognitive intervention need to be integrated with the physical practice plan. Record-keeping using diaries or other forms will show athletes the success rate.

When athletes can consistently perform skills and routines in practice, the confidence will be there for competition. My experience is that we are pressured to meet the standard of a judging system and, therefore, often have routines which have a low percentage of "practice" success. When an athlete can perform a routine ten out of ten times in practice, success is more probable during competition. One needs a challenge for motivation; therefore it seems that solid routines should be used in competition and there should be additional goal skills that keep the practice fun. These skills are not included in routines until they can be done consistently. Often I think we say a team "chokes" when really they have not had a high enough percentage of practice success to expect competition success.

For the athletes and/or team that really chokes, I would recommend a more intense relaxation training program and greater emphasis on self-confidence training. The athlete must be convinced of the benefit of such a program and really want to make a change in the pattern of performance. It might also be helpful to attempt cognitive intervention and problem-solving techniques. For example, to increase self-confidence, a self-suggestion would be to believe in oneself and have the gymnast say, "I have been given talent; I will use this talent to the fullest extent." For problem-solving I would ask the gymnast to write a list of irrational thoughts, for example, "Here comes the trick I missed in warm-ups." I would ask her to give a potential coping technique for the irrational thought, such as, "Blank my mind. Do what I know and understand. Let myself go into automatic and just don't think." Sessions on self-hypnosis or sessions with a professional hypnotist might also be considered to assist the athlete or team that truly chokes.

Goal-setting My approach to goal-setting is to have each individual fill out a questionnaire which indicates physical goals for each event. These skills are broken into practice, competition, and dream goals. Practice goals are those skills which one can do alone but which need more practice time to maintain or to perfect. Competition goals are those skills one wishes to perform in competition that season. Dream goals are skills one really wants to do but which are probably unrealistic for that season. Routines are evaluated in the same manner. Athletes also indicate positive and negative training and competitive attitudes and establish goals for increasing the positive attitudes and decreasing the negative ones.

Coaches review the questionnaires and then meet with each athlete to determine time lines and redirect any inappropriate goals. Team meetings are held to discuss team goals.

Extrinsic Rewards We have not done much with extrinsic (tangible) rewards. Many of our athletes are scholarship athletes and this is a "pre-awarded" extrinsic award. However, there is no threat of loss of this award. Our departmental policy is that the scholarship is renewed for all four years unless an athlete decides to retire or is academically below a 2.0 anytime after the sophomore year.

Our conference declares an athlete of the week, which gives the athlete press coverage and a paper certificate.

Positive reinforcement such as praise, hugs, and general verbal approval are probably the most-used extrinsic reward in our gym. We often will take a day off during the season if we have had a particularly good meet.

Nonverbal Cues Body language is always in use as a nonverbal cue whether conscious or not. Focused attention from a coach or an attitude of disinterest are easily conveyed. Smiles, frowns, enthusiasm, shaking of the head, clapping hands, walking away, turning around, hugging, thumbs up, etc., are all occurring constantly.

Sport Psychologist We do not have a sport psychologist available to work with the team. Unfortunately, we use the university counseling center only when problems exist. We do, however, use literature and audiotapes to supplement the training program. I have a doctorate in education with the area of emphasis being motor learning and sport psychology. However, I definitely believe that working with an outside sport psychologist would be extremely beneficial. My direct involvement with the athletes in the practice environment can sometimes be very beneficial and sometimes detrimental to the mental training program. Issues that might be discussed if I were not also the coach are often deleted by the athlete during discussions.

Psychological Methods   To increase learning, performance, and motivation, we use specific techniques which include maintaining a positive attitude, enthusiasm, empathy, interest, and concern for each individual. Communication and total involvement of team members in the decision-making process is essential. It is also important to establish guidelines, develop general and specific goals, and reevaluate throughout the year. The ability to establish an organized plan, keep records, and be consistent will greatly assist in increasing learning, performance, and motivation. We often seem to establish great plans and then do not consistently follow through with them. Our athletes have been told what to do and how to do it for most of their career prior to reaching the collegiate level. It is difficult to wean them from this pattern and encourage them to be involved in decision-making. I really believe this is extremely important, and intrinsic rewards must take precedence over extrinsic rewards.

Mental Qualities   The gymnast who has established goals and is intrinsically motivated seems most compatible with my style of coaching. Those individuals with the ability to communicate both positive and negative feelings and make suggestions for continual improvement seem to be successful.

It is really impossible to discuss specific qualities that I find desirable in a gymnast, since the personalities of each individual vary greatly. The most common denominator is an enjoyment of the sport and a desire to improve. A positive approach and a good sense of humor are desirable.

chapter 10

Softball

SHARON BACKUS

Profile

Sharon Backus is the head softball coach at the University of California, Los Angeles (UCLA). Backus has established UCLA as having the number one women's softball program in the nation during her ten-year tenure. UCLA has won three NCAA softball championships and has attended the College World Series seven times. UCLA's record under Backus's coaching is 336–91–3.

Backus was an outstanding American Softball Association (ASA) player. She was a five-time ASA All American selection. Backus was NCAA Coach of the Year in 1982, 1984, and 1985. In 1985 she was inducted into the ASA Hall of Fame as one of softball's most honored players and coaches of all time.

Psychological Coaching Methods

Mental Preparation Approximately 25 percent of the team practice involves communication and concentration. Thus the other 75 percent of mental preparation occurs off the practice field. The players mentally prepare the evening before, not just prior to each game. There are no specific drills we use for concentration. I do not use imagery techniques or relaxation techniques in my coaching. Many of my athletes utilize these techniques individually.

Motivation   The overmotivated player is the athlete who is usually a joy to have on the team. However, in the game of softball, where hitting is such a critical part, the overly motivated hitter becomes somewhat frustrated because of her high expectations. She is the type of individual who expects to hit well three of the four times at bat, which is very difficult to do in fast-pitch softball.

I try to educate the individual, as well as the team, in realistic goal-setting and knowing the odds in the game of fast-pitch softball. I focus on the area of hitting because the players want to do so well that they are their own worst enemies. I believe the most important thing is patience and a good attitude.

Undermotivation in players is very difficult to remedy. What I try to do with the team is develop a belief system that consistency is most important regardless of the opponent. With an excellent team, undermotivation is more of a problem than over-motivation because the athletes frequently take their opponents for granted. This occurs because we have a lot of talent and they know we can beat many of our opponents and not really prepare.

I concentrate on always having them ready for each competition. I identify the areas on which the athletes need to work. Knowing that they are not perfect and that there is always something on which they can improve aids in motivating them.

Probably the one thing I do the most is challenge them in practice. I provide a competitive atmosphere because I have found, in dealing with physically talented athletes, if you constantly challenge them they will become self-motivating individuals. They become undermotivated when they are not being challenged. So in practice I always have them have a goal whether it is trying to hit eight out of ten times or trying to field thirty ground balls without mishandling the ball. They are always competing against themselves.

Individually I try to identify any specific problem affecting them, whether it be on the field or in the classroom or a personal problem. If it starts to affect their play I usually bring them into the office and discuss their problem and help them find a solution.

I also try to establish the belief that there is always a reason to give 100 percent. At UCLA it is very easy for our athletes to give 100 percent when it comes time to play. UCLA means a great deal to them. It is an outstanding university where they feel a great sense of pride, so frequently they will win not only for themselves and the team but for the university.

Optimal Arousal   I help my athletes achieve optimal arousal by handling my team as professionals, if I can use that term loosely. I educate them about their opponent's strengths and weaknesses. I discuss my expectations of them for that given day or that week, depending upon the opponent. I always make sure that they are aware of our wins and losses; by this I mean that I want them to have a good perspective as to where we are in the season. We key on games that will affect our seeding and on conference games. We also divide the season into two parts—our pre-national season and then our national season.

As individuals I challenge the athletes to prove their talent and ability, yet I always try to maintain the challenge in a very positive way. I never try to be demeaning to the team or the individuals. There is always a constant positive base.

Emotional Differences   How can you coach for individual emotional differences? As individuals, they are all treated differently but they all know they are treated fairly. I constantly tell them that although they are all a piece of the pie, one may be strawberry, apple, or pumpkin. This seems to work well, it pulls them together knowing that they are a piece of a common pie, one common entity. This develops a strong bond. They all know that they are only as strong as their weakest link.

I really concentrate in the area of players developing a level of respect for one another. I make it very clear that they need not be best friends off the field. But there does need to be a common respect for each individual despite their various differences and backgrounds. When we get on the field there has to be a common bond and respect level. I can honestly say that, because there is that common respect, we have never had too much of a problem even though we have carried fifteen very talented athletes.

Because there are differences between individuals, I communicate differently with certain people on the team. Some athletes you can constantly yell at and verbally reprimand and get the best out of them. Other athletes you have to set down, be calm-headed, and not upset them too much to get the best out of them. I try to identify the proper manner in which to reach each individual.

Athlete or Team That Chokes   I have always felt that choking is a result of insecurity and a fear of failure. I have had players who were known as "chokers." I try to deal with them individually and try to identify where their fear comes from and when it is initiated. I try to provide a means for them to relax. I try to provide different ways for them to concentrate. For example, they may be focusing on how well the pitcher is throwing the ball while they need to focus on how well they have been hitting in practice.

As a team I try and improve their self-esteem—where they have come from and where they are now. They obviously have been doing things right because they are on this team. Coming to UCLA awes many individuals. I encourage them to believe that they have done many things right to get here. They will not lose what they have had by putting on a UCLA uniform.

I increase their confidence level by providing a constant pressure environment in practice so they can see themselves execute. It is so important to develop their confidence, for them to know that they are capable of executing when the pressure is on. For example, I will put a runner on third base and tell the hitter to place the ball into right field. To see themselves do this really helps when it comes time for a game situation.

Goal-setting   Goal-setting is very important in our program because the athletes have so many academic pressures. It is not necessary for them to get all "hyped up" for a game in February when they have two more academic quarters before we even try to reach the final rounds for nationals.

I identify each game, its importance, where it fits in the season, and what I want them to accomplish at that point in the season. The individual and team goals are basically the same—identifying the games that are going to be important as a team. These are the games that they really need to come prepared to play. I also identify the areas that we need to improve; these areas depend upon where we are in the season.

Extrinsic Rewards   We do not use many extrinsic rewards. Perhaps the players think about the championship ring that they received after winning the 1985 nationals and this serves as an extrinsic reward for them. I believe, however, that in more than 80 percent of our athletes motivation is intrinsic; it comes from being part of the UCLA defending champions and the opportunity for an education. There are so many positives for attending UCLA that we do not need many extrinsic rewards. Not giving extrinsic rewards removes singling out one individual or a team judging their teammates.

Nonverbal Cues   We use nonverbal cues as a team to give game signals. I also demonstrate correct technique.

Psychological Methods   In general I challenge the players and make them want to increase their performance level. Constant challenge is really what gets them going; it builds confidence because they are successful within my challenge most of the time. I also need to reprimand them when they fall short or if they have a tendency to get lazy, which they do particularly when they view their opponents as easy. When they fall short or are lazy, I sit them down and say "there are no free lunches."

If something is not right in the learning performance, I try several changes: alter game strategy, change the order of the lineup, and bench an athlete as a disciplinary action or as an example to others as to what I am trying to obtain.

I try to give special and specific verbal support for outstanding play and for great desire and drive in individuals. However, generally the accolades are to the team in a team environment.

chapter 11

Swimming

REBECCA RUTT LEAS

Profile

Rebecca (Becky) Rutt Leas is head coach of women's swimming at Clarion University in Clarion, Pennsylvania. Leas has coached the Clarion team since 1979. Clarion's women's swimming team has been the Division II National Champions in 1980, 1981, 1982, 1983, 1984, and 1986. They placed third in 1985. Leas's teams have a 67–10 record and are the most winning collegiate women's swimming team in the country at any division level.

Psychological Coaching Methods

Mental Preparation Approximately 90 percent of an individual's practice time is spent in mental preparation right along with the physical preparation. Basically, practice should be a simulation of the competitive situation. The success of an athlete is how well she concentrates and how well she replicates the competitive situation in her practice. If a swimmer allows her concentration to lapse, then her performance will suffer because she is not performing the drills to the level necessary to perform well in the race.

I strongly believe that the ability to concentrate is very important in swimming, and I talk a lot about concentration with the team. Ultimately, it is up to the individual and how motivated she is, how goal-oriented she is, and how dedicated she is to a successful program.

With the team as a whole, I try to educate them on the importance of mental preparation. This takes the form of knowledge about stroke technique, strategy, nutrition, and diet. The underlying principle is that knowledge is power.

I work with athletes individually on how to improve, why they are not improving as fast as they would like, how to concentrate better, motivation, and goals of the individual and the team. As a group, we spend quite a bit of time on this: at the beginning of the year we spend three two-hour sessions on this topic. On a day-to-day basis, we spend anywhere from five to fifteen minutes on this before or after our practice session, perhaps discussing what we want to do or what we have done. We spend more time on this than most of the other Division II NCAA teams. Quite frankly I think this is one of the things that has helped us be as successful as we have been.

Mental Concentration   The key to outstanding swimming performance is the ability to concentrate. The mental practice that we utilize to develop concentration is directly connected with our practice sessions in the water, where the goal is perfection in stroke technique. A swimmer may be highly motivated and have great desire, but she first must have good stroke technique.

We work specifically on distance per stroke, which involves trying to get as much distance as possible per arm stroke in a given length of swimming and still maintain a high rate of speed. A person who can swim a length in ten seconds using eight strokes is far better off than if she swims the same distance in the same time in twelve strokes.

We also work on "quality sets." For example, we do ten 100's on 1:25 or 1:30. The swimmer is to swim these as close to race time as possible. This puts a tremendous stress on the swimmer and it is very painful. But it is very necessary for her to identify with that pain level when she gets into the races.

We also have endurance sets, which are less painful. In these sets we may go twenty 100's at a lower rest interval, say 1:15. In these, the swimmer is just supposed to hold an average time and not let it go too high. Here we are striving for the endurance effect. In fact, if the swimmer goes too fast in the endurance part, she can break herself down too much and hinder her competition performance.

Imagery Techniques   I believe that imagery technique is very important in swimming. I talk with athletes individually and as a group about thinking while they are swimming. I ask them to think of themselves as strong and smooth in the water, also, if they have any free time during the day, to think of themselves swimming very efficiently in the water—actually to visualize themselves swimming ten strokes per lap and doing that in twelve seconds flat in their particular stroke. This seems to be very beneficial. We do some work out of the water where I use a stopwatch. I start them and have them visualize swimming a lap in the time they want to swim it. If they say they want to swim it in fifteen seconds, I time them for fifteen seconds and they swim it in their mind and then tell me to click the watch off. We see how close they come to the actual time. We see how close they come to feeling that performance in their mind. This does help a lot for pace, especially in the longer and middle-distance events.

I ask them to think about breathing freely and getting their air without any difficulty—basically to think about operating in a really smooth, efficient manner.

We also do mental rehearsals of starts. The idea is that you get on the blocks with a really calm, confident state of mind. The swimmer is under control and has a readiness to explode off the blocks at the slightest sound. Turns and finishes are also rehearsed, both out of and in the water. The swimmers are supposed to be thinking about the turns and finishes while in the water. One of the problems in swimming is the repetition. In a two-hour swim practice, a swimmer could execute 300 to 400 turns. If the swimmer does not concentrate and does not take that opportunity to work on turns, she is actually practicing something poorly. She is ingraining a poor habit in her body's memory. Swimmers are notorious for doing this. The more successful swimmer overcomes the boredom and does all of these skills at a better level all the time.

Relaxation Techniques   Of all the psychological tools that I use in coaching, I use relaxation techniques the least. I give handouts on mental and emotional relaxation techniques and we talk about these techniques. But actually working with them as a group and doing relaxation techniques is not part of our program. We put in four to six hours a day training, which is necessary for the level of swimming we wish to achieve. I do not believe in adding any more time to the practice schedule, so I do not take time for relaxation techniques.

Motivation   Overmotivation is not usually a problem during the regular season. Occasionally, a new swimmer will try to show off during the first two weeks of practice, but once we start to practice twice a day the swimmers are too tired. There are times when you get a person who stays in this state into the competitive season. I usually give that swimmer a longer and harder warmup prior to competition. These swimmers are usually leaders on the team and do wonderful practices. But they get a little nervous prior to a meet and the harder warmup seems to help a lot.

In post-season championships, such as the conference or nationals, overmotivation becomes a problem. The variable is fatigue, because at this point in time none of the swimmers is fatigued. They have been rested and they are ready for their peak performances. The last three weeks prior to the championship we release their extra energy through "craziness" and more humor during practices.

Undermotivation is the biggest problem for the sport of swimming. This becomes a problem usually in mid or late season when fatigue becomes a factor and the general rigor of the program takes its toll. This is particularly so for college women because they start to question whether they want to be a competitive swimmer. They see what their friends are doing, such as going out to parties on Friday night, when they have to go to bed early to get ready for an early, three-hour Saturday morning practice or a meet. It is very important at this time that we sit down and talk and reemphasize our goals. I try to get everyone "fired up" about our chances of going to nationals, because that is what our team is all about. Going to nationals is the end result.

In coping with daily undermotivation, we take anywhere from five minutes to half an hour to talk about this, especially if I see some serious signs where we are not performing well or are exhibiting behavior that I deem counterproductive to the team goals. I believe it is up to the coach to be aware of and deal with this problem. It is the coach's responsibility to be sensitive to individual and team signals and then to act on these signs.

Optimal Arousal In my approach to achieving optimal arousal, I do not want to get my athletes overaroused for dual meets during the season. I know some coaches who rant and rave and do fantastic locker room scenes before dual meets that are really not important. In other words, the other team is not really that good or the meet is just not that important, because your team can easily defeat the other team. Swimming is a sport where you tear the athlete down and have them try to perform as fast as possible while torn down. You then rest them and have a taper at the end of the season. So I like to play it low key during the season. If I think we need to get up for a particular meet, then I do what is necessary to accomplish that goal. I do not have a set program that I do in the locker room for every single meet. I believe that variety and surprise is important.

I have more team meetings if I want to get my team aroused for a particular meet. There are teams on our schedule, particularly Division I teams, that I like to do well against. In addition to more team meetings where we talk about goals, I might also back off a little on their yardage. I might also decrease the intensity of the yardage rather than decrease the yardage. If it is a really big meet, then I will do my "song and dance" routine in the locker room to try to get them aroused. This is always different each year with each team because each team's personality is different, and what would work for one team would not necessarily work for another. It is important for me to get to know each team each year, particularly the freshmen and the sophomores.

Emotional Differences I ask my athletes to help me deal with their individual differences. I tell them that I know there are individual differences and, if they need more compliments, or whatever, to tell me. I do not find my women swimmers very assertive in asking for help. I would like them to be open and tell me what they are feeling, but they do not seem willing to do that.

I think that coaching college women is very difficult. They are more apt to complain, and yet they will not ask for help. I find it very useful to ask questions. It is also important to look at facial expressions and to read body language. These have been very important to me. Most of the mental and emotional obstructions to a good practice have to deal with things unrelated to swimming, i.e., social, home, or academic problems. I try to get them to take their frustrations out on the water. I do not let them walk away from practice because of problems with their boyfriends, etc. Generally, once they get into the practice it turns out to be a good practice.

Athlete or Team That Chokes Choking is a very difficult problem but I have had a minimal problem with it. For individuals who do choke, a last-ditch approach is to give them a longer warmup and put them in the race a little tired. I do not like to do that because they will never reach their peak performance, but it is better than if they choke and fall apart completely.

The success of a swimmer is dependent upon how she does in practice. If she is fast in practice, she can swim fast in competition. If she swims slowly in workout, she will swim slowly in the meet.

The swimmer who chokes up or does not swim faster in a meet than she does in workouts or one who exhibits no improvement is one who puts tremendous pressure on herself. One swimmer I have now who chokes receives tremendous pressure from home about her performance. Swimmers who equate their self-status and self-image with whether they do well or poorly have this problem. In other words, they are not evaluating their performance; they are evaluating themselves. If they do badly in the meet, they are bad persons; if they do well, they are good persons. It is a difficult thought pattern to get this person out of; it may take three or four years or perhaps it will never happen.

Goal-setting   Goal-setting is very important in the sport of swimming. It is concretely related to the performance of the individual and the team. Swimmers whom I get into my program have gone through yardage programs but have not been taught how to think, how to set goals, and how practice relates to meets. At Clarion our swimmers compete their best their senior year because they are taught how to think.

At the beginning of the year we sit down as a team to form the goals for the year. We decide what we want to accomplish that season, what level of commitment we are talking about, what kind of specific behavior we think is necessary to achieve those goals—for example, going out the night before a meet; what time we think we should get to bed; behavior relating to drugs, alcohol, smoking, and sex. All these sorts of behaviors we talk about at the beginning of the year. I want to know where the team stands on these things so I know what to expect on a daily basis. It is not a magic cure, but it is beneficial.

Setting daily goals is very beneficial. Even our pre-season running is a good example. Many swimmers come to us who have not run, and they do not realize how much running can contribute to their performance in the water. We get them to realize that, if they can run three miles in twenty-two minutes or less, their cardiovascular fitness will be at a higher level when they get into the water. Some accept this at the beginning; others take a while to be convinced of the benefits to the overall program.

Extrinsic Rewards   I make use of extrinsic rewards but not to a great extent. This past year I started having the best-swimmer- or -diver-of-the-meet award. I gave the winner a T-shirt, pair of goggles, or a painter's hat. This was done in a team meeting setting to reward the individual for her outstanding performance and hopefully to motivate other individuals to achieve that award. I have had swimmers win this award who were not the best swimmers. It can be awarded to anyone depending upon their performance.

Sometimes in a practice session, if someone had a particularly outstanding set, I will give them some candy. Nothing elaborate—small Tootsie Rolls.

At the end of the year we have a banquet where we give out awards. I do not think awards are effective in motivating a person during the season for a particular meet. I give a most-valuable award and, most importantly, a coach's award that recognizes good grades and team-oriented behavior as well as performance. My top people may not win this award because they may not have good grades or be team-oriented. I also give a courage award. This is given to someone who has surpassed what the average person would be able to tolerate regarding pain. For example, I had a diver in NCAAs who hit the board with her hand, tore her fingernail off, and broke her knuckles. She was told that she would never have that fingernail again and she was not to get in the water. Her hand was bandaged and she dived the next day on the three-meter board. She said that she had practiced all year and was going to dive; her parents approved so we let her dive. I rewarded her for this courageous behavior and she received the award that year. I have also given this award to a swimmer who had had shoulder problems since she was in high school, but she endured the pain and swam through her senior year to achieve her goals.

The majority of the time I would like athletes to swim fast because they enjoy swimming fast and not because of some little reward.

Nonverbal Cues   I give nonverbal cues in the form of signals in practices and meets. Many coaches do not approve of this, particularly during meets. My swimmers, especially distance swimmers, rely upon this during meets. My distance swimmers like to have that communication with me. I think in part it is the level of pain and they know that I am with them. I make eye contact, I talk with them through signals, and they like that. I believe that it gives them security.

We have won races because of signals. We use signals to pick up the swimmers' kicks, to get their elbows up, in the breaststroke to keep their elbows in, to change the pitch of the wrist, pick up the pace, change head position, change hip and chest position in the backstroke, change hand entry in the backstroke, finish the kick in breaststroke, and streamline in all of the strokes. We especially use signals dealing with relaxation before and after the swimmers get up on the blocks.

We have a whole signal system we use on our team. My swimmers like it, so I use it.

Sport Psychologist   I would like to make use of a sport psychologist, but at Clarion we have access only to a clinical psychologist that is there for general student body use. The only way we make use of the school psychologist is if the athlete has a problem, i.e., parental, boyfriend, etc. In the past I have had swimmers who were anorexic and I required that they see the psychologist in order to stay on the team.

We do not have someone available to work with the team and individuals on positive things. I make use of sport psychologists' articles and make them available to my swimmers. We talk about the different techniques and it is helpful to a degree. I would prefer to have someone work directly with my team.

Psychological Methods   The basis for increasing learning, performance, and motivation is knowledge. Knowledge is power. The more the swimmers know why we are practicing the way we are, the physiological aspects, their diet and nutrition, the better they are going to be and the more motivated they will be.

I also make use of the alumnae of our team. They write very motivational letters to the team. We read them and many times it may bring tears to the eyes of the team members. They are very inspirational to the swimmers, especially before our postseason meets like conference championships and NCAAs.

We try to utilize anything that will give us more control over our performance and our environment. Again, I think information is the key. It is important to educate the athletes so they know the why of what we do. I believe this is a very important factor in why our swimmers see improvement over the four years that they are in intercollegiate competition.

Mental Qualities Individuals who I feel have been highly compatible with my coaching style are swimmers who, with minimal encouragement, are up on a daily basis, in terms of practice performance, and who are willing to pound it out and push themselves to that point that swimmers must. But, in turn, they also seem to appreciate it when I reward them with a word at the end of a set. They are courageous people, aggressive, and they emulate the male approach to the sport more so than the typical female approach. We refer to this as "getting animal." They are very aggressive, assertive, are not afraid to "go for it," and are not afraid of the pain at the end. They are willing to go that extra stroke.

I enjoy a team sport mentality. The swimmers who have had experience in team sports understand that approach better than those who have had only swimming experience. The swimmers who get into the rah-rah approach I really enjoy coaching the most. I want a swimmer who has a drive to win and who becomes the overachiever.

Basically I think that swimming should be fun. There is a great deal of hard work in swimming, but one of the results is enjoying the sport. I work hard at getting my teams to have a lot of team spirit and in turn I think they enjoy the sport more because of it.

KAREN MOE THORNTON

Profile

Karen Moe Thornton is head women's swimming coach of the University of California, Berkeley. While at Berkeley, Thornton's teams have had a dual meet record of 46 and 29. Her teams have finished in the top twelve for the last seven years; three of those finishes have been in the top four.

Thornton swam for the Aquabears Swim Club, Santa Clara Swim Club, and University of California at Los Angeles. She was on the 1972 and 1976 Olympic teams. She is a gold medal winner and has achieved four world, two Olympic, and nine American swimming records. While at UCLA she was a Collegiate All American three times.

Psychological Coaching Methods

Mental Preparation The team spends one to two hours a week on mental preparation out of about twenty hours of training. The amount of additional time each individual spends on her own varies greatly from none to thirty minutes each day.

Mental Concentration For mental concentration we do basic meditation drills. These are concentration drills based on breathing with a mantra or counting. We also do relaxation drills with, for example, a special focus on a favorite flower or beach scene.

We introduce several different kinds of drills for relaxation and concentration control each year and then let each swimmer use the one(s) that she feels works best for her.

Imagery Techniques We use imagery techniques a great deal with our relaxation. The types of images we conjure up include general ones: stroke or turn technique; race pace; feelings such as power, confidence, calm, and control. Specific images that we use are goal time, site of competition, making specific senses more vivid (we work on improving ability to hear, smell, taste, feel, and see all parts of situations), and reacting to competition.

These are done after each swimmer gets relaxed using her favorite method and with a guide describing the situation. We encourage each athlete to do imagery on her own with her specific situation including goals and problem-solving.

Relaxation Techniques We use relaxation techniques extensively—as a prelude to imagery work, as arousal control, and before affirmations.

Motivation In dealing with overmotivated or overaroused athletes, we try to determine the cause and isolate why the athlete cares too much. Often this is a fear of consequences if she does not reach a goal. We try to put the situation back into perspective, that is, we try to place the sport into perspective for the athlete's entire life. We also help each athlete keep focused only on the present and on the process rather than on past experience or expected outcome. Focusing on having fun also helps tremendously. If an athlete is feeling too much pressure to succeed or to avoid failure, it helps to keep the performance and its evaluation separate from the performer and her identity. We try to accomplish this through discussions in team and individual meetings and, if necessary, through relaxation.

If any athletes are undermotivated, they should not be in the program. We seldom have this problem at meets because everyone is encouraged to evaluate why she competes regularly and, if she finds she is no longer motivated, then she moves on to another area in her life.

Sometimes undermotivation occurs during training when the swimmers are really tired. Then it helps to refocus on goals, perhaps establishing new short-term goals and creating situations where each athlete can experience success.

Optimal Arousal To help our athletes achieve optimal arousal for competition, we first try to help them define their own optimal arousal level. We do this by noting arousal levels at various competitions and then drawing a correlation with their performance at that competition. Once this optimal level has been determined, we can use it as a goal for them to try and reach.

At some competitions the athletes will need to get more aroused. This is done by doing more cheering and jumping up and down (playing, dancing, etc.). We also get them more aroused through a meeting in which we stress the importance of their performance; that is, we put more emphasis on the competition. Conversely, if an athlete is overaroused, we try to calm her down with relaxation techniques or by reducing the emphasis on the competition, finding ways to make the competition seem less important.

Emotional Differences I coach for individual emotional differences by dealing with the swimmers as individuals. I try to remember that all the athletes are at different arousal levels and also *need* to be for each to perform her best. In team meetings I try to stay businesslike and stress the facts in unemotional ways. I try to talk to each athlete individually. With the individual approach, if I know the athlete has a tendency to be overaroused, I can calm her down and, if necessary, get someone else more "psyched up" without affecting anyone else adversely.

Athlete or Team That Chokes In dealing with an individual that chokes, let's first assume that the coach is not at fault for putting too much pressure on the athlete. To break the chain of chokes under pressure, you have to determine the cause. This can be difficult to do, but it is the only way to help turn the athlete into a winner under pressure. Fear of success, fear of failure, fear of reprisals, unrealistic goals all are examples of causes for choking. I think it helps to get the athlete to talk about her choking. Identification of the problem is half the battle. Usually the athlete does not have enough confidence, so you need to work on improving self-image and increasing self-esteem.

Goal-setting When we set individual swimmer's goals, we talk about goal definition. I believe that all of us have goals in any area in which we are challenging ourselves. Through introspection, these can be clarified and defined. Often athletes set goals that they feel they should set and then have difficulty reaching them because they do not own them. These goals are not their goals but rather those of their parents, coach, or teammates. Once goals have been defined, the specific areas to work on need to be defined and short-term goals need to be set.

Team goals are set in team meetings through discussions. Only after an athlete or coach suggests a goal and all team members say they can support it does it become a team goal. These goals can be in all areas: academics, national finish, health, dual meets, support, etc.

Nonverbal Cues I do make use of nonverbal cues in my coaching. The nonverbal cues I use are reminders about stroke techniques. Basically I mimic the motion myself, such as rolling shoulders more on backstroke, hand pitch on entry, finish of the stroke, or keeping elbows up on freestyle or fly.

Sport Psychologist We use a sport psychologist occasionally as a guest lecturer. We also listen to various tape series, believing that we can learn something from almost anyone.

Mental Qualities Mental qualities that I look for in an athlete tend to focus on their inner strength. Athletes need to be willing to look inside and evaluate their internal motivation as well as analyze the development of their self-image and self-esteem. They need to be primarily self-motivated rather than being motivated by and swimming for someone else such as a coach or parent.

chapter *12*

Tennis

LIZ DUDASH LAPLANTE

Profile

Liz Dudash LaPlante is head tennis coach at the University of California, San Diego. While at UCSD, LaPlante compiled a 109–63 record. Her teams have placed in the top five four times in the last four years. In addition, the UCSD women's team has won the 1986 NCAA Division III National Team Tennis Championship title.

Psychological Coaching Methods

Mental Preparation   It's very difficult to say what percentage of practice time is spent on mental preparation for the match. Many of the drills do require concentration that should be preparing the players for the match. I rarely do just "mental drills." The focus in practice is on playing drills that force the players to concentrate extra hard to accomplish the drill.

Mental Concentration   I always stress concentration as much as possible. I rarely allow the players to just hit. They usually have some goal in mind which forces them to develop mental concentration.

Examples of drills I use that help develop mental concentration are: must hit the ball fifty times in a row before going to the next drill; must hit every ball past the service line; must hit certain strokes in a direction, i.e., all crosscourt or down the line.

131

Imagery Techniques At times, I use relaxation techniques for imagery training in practice. Occasionally I will have team members lie down for five to ten minutes, relax, and imagine themselves hitting picture-perfect shots. I prefer that the team use time away from practice for imagery. I stress they do this (imagine themselves hitting picture-perfect shots) by themselves before they fall asleep or as a study break.

Relaxation Techniques I do not have any specific techniques for teaching relaxation to my athletes. I constantly talk about relaxation and concentration to the team, and work with certain individuals who need help in relaxation and concentration.

Motivation The process of dealing with the overmotivated player varies according to the individual personality. If I feel the overmotivation is hurting her performance, I talk to her and try to help her put things in perspective, try to help her determine if her goals are attainable. If they are not, I try to help her rethink her goals and set ones that she can obtain.

The undermotivated player is not a problem for me at one level. If someone is not motivated, they do not stay on the team. I deal with a temporary undermotivation problem on an individual basis and relate it back to goals, working with the individual to establish some goals.

Optimal Arousal Achieving optimal arousal for competition is not a problem for UCSD. Each match is important and the players' knowledge of this fact helps them get ready for their opponents. An important factor in getting them aroused for competition is the fact that they have qualified for nationals for the past five years and the women always have this on their minds and know they cannot afford to lose.

Knowledge of their status in collegiate tennis is not the only factor that prepares the team for competition. I always talk to the team before the match, discussing the opposing team's lineup and their strengths. Also, the practice the week of competition prepares the team for the match.

Emotional Differences Coaching for individual emotional differences is probably the hardest part of coaching and I have had my share of problems handling certain players. There is no magic or coaching trick for this particular problem. The key to coaching individual differences is to try to understand these differences. Understanding combined with the realization that it is difficult to change players' personalities is my approach.

Athlete or Team That Chokes Since I used to be a player who choked occasionally, I sympathize with the players who may do the same. The player who chokes needs hours of practice matches and she needs to gain as much confidence as possible.

The player who chokes and thus loses consistently is moved from her place in the lineup. When she can bring her game up, she moves back up the ladder.

Goal-setting I have players who set goals but I do not consider goal-setting as a real coaching technique. I have each player write down her team and individual goals in the beginning of the season. Midway through the season she reviews these goals to see where she stands and set new ones.

I don't consider goal-setting to be a real coaching technique because each player knows she is to put out 100 percent during practice and matches. With this as a basic understanding, I cannot expect too much more if she accomplishes 100 percent output.

Extrinsic Rewards We make use of extrinsic awards as a motivator against weak opponents. When we are playing a really weak team, I offer the "bagel incentive." If a player wins 6–0, 6–0, she gets a bagel. This may not seem like much, but all the women try so hard to get a bagel that if they lose one game they are disappointed.

Nonverbal Cues I use nonverbal cues—basically clapping and thumbs-up signs—to communicate to my players in practice and competition.

Sport Psychologist We use a sport psychologist two times a season. I use a sport psychologist from the university to talk to the team. This usually occurs in the beginning of the season and just before nationals.

Psychological Methods The psychological methods I use to help motivate my athletes are handing out articles on the subject and talking about it in general during practice. I have been very fortunate in that I have had little problem motivating players. Whether they come highly motivated or I do something to make them so, I do not know.

The methods I use to increase learning and performance are trying to be as organized as possible and setting up motivational practices. This hopefully allows each player to reach her potential, mentally and physically.

Mental Qualities The mental qualities that I find highly compatible with my coaching style deal with the players' desire to win. I personally do not like to lose and try to pass this on to my players. I never put them down if they lose, as long as they have tried their hardest. Since my team has been highly ranked the past four years, I have had the pleasure of coaching highly skilled and motivated players. I always try to give them 100 percent of my attention and I have found that most of my team members give the same back.

CAROL PLUNKETT

Profile

Entering her tenth season in charge of the Aztec women netters, head coach Carol Plunkett has been the driving force behind San Diego State University's ascendency among the perennial national women's tennis powers. In 1985, she was voted National Coach of the Year by the Intercollegiate Tennis Coaches' Association (ITCA).

Eight times in the past nine seasons, the Aztecs have been ranked among the top ten schools in the country. Each year since the inception of the NCAA Championships for women in 1982, San Diego State has advanced to at least the quarterfinals of the tournament. In 1984, the Aztecs achieved their highest placing ever with a fourth place finish.

Since Plunkett came to the university in 1977, San Diego State has won more than 70 percent of its matches, compiling a 186–75–1 record in the past nine years. Six Aztec players have earned All American honors in that span, including Micki Schillig, a singles finalist in the first NCAA Women's Championship in 1982.

Plunkett graduated from Oregon State in 1965, having earned a bachelor's degree in physical education. She went on to acquire her master's degree also in physical education from the University of North Carolina in 1967.

Plunkett came to San Diego State after serving as an instructor at Colorado State University from 1974 to 1976. Prior to that, she taught at North Carolina, the University of Rhode Island, and Eastern Oregon State College.

Plunkett has served on the Intercollegiate Tennis Coaches' Association Board of Directors and the NCAA Executive Tennis Committee and has been NCAA Western Regional Advisory chairperson. In addition, she has been active in the San Diego area in community tennis and Adidas Sports Development Clinic guest instructor. In 1986, Coach Plunkett was selected as the Pacific Coast Athletic Association's Coach of the Year.

Psychological Coaching Methods

Mental Preparation Approximately 75 percent of practice time is spent on mental practice. We do not isolate mental practice from physical practice but rather combine the two. For example, when drills are started at the beginning of a practice period and these are consistency drills, there is a set number of accomplishments that are maximums in number. The player works on footwork, skill, and concentration in achieving the maximum number of times the ball will cross the net. In actual play you do not anticipate keeping the ball in play that long, but if you play an opponent who does keep it in play that long it is not skill you're working on but the ability to concentrate and stay with the ball that long.

Another aspect of mental preparation is communication. I work with each student to develop a communication pattern that we will use during a match. In tennis, coaching is allowed only as long as it does not interfere with the match and at changeovers. The coach might say a word or two to the player between points. Thus, when I work one on one with a player during drills and we are working on specific corrections of a stroke or specific things I want her to keep in mind, I ask the athlete what cue, of the ten or so that I said, helped her do the skill correctly. The athlete identifies the cue—"racket back," "knees bent," etc.—and that becomes the coaching cue for that particular athlete. These cues may change from athlete to athlete throughout the team. During a game, if I need to do stroke or skill repair we have already decided what I need to say to that athlete. This helps the athlete recall that ideal-performance state. During a changeover I am making comments that will help the athlete with her own confidence, relaxation, or motivation.

We teach our athletes actual imagery. I use pictures from magazines, ask them to recall in their own minds their favorite athlete, or a time when they felt they had a particularly outstanding performance. I ask them to go through all the sensory modalities to recall that one particular time. We do this in practice and during the one-on-one time.

I even use this in the beginning of practice, when we are doing agility drills, to use the fatigue period of time to lay some suggestions for concentration for focusing.

Overall, I do not isolate out a particular time that we concentrate on mental preparation. Rather this is an ongoing aspect of the practices. Generally I believe that in combination with the skill work we spend about 75 percent of the time on mental preparation.

Mental Concentration   I use specific drills to help develop mental concentration. We use ball drills where players develop the ability to concentrate on the ball, to stay with the ball. The important thing is to develop concentration with which to stay with the opponent and to take weak shots away from the opponent. Drills that help with this are consistency drills. Also drills such as those suggested by various professionals where players stare at a ball. We will have plays where we play points and give the athletes a specific point to play. At any time where the player feels she has lost her concentration, such as just reacting to the ball and not planning the point, we have her stop. I will then ask the athlete to replay that point. Usually I work with only one athlete at a time for this particular drill. The other player is a feeder. Sometimes I have the feeder stop the point and challenge the other player as to what her point plan was. The purpose of stopping the point is to see whether the players were concentrating on the point or whether they were reacting to the ball.

Another set of drills is to give the players difficult drills to perform. The purpose is to give the athletes drills where they have to concentrate, focus on the sequences, and have them in proper order. For example, they start the ball over the net doing one flat ball, one topspin, and one slice. Then they add two topspins, two flat balls, and two slices; then three, three, and three; and four, four, and four. They eventually will be at a point where they have to change the spin of the ball on each hit and keep track of what they are doing. That is what I think is a mental concentration drill. Ultimately we are trying to get the players to focus on the task at hand for every single hit. They do this as a team and they do this as individuals.

I use a lot of one-on-one work with my players through visualization, relaxation, and imagery methods to develop this method of mental concentration.

Imagery Techniques   I use visualization extensively as an imagery technique. I let the athlete choose whatever imagery she can best use. For example, I have one player who does not have a good kinesthetic sense. My best technique with her is to have her look at another player; then she gets the stroke. Some individuals respond best to still pictures. We try to use whatever sensory modalities the player responds to best. Sometimes this is working on a stroke with their eyes closed. Some use recall of an ideal experience where everything worked. In using the recall technique, we want the athlete to concentrate on where they were, colors, etc. This is usually done in the office where I use relaxation or visualization techniques.

Relaxation Techniques   Relaxation is a critical aspect of our program. I believe it relates to working with the athlete who is overmotivated or undermotivated. Breathing is a key factor in relaxation technique, for example, taking a deep breath to the count of four and then letting it go, also the timing of when you use a deep breath to slow down the inner self in order to slow down the outer game. In no-add scoring, which is used at the college level, it is very important that the athlete control the outer game by being in control of her inner self. A deep breath prior to serving can be of assistance in slowing down the inner self. Mental imagery can also play a role at this time where the athlete reviews in her mind the perfect serve.

A player who is overmotivated during a match may reveal this by taking short, rapid breaths. I try to relax this player by standing behind her and taking deep breaths. I will also say, "Now try to relax and take a big, deep breath." I particularly do this during changeovers without actually talking about it but by modeling deep breathing. This works particularly well with players who I work with one on one either through drills or in the office with hypnosis or relaxation techniques.

Some of the relaxation techniques I use are taken from meditation classes I have taken. We work on relaxation techniques in the office. The first few times, it takes several minutes to obtain a relaxed state. We work on reducing this to the shortest amount of time possible. As I have pointed out before, time on the tennis court is of the essence, so I work on key word triggers to get a player to relax in the office or to bring back ideal-performance states, certain key anxiety states, or motivational states. I then can use these key words on the court and have some transfer from the office relaxation work. This works better for some players than others.

Generally I try to get the athlete to focus on the task at hand and not the competitive state, not that particular match, not that particular opponent, and not that particular point. In general, getting the players in touch with a particular thing.

Motivation   We try to externally influence overmotivated athletes and get them to slow down. We have them use the second hand of their watch and use the rules to their full advantage. We also use deep breathing to slow them down.

I believe that overmotivated athletes have a greater difficulty with peak performance for key matches and tournaments. One approach to these players is to give them time off. Give them breaks during practice time, interrupt their drill work to tell them to slow down, or tell them to go get a drink. Also, talk to them and introduce nontennis conversations. Basically I am taking them away from the situation and the setting. I give them very specific self-improvement goals rather than the goal of actually winning. I think they get caught up in the competition rather than in their play, which I believe leads to overmotivation. I try to get them involved in self-competition. If they lose a point and the ball crossed the net only three times, then I tell them to focus on trying to have the ball cross the net four times rather than on trying to win the next point. I give them specific self-improvement goals that will aid in bringing on improved concentration, because what they are doing is gaining control over themselves. Once they have control over themselves, a state of relaxation follows. They then move closer to the ideal-performance state.

The undermotivated athlete is the player on the court who is flat, who just cannot get up for the match. This is the player for whom the match just is going by too fast and she cannot get into the match. This player is more difficult to coach than the overmotivated player. I believe the key here is to get her back to a self-competition state, because she may be bored, tired, thinking of academic concerns, or her social life. The athlete is not focused even though she is trying. I try to give her self-competitive goals. For example, in tennis you want to start the match off with wins. For the person who is having a difficult time, you may change her goal to try to keep the match going until someone on the team finishes with a win. She then has a goal that will help the entire team and her focus moves from winning. The match takes on a different significance; it becomes a cat and mouse game. The issue is not winning the match but prolonging the match. The athlete takes on an entirely different attitude, which sometimes leads to her not only controlling the match but actually winning the match.

Optimal Arousal We approach how to achieve optimal arousal for competition at the beginning of the season and try to determine what works for each individual. We try to schedule less important matches at the beginning of the season so we can determine what works for different individuals. Team competition is very different from individual competition. In team competition there is the pressure of having to win for your team. Some athletes thrive on cheering by teammates or fans; they really thrive on this kind of support. Others panic with cheering. We discuss what feels good for each athlete: "Do you want someone there cheering or do you want someone there just to talk to you?" Some athletes want to be "pumped up" prior to a match and they ask for that kind of talk. Others find that a pep talk before they go on the court gets them too tight and they get too involved with the significance of the match. We will experiment with these situations and have individual sessions with those who need it. We may discuss their opponent, what they need to do, and how important their point is to us. For other athletes, we will go over the same skill evaluation of their opponent but we will say, "If you were to play this person in practice you could beat them easily, maybe in two sets. So try to think of this as a practice match." I review the practice situation and what they had worked on to beat this opponent and try to get them mentally back into the practice. To other athletes I will not say anything at all other than "good luck."

The athletes who get really "pumped up" for a match may not be present when introductions are being made, or may look like they are not paying attention. They have permission to do this because I do not want them to get involved with the excitement of the preliminaries, since that may upset their competitive sense.

We try to work with each individual athlete and find out what works for her and share this knowledge with the rest of the team. A teammate on an adjoining court may, during a changeover, offer a cue of "breathe, move your feet, focus," etc. It really is a year-long experiment as to what works, and finding out what works becomes a team effort.

Emotional Differences I believe there are more emotional differences in tennis players than in any other sport I have ever coached, and I am not sure why this is so. The approach to this diversity is to try to get to know the athletes as people, not just as athletes. With each athlete I have extensive conversations throughout the year about her family, parents, past, academics, plans for the future, and friends. This is not done in a prying way. I also make a point not to be involved in this part of her life; this is just an informational involvement. It helps knowing who her past teachers and professionals were and who she played best under. It helps in my approach to athletes. The most important thing is spending time with each individual athlete, getting to know her and being up front with her as to what I can or cannot do. Regardless of what the person is like, there is no substitute for positive reinforcement. This is true even with the athlete who says, "Why don't you yell at me?" Occasionally athletes express a need for the "bawling out." But even when they do get the "bawling out," I still try to make it a positive approach. Other than keeping the basic tenet in mind, be positive, I do not know how else you coach for individual emotional differences.

Athlete or Team That Chokes There is no perfect answer for the individual or team that chokes. There is no athlete or team who is immune to choking whether it be from a fear of winning, losing, failure, or whatever. The most critical factor is to change the competition to one of self-competition. I try, from the first day that I meet the athletes to when I send them off after the national championship, to make everything on a self-competitive level.

I try a variety of ways to deal directly with the idea of choking, such as getting the team involved in a rap session on choking and discussing different times when they had choked and how they got themselves out of the situation. I let them know it is not something unusual, nothing to be feared, and that they have a lot of team support around them. I let them know that some days they may have no choking and some days they will have all choking. But it is like a barber's pole, a continuum; they are going to eventually, with more and more experience, have fewer moments of choking and eventually they will be able to play their way out of the situation.

I also think that breathing techniques help individuals who choke because choking usually involves either too high or too low an arousal level. Usually the match comes to mean more than it actually does. Dealing with the perspective of what the match is really all about becomes one of the most important things a coach can do.

The most important thing is to find some form of relaxation. Also it is important to get the player back to self-competition and away from the competition of the match.

Goal-setting At the first meeting of the year I have everyone sit down and write out their goals for the year—tennis-related goals, academic goals, personal goals, whatever. I have them write down what they have as goals for this team, what they see they have to do as individuals and as a team to achieve these goals.

When an athlete comes in as a freshman, we do an individual game evaluation of that person. We then tell them what they have to add to their game and that they may not be able to do this until they are a junior or senior. It takes time to make changes and we give them time deadlines to achieve these goals.

I also do a values option with them. A lot of times they have goals that are not really goals; they are what the athletes think they should have as goals. We try to impress on them that, if they say they value something, their actions should reveal that they value it or they probably do not value it. We try to get them to be honest with their values. To assist them in setting their goals, we have some motivational texts that we have them go over. This helps those who are having a difficult time in setting their goals and also helps them identify what really is important to them.

With some athletes, particularly those who are having trouble focusing on a particular direction, we will have them sit down and form goals with us on Monday. This will be what they hope to accomplish that week. On Friday we will review the week to see if they have reached their particular goals, losing weight, studying harder, etc. Then we will establish goals for the weekend, and on Monday we will start all over. If they are not reaching their goals, we will have them modify their goals so they will reach some kind of success. No matter how slow it is to reach a goal, the most important thing is that they reach it.

Some goals set by the athletes are outrageous because they are so difficult to reach. The best approach is to establish short-range goals. We do this both as a team as well as with individuals. We try to establish what we can achieve by Friday. The team offers what we should be doing for that point in the season, whether it be more return of serves, more serves, 50 percent first serve, or whatever. But I let them actually do it and then on Friday maybe we have a contest to see if this is actually occurring.

We use goals a lot as a motivational technique to bring the athletes out of flat periods, to give them a focus and something to concentrate on.

Extrinsic Rewards   There are extrinsic rewards constantly available to tennis players. There are racket, shoe, and clothing companies that want to sponsor players. We get invited to prestigious tournaments as we do better as a team. Some of these tournaments are held at lovely resorts. The team knows this and it serves as an extrinsic motivation. It is inherent within the system; I do not keep it from the individuals.

As a coach I use extrinsic rewards, but they are usually fun things. The rewards might be an ice cream cone to the person who wins a drill challenge. Things that we do together as a team are what is involved. I use extrinsic awards as a fun part of the day, to break up the grueling grind of what is going on.

Nonverbal Cues   I use nonverbal cues in tennis. The coaching time in tennis is quite different than in other sports because there is no time-out to take. The coach needs to give help at critical points or in critical games when there is no way to call a time-out but you need that point in the game. This is the time for the nonverbal cue. We work on these nonverbal cues when we are working one on one or as a team. These cues can be most anything; for example, one of the things I have for "move your feet" is to put two fingers down as if they are walking and move them really fast. The athletes know that they are flat and that they have to get up and move their feet.

Breathing is another important nonverbal cue. I will stand by their court and take a very deliberate deep breath if I want them to slow down. I may also put my hands down if I want them to slow down. If I want them to speed up, I'll pant; I will be right beside their court and do short breathing. If I want a player to get her head up on the serve, I will throw my head back. I will use whatever particular technique we have worked on with that athlete to get her to do the technique correctly, from serving to ground strokes. All of these things are worked on months prior to competition. We work with each individual athlete on each skill, every single stroke they use in the game.

The most-used nonverbal cue we use is the thumbs-up or applauding, or the high sign. We try to emphasize what the player is doing right rather than what she is doing wrong. The encouragement is important whether it be a smile or a nod of the head.

Sport Psychologist   I wish to recognize the services of the late Dr. Mary Ann Tucker, who gave so much information to my team and to me. She taught me many things, among them the importance of sport psychology and having a sport psychologist with the team.

The sport psychologist or the clinical psychologist with sport training can be especially effective using his or her professional skills in counseling in general for the student athlete. This is a common time for the athletes to be going through identity crises and changes that you as a coach do not have the professional skills to deal with. It is ideal to turn these athletes over to someone you trust.

Psychological Methods   If you recruit only those athletes who want to improve in their sport and have an intense desire to begin with and you have athletes who are self-motivated most of the time, the methods you must use are easier than those you must use with athletes who do not have this desire and also perhaps the goal of continuing their sport after graduation. Many of the methods that I use have already been discussed.

Succinctly, my special psychological methods are a well-defined, scientifically based, maximum-conditioning program; the highest level skill analysis in teaching and drilling; a strong understanding of the strategies in the sport; psychology of learning; highly developed communication skills; knowing your athletes as people and understanding their needs and goals; and a program where the coach enjoys young people and teaching young people. Getting the student athletes themselves to understand that competition is a process, not a product, and combining all this into a program are the special methods I use, although they are not psychological methods per se. A sound basic program is one of the best psychological approaches that you can have to any sport. I do not think you can separate psychological methods from any other method. They encompass the whole individual.

Mental Qualities   I like a disciplined, intelligent athlete, one who is somewhat independent, one who has the abilities to follow through, one who is extremely conscientious of her own development. I do not like to deal with a prima donna; I like a humble athlete but a confident one. I like aggressive athletes, players who are aggressive in their style of play, which sometimes makes them aggressive personally.

chapter 13

Track and Field, Cross Country, and Long-distance Running

ELIZABETH REMIGINO-KNAPP

Profile

Elizabeth Remigino-Knapp is women's head track and cross country coach at the University of Connecticut. Remigino-Knapp's teams have been consistent top performers in the five years that she has coached at Connecticut. In track and field they have been New England champions or runners-up in 1983, 1984, 1985, and 1986. In indoor track they were Big East runners-up in 1983, 1984, 1985, and 1986. In 1986 they won the outdoor Big East Track Championship. In 1982 the cross country team took first place in the Big East Championships. In 1984 they were Connecticut Intercollegiate champions and in 1986 runners-up in the New England Cross Country Championships. Remigino-Knapp was a three-sport athlete in college, competing in field hockey, swimming, and track.

Psychological Coaching Methods

Mental Preparation The team members spend 10 to 15 percent of their time on what we call mental preparation. Two times per week we do an intense training session that simulates racelike conditions. We use this more as a mental preparation as opposed to a physiological preparation. We want the athletes to be psychologically prepared for what they will encounter on race day.

141

At the beginning of the training week we discuss what the upcoming race is about and objectives for each race, because each race is different. We talk to the team members and indicate what kind of course they will encounter, who their competition will be, and perhaps, if we can anticipate, weather conditions that must be taken into account. Much of the mental preparation that takes place is preparation for what they will actually encounter so there will be no big surprises.

Mental Concentration We use a specific drill to help work on race composure. This is very much mental concentration during the course of the race. We try to develop this in racelike situations. We use someone, usually our assistant coach, who can run at varying speeds while at the same time talk and actually play games that could stress the individual. A typical situation is where a runner has to make a decision to stay in the race, take the lead, and make a commitment to continue racing. Oftentimes an athlete falls apart during a race; this is usually a mental failure not a physiological failure. Not falling apart mentally is a very big part of distance running. We try to develop this by using a person who can vary the pace of the race, perhaps change what is actually happening in the course of the race by slowing down the pace; sprinting; or, in a 1500-meter, pushing the third lap. We try to get our athletes to attach themselves to this individual and use her in the practice session. The athlete may be actually practicing a weakness. We try to point this out to the team members so they can make a correction.

It is important that they are verbally reinforced for what they are doing. This is done by me or by the leader—the "rabbit." If the athlete can do what we suggest, a great deal of confidence is built up.

The "rabbit" must be someone that the athletes really trust. They must have worked with this person closely and feel that the leader knows what she is doing when she changes the tempo and makes comments that the athletes must react to in their running. Reaction is important; it is mental concentration. Oftentimes you will see an athlete fall asleep during the course of the race; that is, she loses her concentration. It is very important that she not lose the ability to maintain mental concentration.

Relaxation Techniques We do not use relaxation techniques per se. We emphasize relaxation during running. We stress the physiological techniques of relaxation while running. This is very dependent upon running form. Our athletes have their methods of working on relaxation, but we as coaches do not teach a specific technique.

Motivation As a team we do not usually have an entire group of people who are overmotivated. We have individuals who at times are overmotivated and this can be a detriment to their training. Usually individuals who are very driven and achievement-oriented have a tendency to overdo things. The distance runner usually overdoes it by increasing mileage. In essence she does not follow the training workout set up by the coach. I point this out to the athlete and tell her the reasons why I have given her the workout that we have. I then let the athlete make up her own mind. She makes the decision, whether it be right or wrong. We usually have a discussion afterwards as to my rationale for the training and how her personality characteristics have brought about negative results. However, many of these characteristics can be very positive if channeled in the right direction.

I do not set up a guilt trip or "I told you so." I merely point out how this can be a more positive situation for the athlete. Usually it is a learning situation. I have never had a person who would not listen. Usually after they have done it once or twice they get the message that it is not to their benefit to overtrain.

Undermotivation of a team as a whole or with individuals is the biggest barrier that a coach must deal with. It is encountered often with distance runners. The distance runner must train all year, and it is very difficult to be motivated to train all year. One of the things that the coach must understand and get across to their athletes is that there are natural peaks and valleys, both mental and physiological, when a person is training on a year-round basis. There are also many extraneous variables that lead to undermotivation. Many of these are in the form of stress, such as grades, tests, and personal problems when one is in school. Many of these lead to lack of motivation. Many of these forms of stress are difficult for a coach to control. But it is the role of the coach to help the athlete realize that stress is controllable.

I think it is also important for a coach to realize that an athlete cannot give 100 percent throughout the season or throughout her career. It is important that you let the athlete know that you understand many of the stresses that often dictate lack of enthusiasm for the sport, lack of wanting to work hard. Make the athlete aware that she can fit running into her life and that it does not have to be an overwhelming part of it. Much of this is done through communication or role models—either you or her teammates.

Another way to encourage enthusiasm is by setting up success-oriented goals or helping the athlete to achieve these goals. You must remember that each individual is motivated in a different way, and different tactics work for different people. We like to utilize a lot of positive reinforcement.

Optimal Arousal We do not use any special techniques to achieve optimal arousal of our team for competition. However, our team is always ready, psychologically, for our important meets—the championship meets at the end of the season. Our athletes know from the beginning of the season what meets are important. The meets leading up to the championships are really dress rehearsals for what we are trying to achieve. Optimal arousal really hinges on good communication and common goal-setting.

Emotional Differences In coaching, working with individual emotional differences is one of the most important areas in dealing with a team. Track and field and cross country are sports that focus on the individual. As a coach you must take a great deal of time observing and listening to the athlete reacting in many different situations. In this way you can learn a great deal about each athlete; how she reacts will tell you a lot about her as a person. How you deal with her must be different from individual to individual.

In dealing with individual emotional differences, you do not allow a laissez-faire attitude on the team where everyone does what they want. But you must emphasize that you are dealing with the athletes on an individual basis within the structure of the team. You must, as a coach, state very clearly what you expect from each athlete and what her role is on the team.

Athlete or Team That Chokes I have not had to deal with a team that chokes. I have dealt with individuals who have choked. Choking is when one cannot maintain race composure. This happens when a runner cannot view herself as succeeding or lacks confidence in her ability. Also, this can happen when one is not aggressive, is willing to settle for second best, is complacent about the situation—an individual with low self-esteem. Oftentimes there is no commitment on the part of the athlete, and she does not make a decision to push over physiological, psychological, or both barriers.

This is a very difficult situation to deal with because frequently the problem is imbedded very deeply within the person. One of the ways we have successfully dealt with this is simulating many race situations to help build the person's confidence. The individual usually can pinpoint where she chokes and the problem. This needs to be discussed with the athlete as well as how both the coach and the athlete can work together to correct the weakness.

Another way of helping the athlete with choking is to set up goals that will lead to success. These should be small goals where success is possible; also these small goals should lead to larger goals. It is important to positively reinforce the athlete when she does overcome barriers that have led to choking.

Goal-setting   Goal-setting is a very integral part of having a successful team. I do not follow a step-by-step approach to goal-setting. Generally we discuss, with the team, what are realistic goals from the coaching staff perspective. Usually the coaching staff goals and the team goals are the same.

Dealing with goal-setting for the individual is much more specific and can be done step-by-step. Usually this situation is set up with the coach and the athlete. The most important point to emphasize here is that the goals being set up are those of the athlete, not those of the coach. If the goals are set up by the coach and are not the ones that the athlete wishes to achieve, this can create a conflict in obtaining the goals.

Our ultimate goals for the team are stated in the beginning of the season. As we reach these goals they are pointed out and emphasized. It is important that all the individuals involved with the team know their role in achieving the team goals.

When we talk about goal-setting for both the individual and the team, we ask the athletes to specifically state their goals. It is important that they be goals that are fairly realistic to obtain. It is important to set up a plan on how the athletes are going to achieve these goals. The coaches' role is one of facilitator to help the athletes set up their plans in achieving subgoals and then the final goals. Stated within the plans are what the coach must do and what the athletes must do.

The most successful people on our team do not need help in setting their own goals, athletically or personally. But for those who have problems setting goals it takes a great deal of time for both the coach and the athlete. One problem that occurs is when the athlete sets a false goal. She sets a goal that she does not really believe she can achieve or does not want to achieve. This can cause conflict because the athlete and coach are not really working for the same goal. It is important to find out if there are any false goals or ones that cannot be achieved.

Extrinsic Rewards   We use extrinsic rewards to give recognition to our athletes. Most of our rewards come in the form of publicity—public recognition in the newspaper, either locally, nationally, or on campus. We also have rewards that recognize achievement or excellence in certain areas. Much of this recognition is a combination of academic and athletic success and is rewarded by the university in the form of an endowed scholarship.

Mental Qualities   Individuals with mental qualities compatible with my coaching style are those who enjoy being challenged, are goal-oriented, fairly aggressive, have a certain degree of perseverance, believe in working hard both physically and mentally— usually an empathic individual who is very caring about other individuals on the team, and usually a fairly mature individual. This person does not necessarily have to be the most talented individual on the team; she can be of any degree of ability. But I have found that this type of individual achieves beyond their capabilities.

JIM PENNINGTON

Profile

Jim Pennington has coached cross country running for seven years, the last two years at Springfield College. In his first year at Springfield, Pennington earned Coach of the Year honors from both the Eastern Collegiate Athletic Conference and Northeast-8 Conference. In 1986 he was named NCAA Division II District I Coach of the Year by the NCAA Coaches Association. Springfield won the Northeast-8 Conference Championship in 1985 and 1986. Pennington's teams competed in the National Collegiate Athletic Association Championship in 1985 and 1986 and finished tenth and eighth, respectively. For the past two years, his Springfield College team has been steadily moving toward the goal of top NCAA team.

Psychological Coaching Methods

Mental Preparation   The percentage of mental preparation for a cross country meet for the team as a whole is approximately 60–70 percent. I speak with each runner individually about her pace, race strategy, how to run the hills, and keeping an eye out for other team members. I do this several times a week in practice but never in the two days prior to the meet. The entire team is exposed to the above strategies at a team meeting on Monday, at the beginning of the racing week, and then again at our team huddle five minutes before the race.

Mental Concentration   The specific drills that I utilize to develop mental concentration are the following:

1. Uniform color identification of opposing team or several teams. Know the uniform color and design, look for it during the race, and beat it.
2. Trial runs over a similar course in practice, keeping in mind pace, terrain, and opposing teams.
3. Give athletes a detailed map of course to have them memorize key locations and terrain. Develop our team strategy from the layout of the course.
4. Show them pictures of the course and have them memorize what it looks like.

5. Dress some team members in the same color as the opposing school's uniforms and start them out thirty seconds earlier than the rest of the team. The purpose of this drill is to run and catch another team who has gone out very fast in the beginning of the race.

6. Plan a practice that deliberately is extremely hard to complete and challenging to finish. Mentally, this is a very demanding practice, and if the athletes can get through it they have a feeling of being able to accomplish anything.

7. Complete one more interval or a timed mile at the end of a hard practice.

8. On easy days, run relaxed and emphasize relaxation and ease of running.

9. Run with a blank stare on your face as fast as possible or at a certain pace for as far as you can.

Basically I get the athletes physiologically as strong and as fast as each of them can get; then we try to do different things. I keep records of every practice workout, reinforce the idea that this is the work they have done so far, and that their team is the best team around. Also I repeat some of the same workouts every four weeks and show them their differences, particularly their improvements. I quiz them on course strategy and opposing teams. The pace and the strategy for the team is set by the number one runner; I have all others key off her lead. Gradually as each meet approaches I increase the importance of accomplishing certain things at that meet.

Imagery Techniques I use imagery techniques on an individual basis and with the whole team. I utilize several different approaches. Several runners have taken relaxation skill courses at the college and play music with their eyes closed to help relax. While they are doing this I ask them to think all positive thoughts when thinking about racing. If an athlete begins to think negative thoughts, she immediately "zaps" them from her mind.

Some athletes have used another idea I gave them. They write a script of the perfect race or experience, which includes all environmental considerations, movements of body, techniques, and speed of race. They describe feelings, thoughts, and also how they think or actually how their senses operate during the race. Within this exercise they always use "I am" statements, not "I might" statements, in describing pre-event, event, and post-event race thoughts.

Another technique is to set up a practice situation where one group of seven dressed in the opposing team's colors starts out at thirty-second and one-minute intervals prior to the top seven runners. The top seven run until they catch them over a one-mile distance. I ask the top seven runners to imagine seeing themselves gradually catching up to the group that started out first, reaching inside for a little extra, and sprint past them. They are then asked to do the same thing in their minds and also in the race.

Relaxation Techniques I use relaxation techniques in my coaching. I urge the runners to relax and be patient. I also stress that they should not panic but anticipate panic and deal with it by taking long, slow, deep breaths and focusing their thoughts on everything we discussed all week or all season in practice.

One key I have found is not to give a high-powered pep talk the day of the race or the day before. This leads to poor performances and a restless night before the race. I gradually build up the intensity of the season with easy meets at the beginning of the year, particularly a fun, five-mile road race with pizza afterwards. Then, as the season progresses, so does the intensity of the workouts which are done in four-week cycles.

I prefer to have a team talk/meeting on Monday about the upcoming race on Saturday. Each day small comments are made to each team member about each person's role. I also give a lot of positive encouragement, particularly after a workout. On Thursday we have another brief team meeting, which is used as a review of Monday's meeting and a pep talk. The team captains make up posters for the bulletin board and for the side window of the van. Nothing is said on Friday, the day before the race. On race day we arrive one-and-a-half to two hours before the start of the race to walk the course. The runners go out as a team and warm up together; then they split and stretch out on their own. Five minutes before the race we gather together and I say three or four things that reinforce what we discussed in our two previous meetings. We huddle and give a very loud cheer for SC. This we found is very important because we are the loudest team in our cheers. We have found it serves as an intimidator to some other teams or individuals. Coaches of opposing teams have mentioned that their runners heard us cheer.

Motivation   I deal with overmotivation of runners in several ways. Usually overmotivation is caused by fear of failing. I stress consistency to the runners; everyone has a bad race. But if bad races occur over and over again I ask the particular athlete for input on why she thinks it occurs. Sometimes I have her warm up on her own or jog and warm up with a friend. In extreme situations that individual is not allowed to race because she adversely affects the rest of the unit. I then would ask her to see one of our faculty in sport psychology.

I believe most overmotivation is caused by fear or is the result of the desire to want to do well. I try to positively encourage that person and note to the individual and to the team when advances are made in performance or in relaxation. Sometimes negative reinforcement works. I once had a young runner who was very "hyper." I told her, after all effort to control her overmotivation had been tried, that she would never race again. She had caused everyone else to be upset and raised their levels of activity too high. She asked for a second chance and really excelled for the rest of the season and for the next three years.

Another way I help the athlete is to assign her a partner who is like a big sister. The big sister is responsible for helping the athlete cope or giving her insight into her personal experiences. This person is usually an upperclass person on the teams; for example, a freshman has a junior or senior as a big sister.

We maintain a very close team and try to function as a unit. Everything we do in practice is as a team.

Undermotivation is very hard to measure because there are so many factors that could lead to it, such as (1) fear of success or failure so the athletes do the minimum; (2) not running as hard because the athletes want to look good coming in; (3) not wanting to pass another teammate or friend; and (4) a conditioning factor. I try to speak to the athlete and find out the reasons for the problem, since sometimes the coach is the reason for undermotivation. Coaches, I feel for the most part, underprepare distance runners. Distance runners need to feel inside that they have done a sufficient amount of work or have a training base before they can compete at a top level. This I feel is a psychological crutch mainly brought on by advocates of high-mileage workouts.

The method I use for motivating these individuals is a reward system where I announce their performance at the end of the meet. I point out to the whole team the good points of their race. I also give out T-shirts at the end of the year to all those who improved during the season.

Optimal Arousal   I help my athletes achieve optimal arousal for competition in several different ways: gradually building up the intensity of the workouts as the season progresses; gradually building up the level of competition as the season progresses; gradually building up the demands made on the team or on the racing strategy; preparing the team weeks in advance and up to no more than two to three days prior to a contest.

Emotional Differences   The way I coach for individual emotional differences is to look at each runner in pre-practice, practice, pre-meet, meet, and post-meet situations. I look for certain indicators that could be radically different in each situation. I stress consistent thoughts and efforts by each runner. I then fit their individual style to the teams' racing style, so all blend together evenly. If an individual cannot blend in with the group, we have a serious talk to discover how she feels she should compete.

Athlete or Team That Chokes   Teams or individuals that choke are not prepared for new situations that arise. I try to put the athletes through every possible situation I know may occur, and some that may never occur. These trial runs prepare the athletes mentally for any situation that may cause them to panic, thus causing a higher heart rate, higher respiration, etc.

Goal-setting   I set goals individually with an athlete and also in my mind without stating to the athlete what those goals are. I ask them to set short-range weekly goals and season goals. Also I ask them to set realistic long-term goals that can be reached and to update those goals as they are reached. I never set a goal for an individual.

On the team level we set goals as a group for each race. These goals are evaluated at the end of the meet after warmdowns. We discuss how we reached our goals or what contributed to the inability to reach the desired level. We set goals according to the time differences between the first and fifth, first and seventh, and first and tenth runners on our cross country team.

Extrinsic Rewards   I make use of extrinsic rewards. I give a team T-shirt award at the end of the year to all runners who improved during the season. A paper award is given in recognition of outstanding effort. Two picture awards are given: one is the athlete's picture in the school paper and the other is an enlarged, framed picture of themselves.

Nonverbal Cues   I make use of nonverbal cues in several different ways. During a meet I use hand signals to signify pace changes and strategy moves. Prior to a meet, team members wear jerseys of the opposing team's colors. I also use facial expressions for good and bad points.

Sport Psychologist We have several graduate students who have worked with our team for the past two years in counseling, imagery work, or discussion. I ask the athletes to use them as a service, not as a crutch and not to be totally dependent on them.

Psychological Methods My psychological coaching methods are: (1) rewards, (2) positive reinforcement, (3) negative reinforcement, (4) peer pressure, and (5) situation training. The most important psychological approach is that I never give positive feedback until it is deserved or earned. Too many people believe this should be done first. Athletes know when they have done well and there are good points to bring out, such as parts of the race. I stress working on parts so the whole can be achieved.

Mental Qualities Most of my past or current team persons are highly motivated individuals who do not like mediocre performances. They are never satisfied with their performances and when positive reinforcement is applied they reject it. They are also very goal-oriented and have a great deal of personal pride in themselves and the team. They have the ability to relax and work hard and believe in the coach. This is most important. If athletes doubt what you do, you can never get the most out of them. You have to be a "con artist" and make them believe everything you present. They also want to be kept well-informed on their competition.

As a coach I feel these qualities, along with a willingness to learn and change, are most important. Finally, athletes must not be afraid to do speed work. Improvements come with developing a fine balance between speed and distance.

JANE WELZEL

Profile

Jane Welzel has coached cross country running for four years at two different levels, high school and college. In her most recent position, Welzel started a new varsity program at Wellesley College. In her first year she coached the new team to a New England Regional Championship which qualified Wellesley for competition in the National Collegiate Athletic Association Division III Cross Country Championship.

Welzel is a multifaceted athlete, having competed at the University of Massachusetts in swimming, water polo, crew, cross country, and indoor and outdoor track. She is an outstanding runner, having placed fourteenth in the 1984 United States Olympic Trials Marathon.

Psychological Coaching Methods

Mental Preparation A large percentage of the Wellesley College cross country team's mental preparation occurs simultaneously with physical practice. Mental preparation is highlighted in certain workouts. However, I feel that individual athletes contribute the most to their mental preparation by their attitude and commitment to their goals.

Mental Concentration   The drills I use to develop mental concentration are determined by the athletes' strengths and weaknesses. For example, if I noticed that the majority of the team slacked off the pace at the midpoint of the last race, the interval session that week would stress working on pace and making the runners aware of their ability to judge pace when fresh and when fatigued. An example of a workout used to demonstrate this is to have the athletes run a specific pace for intervals of varying lengths.

Imagery Techniques   I use imagery techniques in coaching by having the runners visualize certain competitors or competitive situations. I design drills that simulate the competitive situations in which they may find themselves. I am careful, however, not to create unhealthy rivalries within our team.

Relaxation Techniques   The main relaxation technique I use when the athletes appear nervous is telling jokes or stories to break the tension. During practice, in both easy runs and interval workouts, the athletes work on staying relaxed as they run.

Motivation   When a runner is overly upset about her performance or overly worried about an upcoming meet, I remind her of the reasons she runs and make clear to her that running is something she does; she is not her running. I illustrate this by saying, "I used to think that if I ran poorly I was a bad person and people would not like me." I then illustrate the ridiculousness of this point of view. I reassure her that she is prepared for the race and all she needs to do is run it.

I do not feel I can make a runner want to work out or compete. I try to create an environment in which it is clear that it is the athlete's choice to be here running. If necessary I also remind the runner of the commitment she made to the team and discuss her willingness to keep that commitment.

Optimal Arousal   Achievement of optimal arousal for competition is an ongoing process throughout the season. Initially we establish goals for the season and decide which meets are the most important to run well. Throughout the season I keep the runners aware of their goals and the progress they are making toward achieving them.

Emotional Differences   I feel you must treat athletes as individuals and coach for individual emotional differences. I discuss with each person her strengths and weaknesses and make sure she understands that there is no right or wrong way. I illustrate my point with stories of athletes she has heard of or can relate to so she can see that there are many different methods of working toward her goals. I encourage her to discover what works for her and to be open to new possibilities.

Athlete or Team That Chokes   I make sure the runners who choke are aware that their performance did not reflect their current level of conditioning. I do not make them feel wrong. I just get them to realize, for themselves, that they did not perform up to their ability. We then look at what got in the way of their performing well and make a plan. I try to get them to see that they can learn from a bad performance and that there is no sense in berating themselves. They need to accept the race for what it was, learn whatever lessons it presented to them, and get on with being the runner they are capable of being.

Goal-setting   I set up short-term and long-term goals, both individually and for the team. I constantly remind the runners of their goals. We also reevaluate goals from time to time and make adjustments if appropriate. I make sure the goals are attainable and challenging and contain the element of risk. I feel that the standard should be high enough so there is a risk involved in achieving it (i.e., it is not a sure thing).

Extrinsic Rewards   I do not believe in running or racing for any extrinsic rewards that the coach may offer. The rewards in running are already set; that is, if the team or an individual does well they set personal records or get to go to the championship meets. The individual and/or team receives intrinsic rewards, which I feel are worth focusing on. These intrinsic rewards are a feeling of accomplishment, self-esteem, and self-satisfaction. The runners have the opportunity to set goals and move toward them, meet new people, experience new activities, push themselves to new limits, and learn about themselves.

Nonverbal Cues   I give my athletes nonverbal cues, and sometimes I am sure I am not even aware that I am doing so. I believe that often what you do is heard much louder than what you say. I feel I bring genuine enthusiasm to practice and meets, and that enthusiasm is displayed through my facial expressions, actions, tone of voice, etc.

Psychological Methods   My main goal is to get the runners to appreciate themselves and to acknowledge their commitment. They are the ones responsible for themselves and their running. I believe the better they feel about themselves, the more confident they will be and also the more willing they will be to take risks and push to their limits.

Mental Qualities   Individuals with mental qualities that I find compatible with my coaching style are runners who enjoy running and competing and runners who are motivated by the intrinsic rewards they receive from their participation in the sport.

My coaching style works best when I am in a partnership with the athletes and they use me to assist them in pursuing their goals. Athletes who are not very compatible with my style are the ones who expect me to motivate them and make them runners.

chapter *14*

Volleyball

CHARLIE BRANDE

Profile

Charlie Brande is widely acknowledged as one of the premier "age group" coaches in the nation. From 1978 to the present, Coach Brande has been at the helm of the Orange County Volleyball Club, where his girls' team has captured the national championship in 1978, 1979, 1980, 1982, 1983, 1984, and 1985 and will defend their title in 1986. As the head coach at Corona del Mar High School, Coach Brande won the California State Championship. Prior to his tenure at Corona del Mar, Coach Brande guided both the boys and girls to championship seasons at Newport Harbor High School in 1979 and 1980. His Newport Harbor teams were crowned national high school champions in 1979 and 1980. He has been an assistant coach at the University of Hawaii and at UCLA. In 1982 his UCLA women finished fifth in the country.

Psychological Coaching Methods

Mental Preparation   Our goal is to use the total practice time for mental preparation. Every drill that we do is "concentration"-oriented activity, realizing that mastery of concentration (a key to success in this game) is learned at practice, not at the game.

Mental Concentration   Goal-oriented drills are always utilized especially toward the end of practice when concentration can deteriorate or fail altogether. Even serving

153

drills, which are tough to judge by numbers, are evaluated. I constantly point out that "weak" or "out" serves result from a lack of mental concentration.

Imagery Techniques Imagery techniques occupy an important position in my program. Among the more important are: video equipment, review of technique by player and coach, demonstration of correct technique by coaches, model demonstration.

Relaxation Techniques Mental relaxation is difficult to achieve with a club team that meets only two or three times per week. With a school team that meets every day for three of four months, relaxation through thought can be taught. First, physical relaxation must be achieved. Then the mental relaxation of the players is attained. Once we simultaneously achieve this, individual imagery of successful play is visualized. Finally, successful team interaction is visualized. Best performance is achieved two hours after relaxation techniques are initiated.

Motivation We try to teach that judgment, knowing the right time and place, is absolutely necessary for good play. A major part is to know when and where to "go for it."

From the beginning, it is stressed that "nice try" is not in our vocabulary. To be a part of our disciplined program, a nice try is considered mediocre, not at all appropriate or acceptable for our goals and expectations. Maximum effort on *every* play is the only way that we practice and play.

Optimal Arousal The whole process of the disciplined practice is to prepare for the major event—the game. We have worked too hard not to play hard. The hard practices guarantee a commitment and expected mental attitude when game time comes along.

Emotional Differences "Emotional control" is constantly discussed and stressed. We know that emotional control, rather than an inconstant few "ups" followed by "downs," leads to continued success over a long period of time. To win over and over again requires complete emotional control.

Athlete or Team That Chokes We discuss "choking" as it happens and during future workouts. We start these discussions early in the season so we know how to cope with pressure later in the season when it really counts. This is all part of the mental and physical tough reputation that we as a team and coaching staff have earned.

Goal-setting Every drill we do is goal-oriented. Volleyball is a different sport than most in that the object is not to "get ahead" but to get to fifteen before the other team. A whole new way of thinking needs to be developed through goal-setting.

Extrinsic Rewards We *do not* make use of extrinsic rewards.

Nonverbal Cues Nonverbal cues are an important part of my methodology. Looks and glances are constantly used as a sign of disgust or, more importantly, to provide the constant pressure that we as a team learn to cope with in order to be a perpetual winner!

Sport Psychologist   After the number of years that I have been coaching volleyball, I feel that I am my own sport psychologist. A large part of our success I attribute to our team's understanding of the psychology of successful volleyball.

Psychological Methods   As discussed earlier, I put the players through as many pressure situations as possible. This can be done individually, in player-versus-player performance, or via the team. By playing player versus player, the individual develops the "fight" needed to be successful.

Mental Qualities   A great number of my players have developed the mental and physical toughness that will help them succeed in life (which is a lot more important than the game of volleyball). Every player that has stuck it out in our program has graduated from college (if eligible). One former player has turned into a very good distance runner. When she was asked how she could do this after never having run before, her statement was that from volleyball she learned that she could do anything if she wanted to do it badly enough.

BILL NEVILLE

Profile

Not many coaches can lay claim to having coached a United States Olympic team to a Gold Medal in the 1984 Olympic Games in Los Angeles. Prior to his arrival as head women's volleyball coach at Montana State University, Bill Neville was selected as the assistant coach of the Gold Medal-winning United States Olympic Men's Volleyball team in 1981. From 1981 until the Los Angeles Olympiad, Bill Neville, along with Head Coach Doug Beal, forged the U.S. Men's Olympic volleyball team into the best team in the world.

Coach Neville is widely recognized as a superb volleyball coach and a skilled practitioner of applied sport psychology. He has an outstanding international reputation. Coach Neville served as head coach of the 1976 Canadian Men's Olympic Volleyball team. He has an excellent rapport with his athletes and peers and is a consistent winner.

Mental Preparation   Mental preparation is a constantly ongoing process in our program. The mental aspects are continuously presented, refined, and integrated into virtually every activity and drill we utilize. It is impossible for me to identify specific percentages. However, various drills and exercises are specifically designed for both the team as a whole as well as individual athletes. For example, the setters meet with the coaching staff once a week to discuss and evaluate tactical analysis, in-depth psychological considerations, leadership, communication, and motivational issues. The middle blockers hold similar meetings.

As a coaching staff we utilize psychological and motivational profiles for each athlete. Each athlete has specific behavioral assignments she must practice, and these are evaluated both on and off the court.

Mental Concentration Because volleyball has no time limit and the victorious team must score the winning points in order to win, the ability to concentrate and have the "patience of an Apache" is essential. Most of our drills are designed with *no time limit*; drills are measured by production; e.g., successful attempts in total or in a row are common determinants signifying the satisfactory completion of a specific drill.

Volleyball is an exercise in frustration as well as exhilaration. Successful teams must maintain an emotional balance. The players cannot allow themselves the luxury of too much exhilaration nor the doldrums of frustration. Drills are designed to practice the mental concentration necessary to deal with the unique aspects (mental and physical) of volleyball. For example, one team drill is referred to as the "wash drill." Without belaboring the details, the essence of the drill is that it's team-oriented, extremely competitive, can be frustrating, can be very rewarding, is risky, and magnifies and encompasses all the elements the team faces in actual match play. The focus is on concentration and patience. Two teams play each other. Team A serves team B. The ball is played to its natural conclusion. When a team successfully wins "that play" they have "add" (example: team B gets "add"). Immediately after the first play is terminated, the coach tosses a free ball to the serving team (A). That ball is played once again to its natural conclusion. If team A wins, it is a "wash" (team B, 1; team A, 1). However, if team B had won this second play, they would score a point. The drill continues with the two-play series (a serve and a free ball) with the serve alternating between the two teams. The teams do not rotate until one team wins a rotation by scoring six points (a point is scored when the *two plays* are won consecutively by one team). When a rotation is won, the team gets to rotate. The other team cannot rotate until they win a rotation. To win the whole game a team must win in all six rotations. I think the "wash drill" is the single best team drill for developing concentration, emotional control, and patience. The 1984 Gold Medal USA Olympic Men's Team utilized the "wash drill" in final training prior to the Olympics. The drill lasted more than four hours and was considered a more intense competitive experience than the Gold Medal final against Brazil!

Several individual drills and other team drills we designed with the same philosophy: score two in a row to get one.

Imagery Techniques I am not sure our techniques follow accepted traditional guidelines. We begin teaching our players to "see themselves" through video. Then we have them visualize what they have seen (which must be correct, of course). We talk about "feeling success." The players are encouraged prior to a match, while serving or at practice, to *mentally* review the good feelings of success. One exercise we have them do each morning is to look at themselves in the mirror and say, "Let's make this day the best it can be." Then they do a specific number of push-ups and sit-ups to symbolize their daily recommitment to excellence.

Relaxation Techniques We do not use formal relaxation techniques. However, we try to help individuals who appear unable to relax. If the perceived tenseness is manifested in physical tightness, we use differential relaxation. Again, we integrate the technique within the drills. If players have a propensity toward mental tenseness (self-doubt, lack of confidence, a "mission complex"), we take them through exercise, focusing on the role of athletics in their lives. We have found self-confidence comes from intense preparation which emphasizes a "family support group" feeling on the team. These success-oriented drills and practices enhance the ability of the players and team to relax. I believe *team relaxation* comes from the security and confidence of *thorough* team and individual preparation.

However, if individual players have specific problems of relaxation, we address them and determine the reasons for anxiety and what must be done to solve the problem. We do not use preprogrammed "all team" relaxation techniques such as lying in a dark room with the sounds of a mountain stream rushing over the rocks, backed up by bird songs, blended with a velvet voice describing how we will obliterate our opponents!

Motivation   We initially interview our players to get a good idea of why they play volleyball. Are they trying to prove something? Do they play for the joy of playing? For their parents? We as a coaching staff need to understand why each player plays. More importantly, the player needs to understand why she plays. In 1975, as part of the selection process of the Canadian Olympic team, I interviewed all the players. A key question was "why do you play?" One player described that only volleyball was important to him. It was what he lived for. I cut him. He was stunned, assuming I would want a player that is so devoted to volleyball. He was wrong. Someone with all his eggs in one basket is desperate. All the "eggs" can get broken at once. I told him to develop other parts of his life, put volleyball in perspective, and cultivate a wider range of interests and opportunities. Then I told him to come back. He would be much more stable and content in *playing* volleyball, and not being desperate. I deal with overmotivation with the same philosophy, although I rarely cut college players. The players and team collectively must write about and discuss volleyball and its role in context of their total lives.

Often the player who is undermotivated has been pressured to play by parents or peers because it is the prestigious thing to do. They key is for the player to get comfortable with her real reasons for playing. Many players have a "negative confirmation complex." They continually put themselves into situations where they will fail. (At least they can guarantee something: they're a failure.) I continually create situations where they will gain success and thus obtain the satisfaction of achievement. I continually try to reinforce the good feelings of attaining goals and gradually eliminate the need for negative confirmation. Motivation to achieve will then increase.

Optimal Arousal   Athletes cannot be suddenly aroused for competition. It is an on-going preparation, a life-style development. Every practice is lively and competitive. I want my athletes to be comfortable in an intensely competitive environment. To seek out the big challenges, develop security and confidence in themselves, and give their best effort in the toughest situations are the keys. This mental set is developed in the way in which practice is conducted: competitive drills, positive reinforcement, peer support, emphasizing the joy and fun of competition—each individual's competitive qualities can be tapped in different ways. Therefore, through the team activities, the coaches must discover each player's quirks and idiosyncrasies. Next, an aura of competitive intensity as a team characteristic must be developed.

Prior to any specific competition, the competitive drive must be in place. I believe strongly that using revenge or hate directed toward the opponent cannot be used regularly. Occasionally, rivalries can stimulate arousal. Ultimately, arousal must come from within.

If arousal is based solely on the opposition, the level of intensity will be inconsistent and the team will be susceptible to upsets. If pride, confidence, team and individual goals are the *foundations* of competitive intensity, the team will be aroused from within. Occasionally, the hype of a rivalry will add to the effort. It will get "old" if used too much. Athletes must play for the joy and reward of competition. If they have a "mission," they should become a mercenary, not a volleyball player. Missions are for individuals; volleyball is a team process.

Emotional Differences   Coaching for emotional differences begins with recognizing the individual differences in emotional responses. Likewise, coaches must thoroughly understand their own emotional behavior and how they dovetail with the individual players and the team as a whole. When developing a relationship with each player, the coach must learn how to channel the individual's emotions into a productive level as part of the team. Acknowledging the negative implications, the process is manipulative. It is known as having the knowledge of "what buttons to push" or "strings to pull." It is a necessary and critical part of coaching to be able to harness the emotional energies of the players individually and the team collectively. However, it is a serious responsibility. Emotions in sports, entwined with egos, are very fragile. Certain situations are even more sensitive. Men coaching women and women coaching men present cultural ramifications that may underlie emotional concerns.

Too many coaches seem to be either insensitive or irresponsible in dealing with the emotions of their team. There must be more formal attention given to this important coaching responsibility. "Guilt trips," taking emotions hostage, yo-yoing a player's emotions, etc., should be avoided. Recognizing the legitimacy of emotions, talking about them, having a rule that there is no right or wrong in having a feeling (let's find where a feeling comes from), and keeping open a dialog about feelings are important. We have our players keep "feelings and emotions journals" to help them understand the ebb and flow of their emotions.

This area needs much more research, education, and training, especially with the increase of males coaching females, females coaching males, and high-level competitive pressure and expectations on girls and women. Many coaches avoid the emotional ramifications of competitive sport. However, it is there, it is real, and it is a life lesson. It can be ignored (but still is there), it can be abused (all too often), or it can be addressed (an important lesson).

Athlete or Team That Chokes   I coach the athlete or team that chokes with preventive medicine. Each practice has specific drills designed to put pressure on the athletes and team. We rely on peer support and pressure to help less-confident players to succeed under duress. Many drills require a predetermined number of successful attempts *in a row* to finish. Likewise, in tiring drills the last three points are scored when two successful plays in a row are executed for each point. Individually, we give players specific assignments within a drill that they must complete to get finished. Our goal is to create choke situations in practice so we can assess them and deal with them there. We don't wait until a game in order to discover who chokes or what will cause the team to choke.

Goal-setting   The first assignment the players get in pressure-training is to write the answers to three questions: (1) Why do you want to play volleyball? (2) What do you want to get out of volleyball? (3) What do you want to get out of life? Thus we begin the goal-setting process. We establish team goals collectively (at first, everyone is fairly idealistic). The coaching staff must temper dreams but never stifle or crush them. A rule we have for goals is that they must be reasonable. We evaluate the goals quarterly. We refer to them constantly. (The coaching staff has a copy and each player has a copy of her own goals.)

We use each player's goal-setting program as a basis of communication. We work with each player to adjust the goals relative to the ability or inability to achieve them. We are goal-setting in all aspects of the student athlete's life and continually monitor the progress. Ideally, we would like to set weekly goals but have found it cumbersome. (We encourage the players to outline what they want to accomplish each practice and each week in their journals.)

Extrinsic Rewards   Occasionally, we use extrinsic rewards. It is always a special occasion. We use extrinsic rewards primarily to relieve the tedium of the long weeks and hours of practice. The focus of this type of motivation is to generate fun. Usually, the rewards are the result of a specific competition: rewards over the years have been an ice cream feed, T-shirts, posters, dinners, a day at the beach for the whole team, etc. (Most of the athletic equipment rewards are from my personal collection, accumulated over the years.)

Nonverbal Cues   We have specific hand signals for, for example, tactical adjustments. Certainly, the players learn to read my very animated expressions and body language.

Sport Psychologist   The coaching staff consults with the university psychology professors on specific issues. Basically, logistics limit direct contact with a recognized sport psychologist. We will, occasionally, have players receive counseling. On the national team we had direct involvement of five psychologists. Three dealt with the individuals through individual meetings and questions about themselves. Two psychologists dealt with group dynamics and actually were closely involved with the group.

Psychological Methods   Peer pressure is our most common psychological tool. We occasionally have organized encounter sessions. My coaching staff and I evaluate each other in terms of negative comments and positive comments we make to the team and individual players. We try to "catch" our players doing things right, not just their errors, which often happens in the teaching environment. We try hard to be consistent in our criticism and compliments.

Mental Qualities   My players must revel in the opportunity to compete. They must enjoy a competitive atmosphere. They must be goal-oriented and have a strong work ethic. They must be *team*-oriented. They must have an attitude of competition and thorough understanding of group dynamics and the strength inherent in the group process.

I would rather deal with highly motivated, intense, competitive athletes and teach them the skills of group membership than try to teach nice, easy-going, docile players to be competitive and tough. Frankly, it is easier to make a tough, ol' mountain horse take the bit than make a docile, "milk wagon" pony run a race.

We have had a wide range of mental sets at Montana State over the years. The best have been physically skilled, mentally and emotionally tough.

Philosophically, sport (volleyball) is a great vehicle to teach life lessons and experiences. Values, decision-making, work ethics, performing under pressure, self-esteem, security, confidence, etc., are the rewards of athletic competition long after the scores and championships are forgotten.

RUDY SUWARA

Profile

Now entering his tenth year as head women's volleyball coach at San Diego State University, Rudy Suwara has established a reputation as one of the finest collegiate coaches in the nation.

Suwara has been voted West Coast Athletic Association (WCAA) Coach of the Year four times (1979, 1981, 1982, and 1984) in his career, more than any other coach in the conference. In fact, no other WCAA mentor received the honor more than once in voting conducted by league coaches.

The Aztecs have recorded at least thirty wins each year for the last five years, and have won at an outstanding .789 clip the past four seasons, compiling a 145–39 mark in that span.

San Diego State has captured three first-place finishes and one second-place finish in the WCAA since 1979. Over the past five years SDSU has compiled a 58–20 mark within the league, thus winning 75 percent of its matches against the best teams in collegiate volleyball. In addition, over the past seven years, Aztecs have earned first team All American honors eight times and first team All WCAA honors eleven times.

Currently there are three Aztec alumni playing with the U.S. National volleyball team training for the 1988 Olympics: Toni Himmer ('83), Angela Rock ('84), and Sue Hegerle ('83).

Suwara may have no peer when it comes to developing athletes with little or no previous volleyball experience into outstanding collegiate players. Former Aztec standouts like Mary Holland, a two-time All American at SDSU; Sue Hegerle, past member of the U.S. National team; and Linda Ellers, a walk-on who became one of the WCAA's top players, all came to Montezuma Mesa as relatively unheralded high school players.

Part of Suwara's success in producing outstanding volleyball players can be attributed to his own experience as a competitor. He was a member of the 1968 U.S. Olympic volleyball team, the first U.S. squad to beat the Soviet Union. Suwara has earned All American honors fifteen times in his career and was named to the Volleyball Hall of Fame in 1976. Suwara also played on the 1967 Gold Medal–winning U.S. team in the Pan American Games and with the San Diego Breakers of the International Volleyball Association Professional League.

Suwara still is very active in competitive volleyball. His masters team won the national championship in 1985 for the USVBA senior division. He is also a nationally ranked beach volleyball player.

Born in New York City, Suwara began playing volleyball with his father and brother at a young age. He graduated from the City College of New York, where he was named to the school's Volleyball Hall of Fame in 1965. Suwara got his start coaching as an assistant with the UCLA men's volleyball team for four years. He received his master's degree there in 1972. UC Santa Barbara gave him his first head coaching experience. He lead the Gaucho men's volleyball team to second-place NCAA finishes in 1971 and 1974. His 1974 squad became the first collegiate team to win the USVBA Collegiate and National Open Men's Championship.

In 1976, Suwara made his move to San Diego State, where he coached both the Aztec men and women for his first four years. As men's coach during that time, he compiled a 55–44 record.

Psychological Coaching Methods

Mental Preparation   I devote approximately 10 percent of allocated practice time to specific mental rehearsal and preparation.

Mental Concentration   In order to capitalize on the positive results of mental rehearsal and mental concentration, I incorporate diagrams of our opponent's offense and defense so we can adjust our patterns of offense and defense for best results.

Imagining of successful skill practice and game situations are helpful to the athletes because they are then able to develop a mental picture of successful skill development and to foresee the necessary adjustments they may have to make during the course of a game.

Imagery Techniques   I tell my athletes to think of an opponent's defense and how they will attack it. What do they "see" as the strengths and weaknesses of our opponent in terms of vulnerability.

They are told to see themselves in tense game point situations like serving the game point and mentally and physically practicing the serve that will bring us victory.

Relaxation Techniques   I occasionally tell corny "bad" jokes to have a team laugh and thus reduce their anxiety and stress levels.

We often stretch and do partner massage with the balls which seems to help them relax and focus their attention on the task ahead.

Images of waterfalls, forest trails, and beaches with waves provides a soothing mental picture that helps the team relax.

Motivation   Anxiety is a problem with some of our players. I try to teach them to relax, think positively (e.g., I *can* pass), and to breathe more deeply and slowly.

I try to give them examples of successful players, and help them set reasonable goals. I want them to reach their maximum potential. This is a problem on our team right now with several of our players.

Optimal Arousal   It is hardest to do in long USVBA tourneys, and for weaker opponents. A team goal is to win a game 15–0, a shut-out in volleyball, to play the perfect game.

Emotional Differences   I try to calm specific athletes who are prone to high anxiety. I try to "fire up" the team if they are not going hard.

Athlete or Team That Chokes   I try to put them in tense situations where the team or a specific athlete will prevail in order to build confidence.

I constantly encourage each player to concentrate better, recognize their tension, and overcome it by relaxing and focusing on skill development.

Goal-setting   We have individual goals in jumping, bench pressing, body fat percentage, and grade point average.

We have team goals in National, League, and Regional play.

We have short-term and long-term goals for both individual athletes and the team.

Extrinsic Rewards   Pizza for shut-outs.

SDSU rings for League Champs and graduating seniors.

Nonverbal Cues   Reaching hands overhead-forward "BLOCK-OVER"

(With setter - calls plays: and #1 hitter) (serving targets - on serve)

Hit fist into open palm - means kill the ball.

Sport Psychologist   Dr. Selder in the Physical Education Department works regularly with the Women's Volleyball team utilizing graduate Physical Education students who are majoring in Sport Psychology.

Psychological Methods   Basically I try to keep drills simple and give appropriate feedback, so adjustments and improvement can be made.

I try to both design and run drills in order that the correct technique is attainable most of the time. There is no point to use drills where the athletes are predestined to fail time after time for no *apparent* reason.

Mental Qualities   Highly motivated with high goals.

Good concentration skills and focusing.

Good discipline equals good work habits.

ELAINE MICHAELIS

Profile

Elaine Michaelis is the head women's volleyball coach at Brigham Young University. Michaelis's lifetime coaching record is 412–114–5, which places her as one of the top women intercollegiate volleyball coaches in the country. In addition to coaching volleyball, Michaelis has also coached basketball, softball, and field hockey at Brigham Young.

Psychological Coaching Methods

Mental Preparation   Our volleyball players individually spend 10 percent of their practice and match time on mental preparation. For the individual, this is a specific application. The team as a whole spends 10 percent of its practice and competition time on mental preparation.

Mental Concentration   We use specific drills to develop mental concentration. For example we do serving drills which require a set goal to be achieved before the players can go on to the next practice activity. They must do fifty consecutive serves in the court, with a partner, or hit a target ten times each. Another example is to identify an opponent in practice, which then requires the setter and blocker to organize the offense and defense according to the opponent's position in the rotation. We will assign blockers to block specific hitters certain ways.

Imagery Techniques   Imagery techniques are another form of mental preparation that we use with the team. We visualize courts and areas in which we will play in order to prepare the players for distractions or crowd responses.

We also use imagery to work on skill improvement. We provide a model performance on video and have the athletes visualize the model performance. We pattern skill performance and have them practice it mentally. Following skill errors in performance, we suggest imagery of a successful performance to replace the last image.

Relaxation Techniques   Relaxation techniques are taught in the sport psychology class that athletes take the first two years in the program. During the relaxation sessions, all players do the technique and the psychologist or coach gives feedback at the appropriate time of relaxation.

We remind the players to use relaxation technique in stressful situations such as important serves and pre-game preparation. We incorporate relaxation techniques for anxiety control prior to important matches.

Motivation   In working with the overmotivated player, we use a philosophical approach to put the game and its result in perspective. We use goal-setting, not winning and losing, as the major objective.

In dealing with the undermotivated player, we use responsibility to the team traditions, teammates, and our goals as incentives. We also use arousal techniques to increase performance.

Commitments and contracts are made in pre-season which serve as a foundation for practice and performance efforts. Early practice sessions require high intensity to develop good work habits. Thus we do not have much of a problem with undermotivation.

Optimal Arousal   The first step to help our athletes achieve optimal arousal for competition occurs at the beginning of the year. Philosophically we set team goals and sign contracts as a foundation for excellence. Post-practice and post-game comments always reflect an evaluation of our performance and an effort to keep our basic philosophy a priority.

We teach skills to be used when the effort is not acceptable, for example, jumping, patting stomach, intense warm-up, "go for" extra balls, etc. We use film and strategy sessions to prepare the players for a good mental challenge for the match. We also set match goals. We use motivational remarks in regard to the match and how it fits into our goals and performance objectives. We also use traditions, records, loyalties, and self-satisfaction as incentives.

Emotional Differences   We coach for emotional differences in our athletes. We test and evaluate the athletes in the sport psychology class, which helps them to understand themselves and work on adjustments. I have periodic interviews to evaluate personal progress and inner feelings that determine emotional reactions. We use different approaches with each athlete, which helps them relate and respond to the coach.

We teach the players to accept responsibility for their performance and to put their performance in perspective to their level of achievement and contribution to the team. We define roles on the team and mutually determine the players' contributions and positions. These approaches help control emotions.

Athlete or Team That Chokes   The best approach to coaching the athlete or team that chokes is to try and relieve the pressure by stressing goals and strategies. Philosophically we believe we cannot control winning and losing but we can control our effort and our game plan. Emphasis is placed on what we can control as well as relaxation skills. We keep good relationships between members so everyone feels support, confidence, and acceptance among the team.

We also try to prepare to be competitors in game situations by having stressful drills and practices which require quality performances. We do a great deal of competition in practice.

Goal-setting   Goal-setting is used for personal and team-related objectives. These include academic, spiritual, social, physical training, and technical training goals. They are both short- and long-range goals.

Each game also has specific goals regarding effort and tactical and statistical performance. Each player interprets the team statistics into personal statistics for us to be successful. For example, if we want to hit 28 percent for the match, some players need to hit 30 percent while others must hit 26 percent according to their position and achievement level.

The success of the match is evaluated on achieving the goals rather than the score. Sometimes we are not pleased even with a win.

Extrinsic Rewards   We do not use many extrinsic rewards at our level. We give points for drill performances and give an award for our best practice player. Once in a while we use a treat as a reward. But mostly we use praise in private and public and compliment on good performance. Other extrinsic awards are given by external groups such as all conference and school awards, etc.

Nonverbal Cues   Nonverbal cues are used for positive reinforcement. We use smiles, pats on the shoulder, and looks of acceptance and recognition for a special performance. Also used is eye-to-eye contact on the execution of a personal goal which is understood between coach and player.

We also use signals during the contest for strategy reminders.

Sport Psychologist   We have a sport psychologist hired by the school part-time to teach a class for the athletes their first two years of competition. He also does personal testing and counseling. He observes competition and gives players and coaches suggestions for application of psychological skills.

Psychological Methods   Our overall approach to increasing learning, performance, and motivation is to try to organize practices for the specific application of game skills. All drills begin, continue, and terminate naturally. Practice provides constant pressure to keep concentration high. The basic motivation is to get better and to fulfill our goals. We are a very competitive team, but we enjoy the people and the travel very much. We have a strong sense of fair play and ethical conduct. I believe a coach should help young people become mature and independent in life and in the game. In the educational setting, sport is not the top priority.

References

CHAPTER 1

Hebb, Donald O. 1968. *A Textbook of Psychology*, 2nd ed. Philadelphia: W. B. Saunders Co.

Leonard, Wilbert Marcellus II. 1984. *A Sociological Perspective of Sport*, 2nd ed. Minneapolis: Burgess Publishing Co.

Bryant J. Cratty, *Social Psychology in Athletics*, 1981, p.2. Reprinted by permission of Prentice-Hall, Englewood Cliffs, New Jersey.

Bourne, Lyle E. Jr., and Bruce R. Ekstrand. 1973. *Psychology: Its Principles and Meanings*. Dryden Press. Reprinted by permission of CBS College Publishing.

Cratty, Bryant J. 1970. Coaching Decisions and Research in Sport Psychology. *Quest* Monograph XIII (January):46.

Morgan, William P. 1974. Selected Psychological Considerations in Sport. *Research Quarterly* 45 (4):374–390. Reprinted by permission of the American Alliance for Health, Physical Education, Recreation and Dance, 1900 Association Drive, Reston, Va. 22091.

Fisher, A. Craig, ed. 1976. *Psychology of Sport*, 1st ed. Palo Alto: Mayfield Publishing Co.

Cox, Richard H. *Sport Psychology: Concepts and Applications*. ©1985 Wm. C. Brown Publishers, Dubuque, Iowa. All rights reserved. Reprinted by permission.

Kozar, Bill. 1973. The Effects of a Supportive and Non Supportive Audience Upon Learning a Cross Motor Skill. *International Journal of Sport Psychology* 4 (1):27–38.

Iso-Ahola, Seppo E., and Ken Mobily. 1980. Psychological Momentum: A Phenomenon and an Empirical (unobtrusive) Validation of its Influence in a Competitive Sport Tournament. *Psychological Reports* (April):391–401.

CHAPTER 2

Kroll, Walter, and Guy M. Lewis. 1970. America's First Sport Psychologist. *Quest* Monograph XIII (January):1.

Griffith, Coleman. 1930. A Laboratory for Research in Athletics. *Research Quarterly* 1 (October):34–40. Reprinted by permission of the American Alliance for Health, Physical Education, Recreation and Dance, 1900 Association Drive, Reston, Va. 22091.

Bird, Anne Marie, and Diane Ross. 1984. Current Methodological Problems and Future Directions for Theory Development in the Psychology of Sport and Motor Behavior. *Quest* 36 (1):1, 2.

Landers, Dan. 1982. What Ever Happened to Theory Testing in Sport Psychology? Canadian Society for Psychomotor Learning and Sport Psychology Conference, Edmonton, Alberta, Canada.

Martens, Rainer. 1979. From Smocks to Jocks: A New Adventure for Sport Psychologists. In *Coach, Athlete, and the Sport Psychologist*. Peter Klavora and Juri V. Daniel, ed. Toronto: University of Toronto, School of Physical and Health Education.

CHAPTER 3

George, Judith Jenkins. 1985. Women's Coaching Opportunities Dwindling, Report Says. *The NCAA News* No. Vol (14 October):3.

Leonard, Wilbert Marcellus II. 1980. *A Sociological Perspective of Sport*. Minneapolis: Burgess Publishing Co.

Bryson, Lois. 1983. Sport and the Oppression of Women, *Australian and New Zealand Journal of Sociology* 19 (November):413–426.

Weiss, M., and A. Knoppers. 1982. The Influence of Socializing Agents on Female Collegiate Volleyball Players. *Journal of Sport Psychology* 4:267–279.

Snyder, Eldon E., and Elmer Spreitzer. 1983. Change and Variation in the Social Acceptance of Female Participation in Sport. *Journal of Sport Behavior* 6 (March):3–8.

Anthrop, Joseph, and Maria T. Allison. 1983. Role Conflict and the High School Female Athlete. *Research Quarterly for Exercise and Sport* 54 (2):104–111. Reprinted by permission of the American Alliance for Health, Physical Education, Recreation and Dance, 1900 Association Drive, Reston, Va. 22091.

Salisbury, Jan, and Michael W. Passer. 1982. Gender Role Attitudes and Participation in Competitive Activities of Varying Stereotypic Femininity. *Personality and Social Psychology Bulletin* 8 (September):486–493.

Rosenberg, E., and A. F. Chelete. Avowed Happiness of Members of Sport and Non-Sport Voluntary Associations. *International Journal of Sport Psychology* 11:263–275.

Birrell, Susan. 1978. Achievement Related Motives and the Woman Athlete. In *Women And Sport: From Myth to Reality*. S. L. Greendorfer, ed. Philadelphia: Lea & Febiger.

Wyrick, W. 1971. How Sex Differences Affect Research in Physical Education. In *DGWS Research Reports: Women in Sports*. Dorothy V. Harris, ed. Washington, D.C.: American Association for Health, Physical Education, and Recreation. Reprinted by permission of the American Alliance for Health, Physical Education, Recreation and Dance, 1900 Association Drive, Reston, Va. 22091.

Miller, Donna Mae. 1974. *Coaching the Female Athlete*. Philadelphia: Lea & Febiger.

Sage, George H. 1980. Orientations Toward Sport of Male and Female Intercollegiate Athletes. *Journal of Sport Psychology* 2 (4):358,359.

Bird, Anne M., and Jean M. Williams. 1980. A Developmental Attributional Analysis of Sex Role Stereotypes for Sport Performance. *Developmental Psychology* 16 (July):319–322. Reprinted (or adapted) by permission of the publisher.

Hart, Marie. 1973. On Being Female in Sport. In *Sociology of Sport*, by Harry Edwards. Homewood, Ill.: Dorsey Press.

CHAPTER 4

Miller, Donna Mae. 1974. *Coaching the Female Athlete*. Philadelphia: Lea & Febiger.

Murphy, Patricia J. 1984. Sport and Gender. In *A Sociological Perspective of Sport*. 2nd ed., by Wilbert Marcellus Leonard II. Minneapolis, Minnesota: Burgess Publishing Co.

Dickason, Anne. 1981. The Feminine as a Universal. In *Feminism and Philosophy*, Mary Vetterling-Braggin, Frederick A. Elliston, and Jane English, ed. Totowa, N.J.: Rowman & Littlefield.

Cox, Richard H. 1985. *Sport Psychology: Concepts And Applications*. Dubuque, Iowa: William C. Brown Publishers. Reprinted by permission.

Edwards, Steven W., Richard D. Gordin, and Keith P. Henschen. 1984. Sex Role Orientations of Female NCAA Championship Gymnasts. *Perceptual and Motor Skills* 58 (April):625–626.

Blucker, Judy A., and Eve Hershberger. 1983. Causal Attribution Theory and The Female Athlete: What Conclusions Can We Draw? *Journal of Sport Psychology* 5:353–360.

Owie, Ikponmwosa. 1981. Influence of Sex-Role Standards in Sport Competition Anxiety. *International Journal of Sport Psychology* 12:289–292.

Colker, Ruth, and Cathy Windom. 1980. Correlates of Female Athletic Participation: Masculinity, Femininity, Self Esteem, and Attitudes Towards Women. *Sex Roles* 6 (February):47–58.

Berkey, Ruth. 1972. Psychology of Women Who Compete. *California Association for Health, Physical Education, and Recreation Journal* (January/February).

Morgan, William P. 1972. Sport Psychology. In *The Psychomotor Domain: Movement Behavior*, R. N. Singer, ed. Philadelphia: Lea & Febiger.

Williams, Jean M. 1978. Personality Characteristics of the Successful Female Athlete. In *Sport Psychology-An Analysis Of Athletic Behavior*, 2nd ed., William F. Straub, ed. Ithaca, N.Y.: Movement Publications.

Balazs, Eva K. 1975. Psycho-Social Study of Outstanding Female Athletes. *Research Quarterly* 46:267–273.

Harris, Dorothy V. 1973. *Involvement in Sport: A Somatopsychic Rationale for Physical Activity*. Philadelphia: Lea & Febiger.

Uguccioni, Sarah M., and Robert H. Ballantyne. 1980. Comparison of Attitudes and Sex Roles for Female Athletic Participants and Non Participants. *International Journal of Sport Psychology* 11:42–48.

Landers, Dan. 1970. Psychological Femininity and the Prospective Female Physical Educator. *Research Quarterly* 41 (May):164–170.

Patsy Neal, *Coaching Methods for Women*, ©1969, Addison-Wesley, Reading, Massachusetts. P9.31 (quote). Reprinted with permission.

Lowe, Marian, and Ruth Hubbard, ed. 1983. *Woman's Nature. Rationalizations of Inequality*. Oxford: Pergamon Press. Reprinted with permission.

Female Psychology: The Emerging Self, Second Edition, by Sue Cox. Copyright ©1981 by St. Martin's Press, Inc., and used with Publisher's permission.

CHAPTER 5

Miller, Donna Mae. 1974. *Coaching the Female Athlete*. Philadelphia: Lea & Febiger.

Joseph B. Oxendine, *Psychology of Motor Learning*, ©1984, pp.82, 83, 222, 225, 226. Reprinted by Permission of Prentice-Hall, Englewood Cliffs, New Jersey.

Ausubel, D. P. 1968. *Educational Psychology: A Cognitive View*. New York: Holt, Rinehart & Winston.

Roberts, Glyn C., and Joan L. Duda. 1984. Motivation in Sport: The Mediating Role of Perceived Ability. *Journal of Sport Psychology* 6 (3):312–324.

Russell, C. 1982. The Causal Dimension Scale: A Measure of How Individuals Perceive Causes. *Journal of Personality and Social Psychology* 42:1137–1145.

Weiner, B. 1979. A Theory of Motivation for Some Classroom Experiences. *Journal of Education Psychology* 71:3–25.

Singer, Robert N. 1977. Motivation in Sport. *International Journal of Sport Psychology* 8:1–22.

McClements, James D., and Cal Botterill. 1980. Goal Setting and Performance. In *Psychology in Sports*: *Methods and Applications*, Richard M. Suinn, ed. Minneapolis: Burgess Publishing Co.

CHAPTER 6

Nixon, John E., and Ann E. Jewett. 1980. *An Introduction to Physical Education*. 9th ed. Saunders College/Holt, Rinehart & Winston. Reprinted by permission of CBS College Publishing.

Singer, R. N. 1972. *Coaching, Athletics, and Psychology*. New York: McGraw-Hill.

Eitzen, D. S. 1979. Sport as a Microcosm of Society. In *Sport in Contemporary Society: An Anthology*, D. S. Eitzen, ed. New York: St. Martin's Press.

Lord, R. H. 1979. Volunteer Coaches' Knowledge: Development of a Test. Doctoral dissertation, Texas Tech University. *Dissertation Abstracts International*.

Butt, D. S. 1980. What Can Psychology Offer to the Athlete and the Coach? In *Psychology in Sports*: *Methods and Applications*, R. M. Suinn, ed. Minneapolis: Burgess Publishing Co.

Wooden, J. 1973. *They Call Me Coach*. New York: Bantam Books, Inc.

Botterill, C. 1980. Psychology of Coaching. In *Psychology in Sports: Methods and Applications*, R. M. Suinn, ed. Minneapolis: Burgess Publishing Co.

Thoresen, C. E., and M. J. Mahoney. 1974. *Behavioral Self-Control*. New York: Holt, Rinehart & Winston.

Martens, R. 1978. *Joy and Sadness in Children's Sport*. Champaign, Ill.: Human Kinetics Publishers.

Bandura, A. 1971. Vicarious and Self-reinforcement Processes. In *The Nature of Reinforcement*, R. Glaser, ed. New York: Academic Press.

Tharp, R. G., and R. Gallimore. 1976. What the Coach Can Teach the Teacher. *Psychology Today* 9:75–78.

Orlick, T. D. 1972. A Socio-psychological Analysis of Early Sports Participation. Doctoral dissertation, University of Alberta.

Meichenbaum, D. 1971. Examination of Model Characteristics in Reducing Avoidance Behavior. *Journal of Personality and Social Psychology* 17:298–307.

Bandura, A., ed. 1971b. *Psychological Modeling: Conflicting Theories*. Chicago: Aldine-Atherton.

Mahoney, M. J., and C. E. Thoresen. 1974. *Self-Control: Power to the Person*. Monterey, Cal.: Brooks/Cole Publishing Co.

Lane, J. R. 1980. Improving Athletic Performance through Visuo-Motor Behavior Rehearsal. In *Psychology in Sports: Methods and Applications*, R. M. Suinn, ed. Minneapolis: Burgess Publishing Co.

Titley, R. W. 1980. The Loneliness of a Long-distance Kicker. In *Psychology in Sports: Methods and Applications*, R. M. Suinn, ed. Minneapolis: Burgess Publishing Co.

Suinn, R. M. 1977. Behavioral Methods at the Winter Olympic Games. *Behavior Therapy* 8:283–384.

———. 1980. Body Thinking: Psychology for Olympic Champs. In *Psychology in Sports: Methods and Applications*. R. M. Suinn, ed. Minneapolis: Burgess Publishing Co.

Nicklaus, J. 1974. *Golf My Way*. New York: Simon & Schuster.

Jacobson, E. 1938. *Progressive Relaxation*. Chicago: University of Chicago Press.

Singer, R. N. 1975. *Motor Learning and Human Performance*. 2nd ed. New York: MacMillan Publishing Co.

Meichenbaum, D. H., and R. Cameron. 1974. The Clinical Potential and Pitfalls of Modifying What Clients Say to Themselves. In *Self-Control: Power to the Person*, by M. J. Mahoney and C. E. Thoresen. Monterey, Cal.: Brooks/Cole Publishing Co.

Reprinted with permission from Mahoney's *Cognition and Behavior Modification*, Copyright 1974, Ballinger Publishing Company.

Adams, J. A. 1971. A Closed-loop Theory of Motor Behavior. *Journal of Motor Behavior* 3:111–149.

Oxendine, Joseph B. 1984. *Psychology of Motor Learning*. Englewood Cliffs, N. J.: Prentice-Hall. Reprinted by permission.

Martin, Gary L., and Dennis Hrycaiko, ed. 1983. *Behavior Modification and Coaching Principles, Procedures and Research*. Springfield, Ill.: Charles C. Thomas, Publisher.

Mechikoff, Robert A., and Bill Kozar. 1983. *Sport Psychology: The Coach's Perspective*. Springfield, Ill.: Charles C. Thomas, Publisher.

Bibliography

Ash, M. J., and R. D. Zellner. 1978. Speculations on the use of biofeedback training in sport psychology. In *Psychology of Motor Behavior and Sport*, D. M. Landers and R. W. Christina, ed. Champaign, Ill.: Human Kinetics.

———. 1973. *Aggression: A Social Learning Analysis*. Englewood Cliffs, N.J.: Prentice-Hall.

Bandura, A. 1977. Self-efficacy: Toward a unifying theory of behavioral change. *Psychological Review* 84:191–215.

———. 1977. *Social Learning Theory*. Englewood Cliffs, N.J.: Prentice-Hall.

Bandura, A., and C. J. Kupers. The transmission of patterns of self-reinforcement through modeling. *Journal of Abnormal and Social Psychology* 69:1–9.

Berkowitz, L. 1965. The concept of aggressive drive: Some additional considerations. In *Advances in Experimental Social Psychology*, L. Berkowitz, ed. 2:301–29.

———. 1970. Experimental investigations of hostility catharsis. *Journal of Consulting and Clinical Psychology* 35:1–7.

———. 1978. Sports competition and aggression. In *Sport Psychology*, W. F. Straub, ed. Ithaca, N.Y.: Movement Publications.

Berlyne, D. E. 1966. Conflict and arousal. *Scientific American* 215:82–87.

Bernstein, D. A., and T. D. Borkovec. 1973. *Progressive Relaxation: A Training Manual for the Helping Professional*. Champaign, Ill.: Research Press.

Bird, A. M. 1977. Development of a model for predicting team performance. *Research Quarterly* 48:24–32.

———. 1977. Leadership and cohesion within successful and unsuccessful teams: Perceptions of coaches and players. In *Psychology of Motor Behavior and Sport*, D. M. Landers and R. W. Christina, ed. Champaign, Ill.: Human Kinetics.

Bird, A. M., and J. M. Brame. 1979. Self vs. team attributions: A test of the "I'm o.k., but the team's so-so" phenomenon. *Research Quarterly* 49:260–68.

Bird, A. M., C. D. Foster, and G. Maruyama. 1980. Convergent and incremental effects of cohesion on attributions for self and team. *Journal of Sport Psychology* 2:181–94.

Bird, A. M., and J. M. Williams. 1980. A developmental-attributional analysis of sex-role stereo-types for sport. *Developmental Psychology* 16:319–22.

Borkovec, T. D. 1978. Self-efficacy: Cause or reflection of behavioral change? In *Advances in Behaviour Research and Therapy*. Vol. 1, S. Rachman, ed. Oxford: Pergamon Press.

———. 1981. Stress management in athletics: An overview of cognitive and physiological tech-niques. *Motor Skills: Theory into Practice* 5:45–52.

Carron, A. V. 1980. *Social Psychology of Sport*. Ithaca, N.Y.: Movement Publications.

———. 1982. Processes of group interaction in sport teams. *Quest* 33:245–70.

Carron, A. V., and B. B. Bennett. 1977. Compatibility in the coach-athlete dyad. *Research Quarterly* 48:671–79.

Carron, A. V., and P. Chelladurai. 1978. Psychological factors and athletic success: An analysis of coach-athlete interpersonal behavior. *Canadian Journal of Applied Sport Sciences* 3:43–50.

Case, R. W. 1984. Leadership in sport. *Journal of Physical Education, Recreation, and Dance* 55:15,16.

Chelladurai, P. 1984. Discrepancy between preferences and perceptions of leadership behavior and satisfaction of athletes in varying sports. *Journal of Sport Psychology* 6:27–41.

Chelladurai, P., and A. V. Carron. 1983. Athletic maturity and preferred leadership. *Journal of Sport Psychology* 5:371–80.

Chelladurai, P., and S. D. Saleh. 1980. Dimensions of leader behavior in sports: Development of a leadership scale. *Journal of Sport Psychology* 2:34–45.

Corbin, C. B. 1967. The effect of covert rehearsal on development of a complex motor skill. *Journal of General Psychology* 76:143–50.

Corran, R. 1980. Violence and the coach. In *Psychology in Sports*, R. M. Suinn, ed. Minneapolis: Burgess Publishing Co.

Daniels, F. S., and B. Hatfield. 1981. Biofeedback. *Motor Skills: Theory into Practice* 5:69–72.

Davis, J. H. 1969. *Group Performance*. Reading, Mass.: Addison-Wesley.

Deci, E. L. 1971. Effects of externally mediated rewards on intrinsic motivation. *Journal of Personality and Social Psychology* 18:105–15.

———. 1972. Intrinsic motivation, extrinsic reinforcement. *Journal of Personality and Social Psychology* 22:113–20.

———. 1978. Intrinsic motivation: Theory and application. In *Psychology of Motor Behavior and Sport*, D. M. Landers and R. W. Christina, ed. Champaign, Ill.: Human Kinetics.

Deci, E. L., and R. M. Ryan. 1980. The empirical exploration of intrinsic motivational processes. In *Advances in Experimental Social Psychology*. Vol. 13, L. Berkowitz, ed. New York: Academic Press.

DeWitt, D. J. 1980. Cognitive and biofeedback training for stress reduction with university ath-letes. *Journal of Sport Psychology* 2:288–94.

Dishman, R. K. 1980. Overview of ergogenic properties of hypnosis. *Journal of Physical Edu-cation and Recreation* 51:52–54.

Duffy, E. 1957. The psychological significance of the concept of "arousal" or "activation." *Psychological Review* 64:265–75.

Dweck, C. S. 1975. The role of expectations and attributions in the alleviation of learned help-lessness. *Journal of Personality and Social Psychology* 31:674–85.

———. 1980. Learned helplessness in sport. In *Psychology of Motor Behavior and Sport*, C. H. Nadeau, W. R. Halliwell, K. M. Newell, and G. C. Roberts, ed. Champaign, Ill.: Human Kinetics.

Dweck, C. S., and N. D. Reppucci. 1973. Learned helplessness and reinforcement responsibility in children. *Journal of Personality and Social Psychology* 25:109–16.

Easterbrook, J. A. 1959. The effect of emotion on cue utilization and the organization of behavior. *Psychological Review* 66:183–201.

Epstein, M. L. 1980. The relationship of mental imagery and mental rehearsal to performance of a motor task. *Journal of Sport Psychology* 2:211–20.

Feigley, D. A. 1983. Is aggression justifiable? *Journal of Physical Education, Recreation and Dance* 54:63–64.

Feltz, D. L. 1982. The effects of age and number of demonstrations on modeling of form and performance. *Research Quarterly for Exercise and Sport* 53:291–96.

———. 1982. Path analysis of the causal elements in Bandura's theory of self-efficacy and an anxiety-based model of avoidance behavior. *Journal of Personality and Social Psychology* 42:764–81.

Feltz, D. L., D. M. Landers, and U. Raeder. 1979. Enhancing self-efficacy in high-avoidance motor tasks: A comparison of modeling techniques. *Journal of Sport Psychology* 1:112–22.

Fenz, W. D. 1975. Coping mechanisms and performance under stress. In *Psychology of Sport and Motor Behavior II*, D. M. Landers, D. V. Harris, and R. W. Christina, ed. University Park, Pa.: The Pennsylvania State University.

Fenz, W. D., and S. Epstein. 1969. Stress: In the air. *Psychology Today* 3:27,28,58,59.

Fiedler, F. E. 1967. *A Theory of Leadership Effectiveness*. New York: McGraw-Hill.

Fisher, A. C., V. H. Mancini, R. L. Hirsch, T. J. Proulx, and E. J. Staurowsky. 1982. Coach-athlete interactions and team climate. *Journal of Sport Psychology* 4:388–404.

Forward, J. 1969. Group achievement motivation and individual motive to achieve success and to avoid failure. *Journal of Personality* 37:297–309.

Fosbury, D. 1974. Fosbury on flopping. *Track Technique* 55:1749–50.

Gallwey, W. T. 1974. *The Inner Game of Tennis*. New York: Random House.

Gallwey, W. T., and B. Kriegel. 1977. *Inner Skiing*. New York: Random House.

Garai, J. E., and A. Scheinfeld. 1970. Sex differences in mental and behavioral traits. *Genetic Psychological Monographs* 81:123–42.

Geen, R. G., and E. C. O'Neal. 1969. Activation of cue-elicited aggression by general arousal. *Journal of Personality and Social Psychology* 11:289–92.

Gilmor, T. M., and H. L. Minton. 1974. Internal versus external attributions of task performance as a function of locus of control, initial confidence and success-failure outcome. *Journal of Personality* 42:159–74.

Girdano, D., and G. Everly. 1979. *Controlling Stress and Tension*. Englewood Cliffs, N.J.: Prentice-Hall.

Goldstein, J. H., and R. L. Arms. 1971. Effects of observing athletic contests on hostility. *Sociometry* 34:83–90.

Gould, D., and G. C. Roberts. 1982. Modeling and motor skill acquisition. *Quest* 33:214–30.

Gould, D., and M. Weiss. 1981. The effects of model similarity and model talk on self-efficacy and muscular endurance. *Journal of Sport Psychology* 3:17–29.

Gould, D., R. S. Weinberg, and A. Jackson. 1980. Effect of mental preparation strategies on a muscular endurance task. *Journal of Sport Psychology* 2:329–39.

Gruber, J. J., and D. Beauchamp. 1979. Relevancy of the competitive state anxiety inventory in a sport environment. *Research Quarterly* 50:207–14.

Hale, B. D. 1982. The effects of internal and external imagery on muscular and ocular concomitants. *Journal of Sport Psychology* 4:379–87.

Harrell, W. A. 1980. Aggression by high school basketball players: An observational study of the effects of opponents' aggression and frustration-inducing factors. *International Journal of Sport Psychology* 11:290–98.

Harrison, R. P., and Feltz, D. L. 1981. Stress inoculation for athletes: Description and case example. *Motor Skills: Theory into Practice* 5:53–61.

Harter, S. 1981. The development of competence motivation in the mastery of cognitive and physical skills: Is there still a place for joy? In *Psychology of Motor Behavior and Sport*, G. C. Roberts and D. M. Landers, ed. Champaign, Ill.: Human Kinetics.

Helmreich, R., and J. T. Spence. 1977. Sex roles and achievement. In *Psychology of Motor Behavior and Sport*, R. W. Christina and D. M. Landers, ed. Champaign, Ill.: Human Kinetics.

Hersey, P., and K. Blanchard. 1982. *Management of Organizational Behavior: Utilizing Human Resources*. Englewood Cliffs, N.J.: Prentice-Hall.

Hickman, J. L. 1979. How to elicit supernormal capabilities in athletes. In *Coach, Athlete, and the Sport Psychologist*, P. Klavora and J. V. Daniel, ed. Toronto: University of Toronto Press.

Huddleston, S., and D. L. Gill. 1981. State anxiety as a function of skill level and proximity to competition. *Research Quarterly for Exercise and Sport* 52:31–34.

Inciong, P. A. 1974. Leadership styles and team success. Unpublished doctoral dissertation, University of Utah, Salt Lake City.

Ingham, A. G., G. Levinger, J. Graves, and V. Peckham. 1974. The Ringleman effect: Studies of group size and group performance. *Journal of Experimental Social Psychology* 10:371–84.

Iso-Ahola, S. E. 1977. Immediate attributional effects of success and failure in the field: Testing some laboratory hypotheses. *European Journal of Social Psychology* 7:275–96.

Jacobson, E. 1936. The course of relaxation in muscles of athletes. *American Journal of Psychology* 48:98–108.

———. 1938. *Progressive Relaxation*. Chicago, Ill.: The University of Chicago Press.

Jeffrey, D. B. 1974. A comparison of the effects of external control and self-control on the modification and maintenance of weight. *Journal of Abnormal Psychology* 83:404–10.

Kahneman, D. 1973. *Attention and Effort*. Englewood Cliffs, N.J.: Prentice-Hall.

Kane, J. E. 1964. Psychological correlates of physique and physical abilities. In *International Research in Sport and Physical Education*, E. Jokl and E. Simon, ed. Springfield, Ill.: Charles C. Thomas, Publisher.

Kelley, H. H. 1973. The process of causal attribution. *American Psychologist* 28:107–28.

Korten, D. C. 1962. Situational determinants of leadership structure. *Journal of Conflict Resolution* 6:222–35.

Kroll, W. 1979. The stress in high performance athletics. In *Coach, Athlete, and the Sport Psychologist*, P. Klavora and J. V. Daniel, ed. Toronto: University of Toronto Press.

Kukla, A. 1972. Foundations of an attributional theory of performance. *Psychological Review* 79:454–70.

Landers, D. M. 1980. The arousal-performance relationship revisited. *Research Quarterly for Exercise and Sport* 51:77–90.

———. 1982. Arousal, attention, and skilled performance: Further considerations. *Quest* 33:271–83.

Landers, D. M., and G. Luschen. 1974. Team performance outcome and cohesiveness of competitive coaching groups. *International Review of Sports Sociology* 9:57–71.

Lane, J. F. 1980. Improving athletic performance through visuomotor behavior rehearsal. In *Psychology in Sports*, R. M. Suinn, ed. Minneapolis: Burgess Publishing Co.

Lang, P. J. 1978. Self-efficacy theory: Thoughts on cognition and unification. In *Advances in Behaviour Research and Therapy*. Vol. 1, S. Rachman, ed. Oxford: Pergamon Press.

Layman, E. M. 1978. Meditation and sports performance. In *Sport Psychology: An Analysis of Athlete Behavior*, W. F. Straub, ed. Ithaca, N.Y.: Movement Publications.

Lefebvre, L. M. 1979. Achievement motivation and causal attribution in male and female athletes. *International Journal of Sport Psychology* 10:31–41.

Long, B. C. Stress management for the athlete: A cognitive behavioral model. In *Psychology of Motor Behavior and Sport*, C. H. Nadeau, W. R. Halliwell, K. M. Newell, and G. C. Roberts, ed. Champaign, Ill.: Human Kinetics.

Mackay, D. G. 1981. The problem of rehearsal or mental practice. *Journal of Motor Behavior* 13:274–85.

Mahoney, M. J., and M. Avener. 1977. Psychology of the elite athlete: An exploratory study. *Cognitive Therapy and Research* 1:135–41.

Marston, A. R. 1965. Imitation, self-reinforcement and reinforcement of another person. *Journal of Personality and Social Psychology* 2: 255–61.

Martens, R. 1975. *Social Psychology and Physical Activity.*New York: Harper & Row.

———. 1977. *Sport Competition Anxiety Test*. Champaign, Ill.: Human Kinetics.

Martens, R., D. Burton, F. Rivkin, and J. Simon. 1980. Reliability and validity of the competitive state anxiety inventory (CSAI). In *Psychology of Motor Behavior and Sport*, C. H. Nadeau, W. R. Halliwell, K. M. Newell, and G. C. Roberts, ed. Champaign, Ill.: Human Kinetics.

Martens, R., L. Burwitz, and J. Zuckerman. 1976. Modeling effects on motor performance. *Research Quarterly* 47:277–91.

Martens, R., D. M. Landers, and J. Loy. 1972. *Sport Cohesiveness Questionnaire*. Washington, D.C.: American Alliance of Health, Physical Education, and Recreation.

McClelland, D. C., J. W. Atkinson, and E. L. Lowell. 1953. *The Achievement Motive*. New York: Appleton-Century-Crofts.

Meyers, A. W., C. J. Cooke, J. Cullen, and L. Liles. 1979. Psychological aspects of athletic competitors: A replication across sports. *Cognitive Therapy and Research* 3:361–66.

Morgan, W. P. 1976. Psychological consequences of vigorous physical activity and sport. *Proceedings of the American Academy of Physical Education*.

———. 1980. The trait psychology controversy. *Research Quarterly for Exercise and Sport* 51:50–76.

Morgan, W. P., and D. L. Costill. 1972. Psychological characteristics of the marathon runner. *Journal of Sports Medicine and Physical Fitness* 12:42–46.

Morgan, W. P., J. A. Roberts, F. R. Brand, and A. D. Feinerman. 1970. Psychological effect of chronic physical activity. *Medicine and Science in Sports* 2:213–17.

Moyer, K. E. 1976. The physiology of violence. In *Psychology of Sport*, A. C. Fisher, ed. Palo Alto, Cal.: Mayfield Publishing Co.

Nideffer, R. M. 1976. Test of attentional and interpersonal style. *Journal of Personality and Social Psychology* 34:394–404.

———. 1981. *The Ethics and Practice of Applied Sport Psychology*. Ithaca, N.Y. Movement Publications.

Nideffer, R. M., and R. Sharpe. 1978. *ACT: Attention Control Training*. New York: Wyden.

Novaco, R. W. 1979. The cognitive regulation of anger and stress. In *Cognitive-behavioral Interventions*, P. C. Kendall and S. D. Hollon, ed. New York: Academic Press.

Oxendine, J. B. 1970. Emotional arousal and motor performance. *Quest* 13:23–32.

Paivio, A. 1971. *Imagery and Verbal Processes*. New York: Holt, Rinehart & Winston.

Passer, M. W. 1983. Fear of failure, fear of evaluation, perceived competence, and self-esteem in competitive-trait-anxious children. *Journal of Sport Psychology* 5:172–88.

Percival, L. 1971. The coach from the athlete's viewpoint. In *Proceedings, Symposium on the Art and Science of Coaching*, J. W. Taylor, ed. Toronto: Fitness Institute.

Pylyshyn, Z. W. 1973. What the mind's eye tells the mind's brain: A critique of mental imagery. *Psychological Bulletin* 80:1–22.

Reis, J. A., and A. M. Bird. 1982. Cue processing as a function of breadth of attention. *Journal of Sport Psychology* 4:64–72.

Rejeski, W. J., and L. R. Brawley. 1983. Attribution theory in sport: Current status and new perspectives. *Journal of Sport Psychology* 5:77–99.

Roberts, G. C. 1984. Toward a new theory of motivation in sport: The role of perceived ability. In *Psychological Foundations in Sport*, J. M. Silva and R. S. Weinberg, ed. Champaign, Ill.: Human Kinetics.

Rotella, R. J., B. Gansneder, D. Ojala, and J. Billing. 1980. Cognitions and coping strategies of elite skiers: An exploratory study of young developing athletes. *Journal of Sports Psychology* 2:350–54.

Rushall, B. S. 1970. An evaluation of the relationship between personality and physical performance categories. In *Contemporary Psychology of Sport*, G. S. Kenyon, ed. Chicago, Ill.: Athletic Institute.

Rushall, B. S., and Daryl Siedentop. 1972. *The Development and Control of Behavior in Sport and Physical Activity*. Philadelphia, Pa: Lea & Febiger.

Ryan, E. D. 1970. The cathartic effect of vigorous motor activity on aggressive behavior. *Research Quarterly* 41:542–51.

———. 1980. Attribution, intrinsic motivation, and athletics. In *Psychology of Motor Behavior and Sport*, C. H. Nadeau, W. R. Halliwell, K. M. Newell, and G. C. Roberts, ed. Champaign, Ill.: Human Kinetics.

Ryan, E. D., and J. Simmons. 1981. Cognitive demand, imagery, and frequency of mental rehearsal as factors influencing acquisition of motor skills. *Journal of Sport Psychology* 3:35–45.

Sage, G. H. 1978. Humanistic psychology and coaching. In *Sport Psychology: An Analysis of Athlete Behavior*, W. F. Straub, ed. Ithaca, N.Y.: Movement Publications.

Scanlan, T. K., and M. W. Passer, 1979. Sources of competitive stress in young female athletes. *Journal of Sport Psychology* 1:151–59.

———. 1980. Self-serving biases in the competitive sport setting: An attributional dilemma. *Journal of Sport Psychology* 2:124–36.

Silva, J. M. 1980. Assertive and aggressive behavior in sport: A definitional clarification. In *Psychology of Motor Behavior and Sport*, C. H. Nadeau, W. R. Halliwell, K. M. Newell, and G. C. Roberts, ed. Champaign, Ill.: Human Kinetics.

———. 1980. Understanding aggressive behavior and its effects upon athletic performance. In *Sport Psychology*, W. F. Straub, ed. Ithaca, N.Y.: Movement Publications.

Smith, R. E. 1980. A cognitive-affective approach to stress management training for athletes. In *Psychology of Motor Behavior and Sport*, C. H. Nadeau, W. R. Halliwell, K. M. Newell, and G. C. Roberts, ed. Champaign, Ill.: Human Kinetics.

Smith, R. E., and F. L. Smoll. 1978. Psychological intervention and sports medicine: Stress management training and coach effectiveness training. *University of Washington Medicine* 5:20–24.

Smith, R. E., F. L. Smoll, and E. Hunt. 1977. A system for the behavioral assessment of athletic coaches. *Research Quarterly* 48:401–7.

Spielberger, C. D. 1966. *Anxiety and Behavior*. New York: Academic Press.

Spink, K. S. 1978. Win-loss causal attributions of high school basketball players. *Canadian Journal of Applied Sport Sciences* 3:195–201.

Start, K. B., and A. Richardson. 1964. Imagery and mental practice. *British Journal of Education Psychology* 34:280–81.

Suinn, R. M. 1976. Body thinking: Psychology of Olympic champs. *Psychology Today* 10:38–44.

————. 1980. Psychology and sports performance: Principles and applications. In *Psychology in Sports*, R. M. Suinn, ed. Minneapolis: Burgess Publishing Co.

Thirer, J., and M. S. Rampey. 1979. Effects of abusive spectators' behavior on performance of home and visiting inter-collegiate basketball teams. *Perceptual and Motor Skills* 48:1047–54.

Vallerand, R. J., and G. Reid. 1984. On the causal effects of perceived competence on intrinsic motivation: A test of cognitive evaluation theory. *Journal of Sport Psychology* 6:94–102.

Van Schoyck, S. R., and A. F. Grasha. 1981. Attentional style variations and athletic ability: The advantages of a sports-specific test. *Journal of Sport Psychology* 3:149–65.

Walker, R., R. Nideffer, and W. Boomer. 1977. Diving performance as it is correlated with arousal and concentration time. *Swimming Technique* (Winter):117–22.

Weinberg, R. S. 1982. The relationship between mental preparation strategies and motor performance: A review and critique. *Quest* 33:195–213.

Weinberg, R. S., and M. Genuchi. 1980. Relationship between competitive trait anxiety, state anxiety, and golf performance: A field study. *Journal of Sport Psychology* 2:148–54.

Weinberg, R. S., D. Gould, and A. Jackson. 1979. Expectations and performance: An empirical test of Bandura's self-efficacy theory. *Journal of Sport Psychology* 1:320–31.

Weinberg, R. S., D. Yukelson, and A. Jackson. 1980. Effect of public and private efficacy expectations on competitive performance. *Journal of Sport Psychology* 2:340–49.

Weiner, B. 1972. *Theories of Motivation: From Mechanism to Cognition.* Chicago: Rand McNally.

————. 1981. The role of affect in sports psychology. In *Psychology of Motor Behavior and Sport*, G. C. Roberts and D. M. Landers, ed. Champaign, Ill.: Human Kinetics.

White, R. 1959. Motivation reconsidered: The concept of competence. *Psychological Review* 66:297–323.

Widmeyer, W. N., and R. Martens. 1978. When cohesion predicts performance outcome in sports. *Research Quarterly* 49:372–80.

Williams, J. M. 1978. Personality characteristics of the successful female athlete. In *Sport Psychology: An Analysis of Athlete Behavior*, W. F. Straub, ed. Ithaca, N.Y.: Movement Publications.

Wrisberg, C. A., and M. R. Ragsdale. 1979. Cognitive demand and practice level: Factors in the mental rehearsal of motor skills. *Journal of Human Movement Studies* 5:201–8.

Yukelson, D., R. Weinberg, and A. Jackson. 1984. A multidimensional sport cohesion instrument for intercollegiate basketball teams. *Journal of Sport Psychology* 6:103–17.

Zajonc, R. B. 1968. Social facilitation. In *Group Dynamics,* D. Cartwright and A. Zander, ed. New York: Harper & Row.

Zander, A, 1969. Group aspirations. In *Group Dynamics,* D. Cartwright and A. Zander, ed. New York: Harper & Row.

————. 1975. Motivation and performance of sport groups. In *Psychology of Sport and Motor Behavior,* D. M. Landers, ed. University Park, Pa.: Pennsylvania State University Press.

Zillman, D., R. C. Johnson, and K. D. Day. 1974. Provoked and unprovoked aggressiveness in athletics. *Journal of Research in Personality* 8:139–52.

Zillmann, D., A. H. Katcher, and B. Milsvsky. 1972. Excitation transfer from physical exercise to subsequent aggressive behavior. *Journal of Experimental Social Psychology* 8:247–59.

Index